THE EVERYTHING®
GUIDE TO
CATHOLICISM

Dear Reader,

The research and writing of this book has been for me a labor of love. As a "cradle Catholic," Roman Catholicism has been part of my life from the outset. After short careers in the Navy and the business world, I chose to become a religious priest in the Congregation of Holy Cross. Throughout my life I have been intrigued by the teachings of the church and its history; they have become the bedrock of my life. However, I have noticed, especially as a priest, a lack of religious literacy among Catholics, and many misperceptions concerning the church among people of other faiths. Thus, it is a pleasure to write a book that presents the basics of Catholicism in a way that is understandable and entertaining to you. I hope that your appreciation of Catholicism—historically, theologically, and socially—is greatly enhanced through your reading and study of this volume.

Richard Gribble,
CSC, PhD

Welcome to the EVERYTHING® Series!

These handy, accessible books give you all you need to tackle a difficult project, gain a new hobby, comprehend a fascinating topic, prepare for an exam, or even brush up on something you learned back in school but have since forgotten.

You can choose to read an *Everything®* book from cover to cover or just pick out the information you want from our four useful boxes: e-questions, e-facts, e-alerts, and e-ssentials.

We give you everything you need to know on the subject, but throw in a lot of fun stuff along the way, too.

We now have more than 400 *Everything®* books in print, spanning such wide-ranging categories as weddings, pregnancy, cooking, music instruction, foreign language, crafts, pets, New Age, and so much more. When you're done reading them all, you can finally say you know *Everything®*!

QUESTION

Answers to
common questions

FACT

Important snippets
of information

QUOTE

Words of wisdom
from experts in
the field

ESSENTIAL

Quick
handy tips

PUBLISHER Karen Cooper
DIRECTOR OF ACQUISITIONS AND INNOVATION Paula Munier
MANAGING EDITOR, EVERYTHING® SERIES Lisa Laing
COPY CHIEF Casey Ebert
ASSISTANT PRODUCTION EDITOR Jacob Erickson
ACQUISITIONS EDITOR Hillary Thompson
ASSOCIATE DEVELOPMENT EDITOR Hillary Thompson
EDITORIAL ASSISTANT Ross Weisman
EVERYTHING® SERIES COVER DESIGNER Erin Alexander
LAYOUT DESIGNERS Colleen Cunningham, Elisabeth Lariviere, Ashley Vierra, Denise Wallace

THE
EVERYTHING®
GUIDE TO
CATHOLICISM

A complete introduction to the beliefs, traditions,
and tenets of the Catholic Church from past to present

Richard Gribble, CSC, PhD

Avon, Massachusetts

An Everything® Series Book.
Everything® and everything.com® are registered trademarks of F+W Media, Inc.

Published by Adams Media, a division of F+W Media, Inc.
57 Littlefield Street, Avon, MA 02322 U.S.A.
www.adamsmedia.com

ISBN 10: 1-4405-0409-1
ISBN 13: 978-1-4405-0409-9
eISBN 10: 1-4405-0410-5
eISBN 13: 978-1-4405-0410-5

Printed in the United States of America.

10 9 8 7 6 5 4 3 2 1

Library of Congress Cataloging-in-Publication Data
Gribble, Richard.
The everything guide to Catholicism / Richard Gribble.
p. cm.
Includes bibliographical references and index.
ISBN 978-1-4405-0409-9 (alk. paper)
1. Catholic Church—Doctrines. 2. Theology, Doctrinal—Popular works. 3. Catholic Church—
Customs and practices. I. Title.
BX1754.G73 2011
230'.209—dc22
2010038518

This book is available at quantity discounts for bulk purchases.
For information, please call 1-800-289-0963.

Photos on pages 3, 17, 184, 205, 244 were taken from stock photo CD "Religions of the World" by
Steve Allen, Brand X Pictures © 2001.

Photos on pages 32, 52, 68, 87, 113, 120, 144, 159 were taken from stock photo CD "The Christian
Faith" by LushPix Value © Unlisted Images, Inc.

Contents

Dedication

Stonehill College, a small Catholic liberal arts institution of higher education in North Easton, Massachusetts, is where I call home and the school
where I teach. Since 1995 I have had the privilege of sharing my faith,
both academically and spiritually, with some wonderful students. Since
the genesis of this project came at the request of a former student, it is
appropriate that this book be dedicated to all of my former students at
Stonehill who have helped me to be a better teacher, scholar, Catholic,
and priest.

Acknowledgments

This book would not have been possible without four important people.
First, I want to thank Ms. Hillary Thompson, the one who invited me into
this project and who has guided it from the outset to its completion. Secondly, I wish to acknowledge my spiritual director, Father Richard Segreve,
CSC, who helps me to understand my faith in the complex world. I thank
Father Bob Kruse, CSC, for reading and commenting on this manuscript.
Lastly, I wish to thank my dear friend Sister Tania Santander Atauchi, CDP,
who over the last decade has helped me to deepen my appreciation for
the richness of Catholicism.

The Top 10 Things Everyone Should Know about Catholicism

1. The Catholic Bible contains seven additional books in the Old Testament not found in Protestant Bibles.

2. The pope is elected by a secret conclave of the world's cardinals who are younger than eighty years of age.

3. St. Thomas Aquinas, one of the most brilliant scholars in all history, was referred to as the "Dumb Ox" because of his great size and humility.

4. Pope Julius II was both a warrior and a patron of the arts. He was the one who commissioned Michelangelo to paint the ceiling of the Sistine Chapel.

5. St. Anthony of Padua is the patron saint of those looking for lost items.

6. Marriage is the only one of the seven sacraments in which the minister performing the rite is not the priest or bishop; the bride and groom are the ministers of the sacrament.

7. Between 1409 and 1415 there were actually three popes reigning at the same time: one in Pisa, a second one in Avignon, and the third in Rome. This period was known as the Great Western Schism.

8. The dogma of papal infallibility has been invoked only once since it was proclaimed at the Vatican I in 1870. The occasion was the definition of the Assumption of Mary into heaven by Pope Pius XII in 1950.

9. Elizabeth Ann Seton was the first United States–born canonized saint.

10. Since 1850 Catholics have represented the largest single religious denomination in the United States. Today Catholics represent approximately 23 percent of the population.

Introduction

RELIGIOUS TRADITIONS HAVE BEEN part of human civilization from the very outset. Most ancient peoples for whom we have historical records—the Egyptians and Mesopotamians, along with the great civilizations of the Greeks and Romans—had significant traditions of gods and goddesses, many of whom were immortalized in mythology. Ancient religions in the East, beginning with the Hindus and moving forward chronologically with the Buddhists, Daoists, and Confucianists, sought answers to the basic questions of life: Who am I? Why am I here?

It was the great Western religious traditions, however, that began the concept of monotheism. The Jews, the chosen people of God, were formed when Abram (later Abraham) left his native land of Ur. He journeyed west at the request of God to a land today known as the nation of Israel. This Promised Land would actually become sacred to all three great Western religious traditions: Judaism, Christianity, and Islam. The long history of the Jews, including their sojourn in Egypt and emancipation from slavery at the hands of Moses, their journey in the desert, arrival in the Promised Land, and their eventual development of a monarchy, set the stage for further developments. Later, the prophets proclaimed the message of God to their fellow Jews before, during, and after the infamous Babylonian exile. Eventually the Roman Diaspora in A.D. 70 scattered the Jews from their homeland; they were not to return until 1948 with the formation of the present state of Israel.

Christianity, centered on the life and mission of Jesus of Nazareth, was chronologically the second great monotheistic religion to evolve in the Holy Land. Initially the faith grew slowly, primarily through the work of St. Paul, but with the Edict of Milan in 313, Christianity became the religion of the Roman Empire. In the seventh century the prophet Mohammed inaugurated a revolution on the Arabian Peninsula. Islam, meaning one who submits, spread rapidly both east and west over the next several centuries, becoming dominant in the Middle East and extending as far north as Spain. Jerusalem is sacred to Muslims as the site of Mohammed's "night journey" in 620.

Roman Catholicism is the contemporary manifestation of those first followers of Jesus Christ. Over the 2,000 years of the Common Era, Catholicism has been responsible for the construction of Western civilization. The church was the institution at the forefront in the areas of education, science, art and architecture, structures of international law, economics, and Western morality. During the past 2,000 years, much of what Catholicism teaches, while always consistent with the tradition, has evolved in its understanding.

Catholicism is a complex faith rooted in sacraments, dogma, doctrine, and a highly organized hierarchical structure. This book seeks to present a systematic approach to the study of Catholicism. To that end, this guide is divided into seven sections: History, Revelation, God, Roman Catholic Theology, Study of the Church (Ecclesiology), Spirituality, and Contemporary Issues. It is hoped that you will not only be engaged but challenged while reading this book. *The Everything® Guide to Catholicism* not only presents the teachings of Catholicism, but for those who are Catholic, it provides a challenge to abide more fully in church doctrine.

My hope is that this volume will be the catalyst that will increase your desire to learn more about this fascinating religious tradition. Each of the chapters in this book can be studied at greater length and depth. Certainly there will be some topics that will strike you more powerfully than others. I hope that this guide will inspire you to read more detailed studies in Catholicism to satisfy your interests and assist your faith perspective, both academically and spiritually.

CHAPTER 1

The Apostolic, Patristic, and Medieval Church (0–1400)

History provides a rich context to what Christians believe through the movements, events, and significant personalities that have molded both the beliefs and legacy of the faith. The study of Roman Catholicism, therefore, must begin by providing insight to the 2,000 years of Christian history. This story has been the foundation for Western civilization in the Common Era. The first 1,400 years of Christian history describe a movement from obscurity to a position of dominance in society.

Life, Death, and Resurrection of Jesus

Christian history begins with and is centered on the person of Jesus Christ, whom believers proclaim to be the Son of God and divine. Unfortunately, extant historical sources give us very little information about the historical Jesus. The first-century Jewish historian, Josephus, in his treatise *The Antiquities of the Jews*, provides some information on the career of one named Jesus. A second passage in the same work describes Jesus as the brother of James, possibly James the Just, who became the leader of the nascent Christian community in Jerusalem after Jesus' death. The Roman historian Tacitus in Book 15 of his work *Annals* mentions a certain *Christus* who was crucified by the order of Pontius Pilate during the reign of the Emperor Tiberius. The principal source of information about Jesus is found in the Gospels of Matthew, Mark, Luke, and John. From these latter four texts the basic story of Jesus' life, death, and resurrection, which is central to all Christian thought, emerges.

QUESTION

Why do some scholars challenge the historical accuracy of the Gospels?
The simple answer is that these four accounts of Jesus' life often describe similar events but with many differences in details concerning time, place, and specifics of what occurred. The evangelists sought to explain the events to specific peoples; contemporary historical accuracy was not a significant concern.

Jesus of History and Faith

The question of the historical Jesus has captivated scholars since the late eighteenth century, and it continues to be a question today. What precisely can we know about Jesus from a historical perspective? As discussed in Chapter 5, the Gospels were not written as historical biographies of Jesus of Nazareth, but rather as expressions of faith that sought to present to various communities in antiquity the life and mission of Jesus. This question of the historical veracity of the sources that describe Jesus' life reached its peak in late-nineteenth-century work *The Quest for the Historical Jesus* by Albert

Schweitzer. What Schweitzer said was that, from an academic historical perspective, little can be verified historically about the actual events of Jesus' life save that he was born, lived and traveled in Palestine, was ordered executed, and was proclaimed by his followers to have risen from the dead.

Christianity, and, therefore, Roman Catholicism, while premised on a strong historical foundation, is rooted in faith. The Christ of faith, which affirms that Jesus of Nazareth was the long-awaited Messiah, is the concept of how Jesus Christ was understood by his followers, both during his lifetime and through two millennia of Christian history. Belief in the mission and message of Jesus as the Messiah sent by God as Savior of the world is the foundation upon which Roman Catholicism is based. It is essential to understand that the Christ of faith—that is, how people understand Jesus' mission and message—is rooted in the historical reality of Jesus' life. Pope Benedict XVI, in his book *Jesus of Nazareth*, accurately responds to the perception by some that the historical and faith elements of Jesus cannot be reconciled. He wrote, "Where is the post-Easter faith supposed to have come from if Jesus made no foundation for it before Easter?" In other words, the Christ of faith must be based on a historical Jesus.

ESSENTIAL

The confession of faith by Peter in Matthew's Gospel (16:15–16) is central to idea of the Christ of faith: "He [Jesus] said to them, 'But who do you say that I am?' Simon Peter answered, 'You are the Messiah, the Son of the living God.'" Peter and the other apostles believed Jesus was divine.

What the Gospels Say about Jesus

While the Gospel accounts vary in details, the life, mission, and message of Jesus is clear and consistent. Jesus of Nazareth was born in Bethlehem, in 3 B.C.E. He lived in relative obscurity in Nazareth, the hometown of Mary, his mother, and Joseph, his foster father, until he was approximately thirty years old. For the next one to three years, the Gospel accounts vary. Jesus was engaged in an active apostolic ministry, traveling throughout the regions of Galilee and Judea, and on occasion outside Palestine, proclaiming a message that sought to fulfill the predictions of Hebrew prophets and to blaze a new path that, as Jesus himself says, brings fulfillment to the Hebrew law (Matthew 5:17). During his active ministry, Jesus gathered a select group of twelve men, whom he named apostles. After Jesus' death, these were the ones specifically tasked with evangelization of the nations.

QUOTE

Jesus' final instructions to his apostles before leaving the earth were to evangelize the nations: "Go therefore and make disciples of all nations, baptizing them in the name of the Father and of the Son and of the Holy Spirit and teaching them to obey everything that I have commanded you." (Matthew 28:19–20a)

Jesus' message was highly controversial with the Jewish religious elite, for he challenged their authority and belief in the absolutism of the law. This conflict became so severe that ultimately in 30 C.E. Jesus was sentenced to death and executed by crucifixion at the hands of the Romans, the occupying force in Palestine. The Gospel accounts all agree that this event happened on a Friday and that on the ensuing Sunday morning, Jesus rose from the dead, appearing to his apostles and to others on numerous occasions. After some time (tradition has set this as forty days), Jesus ascended to heaven.

Acts of the Apostles

Commonly called the fifth Gospel, the Acts of the Apostles narrates two important stories: the growth of the nascent Christian community and the

ul. Acts says that shortly after Jesus' ascension, the Holy
ter 10) came upon the apostles and a few other disciples,
community with special gifts to continue the work of Jesus
fear that had gripped the community since the ascension.
speaks of Peter, leader of the apostles, and his initial evange-
. Additionally, we learn of the growth and spread of the com-
as first referred to as Christians in the city of Antioch. Lastly,
hat the tensions between the Jewish religious elite and the
istian community continued until it became clear that Chris-
parate; they could no longer be a group within Judaism.

nistry of St. Paul

ance of the career of Paul of Tarsus, the first and primary evan-
theologian of Christianity, cannot be underestimated. Paul, a
arisaic Jew, well-educated and schooled in the law, experienced
when Jesus appeared to him while traveling to Damascus on a
persecute Christians. Paul spent the next several years prepar-
at became a ministry to Gentiles. Biblical scholars suggest Paul
years 47–60 traveling the eastern Mediterranean on three arduous
ry journeys, during which he established Christian communities.
he went initially to the local synagogue, but then branched out to
he message of Jesus to all who would listen, most notably Greek

ESSENTIAL

he Council of Jerusalem (49 c.e.), it was determined that Gentiles
not need to abide by Jewish law and undergo ritual circumcision
in order to be baptized as Christians. This decision was critically important for the advancement of Christianity since the emerging faith
could now expand on its own and not as a subcategory of Judaism.

All of Paul's letters (save Romans and Philemon, see Chapter 5) were
addressed to Christian communities that Paul founded during these
three missionary journeys. Although not systematic in their theology, the

teachings in these documents became fundamental church doctrine, including instructions on marriage and divorce, the second coming of Christ, church organization, and justification and salvation.

Christianity and the Roman Empire

Initially, Christians were viewed by the Romans as a sect of Judaism and thus tolerated. However, beginning with the reign of Emperor Nero (64–66 c.e.), Christians were persecuted due to their perceived threat to the state, their abandonment of the Roman gods, and their repugnance of military service. Christians were used as scapegoats when external problems such as war and economic failure threatened the empire. Persecutions of Christians were both general and more localized. The campaigns of Nero, Domitian (95), and Trajan (111) were strong but local in character. However, Decius (249–251), Valerian (258–260), and Diocloetian (303–305) conducted general persecutions, leading many to apostatize and creating many martyrs. These persecutions ended in 313 with the publication of the Edict of Milan by the Emperor Constantine the Great. The conversion of the emperor shortly thereafter was transformative for Christianity, as almost overnight the faith went from being forbidden to being the standard religion of the empire.

Orthodoxy and Heresy

Recognition of Christianity in the early fourth century did not mean that within the community of faith all was settled; rather, many disagreements concerning theology arose, most especially teachings concerning God as Trinity (see Chapter 8) and Jesus Christ (see Chapter 9). There was no clear division between orthodoxy—that which is accepted as correct and proper teaching—and heresy—false teachings (heterodoxy). In their attempts to understand and articulate the faith, Christians lapsed into various teachings that over the course of history have been condemned as heretical.

During the patristic church (0–600), these heresies were grouped in two basic categories: those associated with the Trinity and those associated with Jesus Christ. During the third, fourth, and fifth centuries, Christians battled each other in an effort to try to understand the mystery of God. Subordinationism, the idea that the Father, Son, and Holy Spirit are not co-equal; Sabellianism, or modalism, the belief that God appears in different modes throughout history (Creator, Redeemer, and Sanctifier); and tritheism, the belief that the Trinity was actually three gods, were the principal heresies concerning the theology of God. Heresies also arose concerning the person of Jesus. Arianism, which dominated the church in the fourth century, was the belief that Jesus, because he was the only begotten Son of God, could not be divine.

In response to Arianism, in the fourth century, Appolinarius emphasized the divinity of Christ to the detriment of his humanity. In the fifth century, Nestorius went to the opposite extreme, denying that Mary was the mother of God (*Theotokos*) but rather was only the mother of the human Jesus. This meant that at some time, God "adopted" the human Jesus, making him divine. Only in 451 at the Council of Chalcedon was the orthodox teaching regarding Jesus formally defined.

Saints Augustine and Thomas Aquinas

The first 1,400 years of Christian history generated numerous significant personalities, both pious and saintly individuals and others who made significant contributions. Two of the most famous during this period were Saints Augustine (354–430) and Thomas Aquinas (1215–1274). Each of these men became towering figures in the history of Christianity and Roman Catholic theology.

St. Augustine

Augustine was the son of a saintly woman, Monica, and a pagan father, Patricius. During his youth and early adulthood he searched for a way to harness and utilize his brilliant intellect. A teacher of rhetoric, he initially tried Manichaeism, a dualistic philosophy contrasting good and evil, but after some years found it empty of meaning. Eventually he was converted to Christianity, becoming bishop at Hippo (North Africa). Through his voluminous writings, including his autobiography, *The Confessions*, he became known as the "Father of grace," a title he earned through his insistence that the grace of God was absolutely necessary for human salvation. In his long life he gained recognition for his intellect and his courageous fight against two heretical groups, the Donatists and the Pelagians.

St. Thomas Aquinas

Thomas Aquinas was a Dominican friar whose theology, called Scholasticism, based on the philosophy of Aristotle, was dominant in the church for nearly 800 years and continues to be highly significant today. His *Summa Theologica* was his magnum opus; its methodology, theology, and philosophical approach became standard in the Catholic world for several centuries and re-emerged in the nineteenth century as Neoscholasticism.

Catholicism in the Medieval World

The church's integral position in society was fundamental to medieval Europe. It was a time when only those who held orthodox beliefs could be considered worthy members of society. Medieval scholar R. W. Southern aptly has stated, "In a word, the church was a compulsory society in precisely the same way as the modern state is a compulsory society."

Medieval Europe championed the idea that the church could truly claim to be the state; people assumed the church had overriding political authority in all areas. Medieval lords and their feudal system of serfdom were subservient to the power of local bishops and ultimately to the pope. The commanding position of respect held by the papacy provided unity to the diverse cultures and peoples of western Europe.

The church of the Middle Ages produced an intellectually gifted clergy through the rise of universities, which became a significant force in Italy, France, and England in the late eleventh and twelfth centuries. The University of Bologna (1088) is often argued to be the first great medieval university. Movement away from the feudal system to a more urbanized society created a demand for better-trained clergy. Prior to this time priestly education was largely confined to monasteries and cathedral schools. However, with the reform of Pope Gregory VII (1073–1085), a more advanced training ground for clergy was necessary. Higher education was essential to development of the church and advancement in the hierarchy. It also became the training ground for the great theologians including Thomas Aquinas, Bonaventure, and Peter Abelard.

Christianity and Islam

Yet, this was also a time when the inferiority of Western culture to that of the Greeks and the burgeoning Muslim community also became obvious. The Eastern Church, headquartered at Constantinople, produced the vast majority of theologians and other significant thinkers and personalities that advanced the cause of the church. Western Christendom had survived the onslaught of the barbarians only to play second fiddle to Constantinople while simultaneously being beleaguered by its greatest enemy, Islam. Islam began in the early seventh century in Arabia and spread widely and rapidly east and west, and made a significant presence on the Iberian Peninsula and in the Holy Land.

The response of the papacy to Islam was the period of Crusades (1095–1272). This series of military campaigns, led by the Latin (Western) Church, especially the kings of France and the Holy Roman Emperors, was waged to regain control of the Holy Land from Muslims. There were nine numbered Crusades during this approximate 200-year period, but several additional forays, including the Albigensian (1209) and Children's Crusades (1212), plus other battles in Spain and eastern Europe, were waged. Intense religious fervor of this era was an important ingredient to the start of these military campaigns, which generally ended in failure. Several of these Crusades, most notably the Fourth (1202–1204), were diverted from their original goals. While the Crusades were not successful in returning the Holy Land to Christian control, the adverse ramifications of these actions in Christian-Muslim relations continues to be felt today.

Church and State Relations

Theoretically, the appointment of church officials had always been the purview of the papacy, but with the decline of political power in the West, including the papacy, the responsibility and privilege of investiture of bishops, including the selection of the pope, fell to secular officials. This situation left the church powerless to address corruption, especially the practice of simony (the buying and selling of church offices), as bishops answered in matters of authority to the state.

FACT

The Papal Bull, *Unam Sanctum* (1302), issued by Boniface VIII, proclaimed that the church held power of "two swords," the spiritual and temporal. It went on to say, "The one sword, then, should be under the other, and the temporal authority subject to spiritual." This decree ended secular control of church offices.

In 1075, in response to this situation, Pope Gregory VII proclaimed that the pontiff alone held universal power, gaining this authority directly from God. The Holy Roman Emperor, Henry IV, rejected Gregory's claim. Eventually the balance of power shifted to the Church and Henry was forced to repent.

The Orthodox-Catholic Split

Christianity was born and matured during the time of the Roman Empire. The division of the empire initiated by Diocletian in the early fourth century became permanent less than 100 years later. While the West collapsed in the fifth century, the East at Byzantium (Constantinople) continued to flourish. This political division spilled over into the church. Beyond politics, other factors such as language and culture created a greater gap between these powers. Over time the two halves of the church developed different rites and held different approaches to religious doctrines. These conditions laid the foundation for the Great Schism between the Eastern Orthodox and Roman Catholic faiths that continues today.

The primary cause of the split was a conflict over papal authority in the East. During the patristic period, the church was organized with four patriarchs in the East (Constantinople, Alexandria, Antioch, and Jerusalem) and the patriarch of Rome. Conflict arose when Pope Leo IX in the mid-eleventh century claimed authority over the four Eastern patriarchs. In response, the Eastern bishops referred to decrees from earlier church councils, especially Chalcedon (451), which proclaimed the equality of the Bishops of Rome and Constantinople. Additionally, the Eastern bishops rejected the

Latin Church's insertion in 1014 of the *filioque* (and the Holy Spirit) clause into the Nicene Creed, originally written at the first Ecumenical Council of Nicaea (325) and later modified at Constantinople I (381).

These disputes, combined with other differences in practice, including liturgical rites (such as Rome's use of unleavened bread for the Eucharist) and the West's insistence upon celibacy for priests, plus the loss of Alexandria, Jerusalem, and Antioch to Islam, drove the two sides further apart. An infamous verbal conflict between the Patriarch of Constantinople, Michael Cerularius, and legates (personal representatives) of Pope Leo IX led to mutual excommunication orders. Still, despite anger on both sides, the two divisions of Christendom were not fully conscious of a permanent separation. The situation was exacerbated greatly, however, during the Fourth Crusade (1202–1204) when Crusaders from the West, originally destined for Jerusalem, were diverted and sacked Constantinople. Two Councils, Lyons (1274) and Florence (1439), made efforts to find a solution to the schism, but officials in the East eventually rejected the Councils' decrees. The loss of Constantinople in 1451 to the Ottoman Turks made the breach between East and West permanent.

CHAPTER 2

The Reformation and Counter Reformation (1400–1648)

Christianity today is experienced as a multitude of faith communities with a common bond of belief in the Trinity and Jesus as Lord. Christianity began as a united faith, but the Great Schism that separated the Orthodox East from the Roman West broke this unity. The Protestant Reformation of the sixteenth century, however, was the event that splintered Christianity into the types of faiths we see today. The story of this fracture and the church's response are critical to the understanding of Roman Catholicism today.

The Great Western Schism

Since the time of St. Peter, understood by Roman Catholics to be Jesus choice as the first pope (Matthew 16:18), Rome was the host city, or see, for the papacy. However, in 1305, Clement V, a Frenchman from Gascony, was elected pope. Believing that he owed his election to French clerics, he decided not to go to Rome but rather set up his administration in Avignon, France, along the Mediterranean Sea.

Avignon Papacy

Clement's breach of tradition required some rationale. He claimed that Avignon was more centrally located in the empire and, therefore, better for communication. Additionally, the need for connection to the French court made Avignon a most appropriate location for the pope. Lastly, Avignon enjoyed much better weather and was a generally more pleasant place to live than Rome.

Clement died in 1314, but the next six successors to the papacy, all Frenchmen, continued his rebellion and remained in Avignon. This domination, the ties of these men to their native land, and the perception that there was no ostensible reason to return to Rome kept the papacy in Avignon until the reign of Pope Gregory XI (1370–1378). Although Gregory remained subject to the influence of the French court, political and economic turmoil in Italy (which threatened papal lands in that region as well as allegiance to the pope himself) forced Gregory to consider a return to Rome. Additionally, the pope was influenced by St. Catherine of Siena, who convinced him to return to Rome in 1376. The Avignon papacy had ended.

The Schism Begins

The end of the Avignon papacy did not bring peace but rather was the initial salvo in the greatest split in Western Christendom's history. During its sojourn in Avignon, the papacy had earned a reputation for corruption, and when Gregory XI died in 1378, the citizenry of Rome demanded a Roman be elected pope, especially after seven successive French pontiffs. The Archbishop of Bari was elected and took the name Urban VI. However, not long after the Cardinal electors concluded their work, they began to regret their decision. Urban was overbearing and prone to violent anger, and appeared to be mentally unstable. Therefore, claiming they had made a mistake, the Cardinals elected Robert of Geneva as a new pope. Taking the name Clement VII, he returned to Avignon. Meanwhile, Urban refused to abdicate, as he was a validly elected pope. The Western Schism had begun.

Solving the Crisis

Between 1378 and 1409, the two rival popes with their loyal constituencies continued to reign in Rome and Avignon. This intolerable situation was eventually addressed in 1409 when a council was called at Pisa to bring unity to the papacy. The council deposed both reigning popes, Benedict XIII in Avignon and Gregory XII in Rome, and elected a new man, Alexander V. Alexander lived only a very short time and was replaced by John XXIII. However, Benedict and Gregory, believing their elections to be valid, refused to leave, thus creating a situation with three popes: one in Rome, a second in Avignon, and a third in Pisa.

FACT

The Council of Constance produced *Sacrosancta*, a document that claimed the council held authority immediately from Christ and, therefore, held power even over the pope. This claim of jurisdiction was essential in deposing the three reigning popes, leading to the election of Martin V.

The Western Schism ended as a result of the Council of Constance (1414–1418). In 1415, John XXIII was deposed. Gregory XII in Rome agreed to step down so long as a Roman was elected to secure the legitimacy of the Roman line. In turn, Benedict in Avignon, without sufficient support, was excommunicated. The Council of Constance then elected Martin V to be the rightful successor to the chair of Peter. The Western Schism finally ended.

The Catholic Reformation

The Avignon papacy and the Western Schism provide a general but accurate picture of the state of Christendom at the dawn of the sixteenth century. The unsettled conditions of the church, which these events illustrate, were found in other areas as well. During its 1,500 years of history, multiple abuses had gradually crept into the church. Some of these common abuses were the buying and selling of indulgences, benefices, and bishoprics (office and responsibility given to a local bishop), the widespread practice of simony, and the granting of dispensations based on payment. Additionally, significant problems with the clergy, including immorality, ignorance, and lack of training, and the refusal of many bishops and pastors to reside in their diocese or parish, were common and widespread. These problems led to an almost universal cry for reformation within the church.

Christian Humanism

The problems and abuses present in the church of the sixteenth century required resolution. Long before famous personalities such as Martin Luther and John Calvin pressed for reform, Catholics, understanding within their own ranks the need for change, made significant efforts toward reform. Christian humanism, a scholarly path that sought to correct problems by using ancient texts as the guiding principle for religious reform, was the first approach to correct the problems.

Three of the most famous Christian humanists were Erasmus, Cardinal Francisco Ximenes, and John Colet. In his day, Erasmus was an ecclesiastical superstar using satire to comment on church policies and the hierarchy. One of his most famous books, *In Praise of Folly* (1511), raised the concern of many church officials because of its biting criticism of many church practices, but people knew he was correct and understood it as an effort to reform morals and structures of Christian society. Cardinal Francisco Ximenes, Primate of Spain (1495–1517), led a team of scholars that completed the Complutensian Polyglot Bible, providing the Scriptures in Hebrew, Greek, and Latin. John Colet, an English theologian, was one of the first to engage in scriptural exegesis (analysis of the Bible). He saw the Scriptures as a guide to life and the road to a renewed theology and revival of Christianity in his day.

Reform of Policy

In addition to Christian humanism, Catholics sought reform through changes in policy. Nicholas of Cusa, Cardinal Archbishop of Trier (1400–1464), initiated a campaign to reform the German Church. He set up regulations to control both clerics and laity and enacted laws to counter simony and concubinage. He enforced the powers of local bishops and assured papal bulls and other documents were followed. Gasparo Contarini, a layman elevated to the position of cardinal in 1535, headed a team appointed by Pope Paul III that identified abuses and made recommendations for their correction. Their report, the *Consilium de Emendanda de Ecclesiae*, outlined numerous abuses and suggested answers could be found by reform within the church.

QUESTION

If the cry for reformation was loud and long in the first days of the sixteenth century, why did an official papal response take so long?
Basically, the popes realized the need for change must start with them, and many were unwilling to reform. Contarini's report of 1537 noted papal responsibility for the situation and the need for immediate change.

Formation of New Religious Orders

The Catholic Reformation was also manifested through the inauguration of new religious orders. Like monasticism and the mendicant orders in earlier centuries, which sought to address specific needs, new communities arose in the early sixteenth century to initiate reform among priests and religious. The Capuchins and Conventuals, derivatives of the Franciscans founded in the thirteenth century, sought reform within this particular religious congregation. The Oratory of Divine Love (1516), Theatines (1524), and Barnabites (1533) were new religious congregations that sought pastoral and parochial renewal.

The Protestant and Radical Reformers

The Catholic Reformation sought to eliminate abuses and steer Catholicism and the papacy toward calmer waters, but other forces in the sixteenth century saw greater reform and a new direction for the church. Collectively known as the Protestant Reformation, these groups, led by powerful and charismatic individuals, broke free from Roman Catholicism, leading to the plethora of Christian groups present in the twenty-first century. The Protestant reformers initially sought only administrative change within Roman Catholicism, but gradually when their appeals for change fell on deaf ears, their protests became stronger and highly theological, creating a deep split between these new groups and Roman Catholicism.

The Reform of Martin Luther

Martin Luther was an Augustinian friar and professor of Scripture at the University of Wittenburg. As a result of his study of Scripture, he began to agonize over the question of personal salvation: What was necessary to be justified to God? During his famous "Tower Experience" (1512), Luther, using his expertise in Scripture and concentrating on Paul's letters to the Galatians (2:16) and Romans (3:28–31), concluded that justification was not based on works but rather on faith alone. Thus, Luther established the first half of his famous twofold battle cry: *Sola fide, sola scriptura* (faith alone, Scripture alone).

Conscious of the many aforementioned abuses present in the church during his day, especially the buying and selling of indulgences, Luther responded on October 31, 1517, with the publication of his Ninety-Five Theses. Luther's document sought to articulate and seek resolution to abuses that centered about indulgences and abusive papal power. Over the next few years Luther sought to defend his position against church authorities who considered his position, especially his rejection of papal authority, to be heretical. Luther was ordered to recant his position at the

Diet of Augsburg (1518), but he refused. Finally on January 3, 1521, he was excommunicated. One final opportunity for resolution at the Diet of Worms (April 18, 1521) also failed; a permanent break was now evident.

ESSENTIAL

Luther was successful while earlier reformers failed for numerous reasons. His views were widely published through the use of printing. He appealed to economics, pointing out that indulgences were expensive. He used the vernacular language in Scripture, because average people could not read Latin or Greek. He also appealed to German nationalism. Finally, people were attracted to his charismatic personality.

Luther's initial call for administrative change was extended to theological reform through his famous treatises of 1520. In his "To the Christian Nobility of the German Nation" and "The Babylonian Captivity of the Church," Luther vehemently attacked the papacy, suggesting that papal control had denied the state temporal authority and usurped powers from bishops and the laity. Theologically, he rejected the concept of transubstantiation (see Chapter 11) and the principle that the Mass was a sacrifice. Eventually, Luther rejected the sacraments, save baptism, Eucharist, and (to some extent) penance.

John Calvin and the Reformed Tradition

John Calvin, a layman living in Geneva, came to prominence in 1536. Like Luther, he too sought to reform Roman Catholicism, concentrating on a return to moral order. Coming after Luther's official break, from the outset Calvin sought a new direction outside Roman Catholicism. He gained a loyal following even more from his exemplary and disciplined life than from his teaching.

Calvin's revolt, referred to as the Reformed Tradition, became the norm for Protestantism outside those loyal to Luther. His theology moved further away from Roman Catholic teaching. Calvin was an advocate of predestination, the concept that Christ did not come to die for all but only for the elect. He moved beyond Luther's teaching on the Eucharist, seeing the bread and wine as simply symbolic of Christ; the Catholic teaching of Christ's real presence was rejected. The Reformed Tradition placed a high importance on moral discipline while seeking an austere simplicity in worship.

The Radical Reformers

Radical Reformers were a third branch of the Protestant Reformation. Believing that Luther and Calvin had not moved sufficiently far from Roman Catholic theology and practice, the Radical Reformers broke from the Lutheran and Reformed communities to form small communities throughout western Europe. Rather than dominating certain regions or countries, as did Lutheranism and the Reformed Tradition, Radical Reformers formed small isolated groups that existed within the dominant Catholic, Lutheran, or Reformed communities.

The theology of the Radical Reformers was consistent with their isolated and extreme position. These groups practiced adult baptism, advocated separation from the world, condemned the use of force and taking oaths, rejected military service, and refused to pay taxes that supported beliefs contrary to their thinking. Radical Reformers, seen today in the Amish, Moravian, and Mennonite communities, were often hated, a reality that only exacerbated their isolated position.

The English Reformation

King Henry VIII in England seemed the most unlikely of religious reformers. His initial denouncement of Luther's revolt gained him the title "Defender of the Faith" from Pope Leo X in 1521. Yet by 1532, Henry found himself in deep conflict with Rome. Married to Catherine of Aragon as a result of a special dispensation from the pope, Henry wanted to dissolve his marriage because his wife had not produced a male heir. When the pope rejected Henry's claim that his marriage to Catherine was unlawful, he proceeded to move away from papal authority and in 1534 through his *Act of Supremacy* declared himself head of the Church in England.

The English Reformation was initially based on power and control; there were virtually no theological differences with Roman Catholicism. As time passed and the separation widened, however, theological and disciplinary differences, for example clerical celibacy, became more evident. Even today, the Anglican faith (called the Episcopalian Church in the

United States) is the religious tradition most closely aligned theologically with Roman Catholicism.

The Counter Reformation

The four branches of the Protestant Reformation generated a significant response from Roman Catholicism. The Catholic Reformation had sought to reform those administrative problems and abuses that over the centuries had become accepted practice in the church. The Counter Reformation, however, was a deliberate rejection, a counteroffensive against the theological positions held by various Protestant groups. The frontal assault of Protestantism was answered by Roman Catholicism with a two-front counterattack: the work of the Society of Jesus, commonly known as the Jesuits, and the Council of Trent (1545–1563).

The Society of Jesus

The Society of Jesus was an instrumental force in the Counter Reformation. The society was founded by St. Ignatius of Loyola, a former soldier who was transformed to a vocation to serve God while recovering from wounds received in a battle. Initially frustrated in his attempts to become a priest, he was eventually ordained. In 1534 he and six compatriots joined together in a brotherhood with the desire to place themselves at the service of the pope. Six years later in 1540 the Society of Jesus was officially recognized as a religious order.

The Jesuits grew rapidly, numbering over 1,000 members by the time of Ignatius's death in 1556. They were highly influential due to their extensive work in education. With the Protestant Reformation raging all over Europe, the Jesuits were a significant counterforce that sought to re-establish the authority of the papacy and to uphold Roman Catholic theology. As educators of future priests, members of the hierarchy, and the elite of society, the Jesuits had the position and the ability to stand against the tide of the Reformation.

The Council of Trent

The Council of Trent, conducted in three discontinuous sessions between December 1545 and December 1563, was unquestionably the most significant council of its time, and possibly the most significant of the twenty-one councils in history. Catholics believed that substantive reform could only come through a council, but opinions on who should call such an assembly and the unwillingness of popes to initiate reform delayed action. When reform came, opinions varied on a basic question: should the church accommodate Protestants or reject their ideas? In many ways the Council of Trent was a triumph of conservatives and militants over more conciliatory and liberal forces.

QUOTE

At Trent session IV, April 8, 1546, the Council Fathers stated, "This discipline [the teaching of Christ] is contained in written books and unwritten traditions, which were received by the Apostles from the lips of Christ himself . . . and were handed on and have come down to us."

The council addressed the two primary categories of the Reformation separately. The bishops believed that the administrative and discipline questions raised by the Protestant Reformers had merit, especially when the Catholic Reformation, prior to Luther's revolt, had recognized the same problems and sought their resolution. In an effort to strengthen and standardize clerical training, the council mandated that all dioceses establish seminaries to educate clerical candidates. Clerical discipline was addressed by maintaining residency requirements for priests and bishops in their respective parishes and dioceses. Bishops were given greater supervisory roles and power to adequately supervise priests, religious orders, and church holdings. The buying and selling of indulgences was eliminated.

The council's reform in areas of administration and discipline was balanced by a strong rejection of the theology proposed by the Protestant reformers. The council declared that faith alone was insufficient for justification; faith accompanied by manifestations of love and work was necessary for salvation. Luther's notion that Sacred Tradition (see Chapter 5) had no place in Revelation was rejected; Scripture and Tradition were part of Revelation. The council upheld the validity of the seven sacraments and rejected all ideas that the Eucharist was not the real presence of Christ. In short, the Council of Trent removed or reformed many administrative and clerical discipline abuses but held fast on all Roman Catholic theological principles, rejecting totally the ideas of the Protestant reformers.

The Era of Exploration

The church of sixteenth-century Europe was under siege with both Catholics and Protestant reformers seeking change, but during the same period of history the church expanded its horizons radically through extensive missionary efforts to the East and the New World. Inspired by the Gospel exhortation to go to all nations and baptize, missionaries encountered new cultures and religions in the East and discovered native peoples in the New World. These brave religious did not see their work as voluntary but rather as a requirement in their role as disciples of Christ.

Missionaries to India, China, and Japan

During the sixteenth and seventeenth centuries, Jesuit missionaries sought converts in the East while introducing Western knowledge to the region. St. Francis Xavier, one of the founding Jesuits, left Europe in 1540 in response to an invitation from King John III of Portugal to restore Christianity to European colonists in Goa on the southern Indian subcontinent and to evangelize local peoples in the same region. Somewhat successful in India, he moved on to Japan, finding greater success. He died on December 3, 1552, en route to China to continue his missionary endeavors. About a half century later another Jesuit, Robert de Nobili, also came to southern India. He pioneered a new theory of evangelization, inculturation, adopting many local customs and ideas not contrary to Christianity in order to find acceptance with the local people. The practice was controversial but highly successful.

Missionaries to the New World

Columbus's discovery of the New World at the end of the fifteenth century brought a new vista for Europe and new opportunities for Christian evangelization. From the outset, Christian missionaries accompanied various explorers and Spanish conquistadors in their quest for fortune and fame. Franciscan friars were integrally involved in efforts to evangelize the native peoples in Mexico, South America, and the west coast of North America. Their method of acculturation operated on the principle in missionary work that nothing in pagan native culture was of value. Rather, the missionaries sought to create a "tabula rasa" (blank slate) in the native population that could then be redrawn on the lines of Spanish Catholicism.

The newly founded Jesuits sent missionaries to the New World as they were simultaneously sending them to the East. French Jesuits arrived in the Great Lakes region of North America in the mid-seventeenth century. Using the inculturation method of Robert de Nobili, these brave missionaries obtained few converts among the North American native tribes while generating several martyrs. Living like the people they sought to evangelize, these missionaries gained much respect in the annals of North American church history.

CHAPTER 3

Revolution and Restoration (1648–1962)

The Reformation and Counter Reformation periods of church history were transformative in the creation of a diversity of Christian denominations. The battles the church faced in the sixteenth century found new manifestations, both internal and external to the institution, over the next two centuries. Disagreements over local versus universal church authority as well as theology occurred simultaneously with the French Revolution and the Napoleonic Wars. These wars transformed the face of Europe, forcing the church to adapt in order to survive.

Gallicanism

The tensions created by the Reformation and the ongoing battle of the Thirty Years' War (1618–1648), a battle between Catholics and Protestants in the Holy Roman Empire, continued in the church toward the close of the seventeenth century. This tension was manifested most clearly in the rise of national churches, collectively referred to as Gallicanism, but given other names in various countries. The Western Schism and the Reformation greatly weakened the power of the papacy from the time of Pope Gregory VII and his triumph over Henry IV during the Investiture Crisis. The Council of Constance proclaimed the authority of the council over the pope, a necessary step in order to end the Western Schism. As a result, national churches, with authority held by local bishops and not the pope, arose with the French Church as the leader. In 1682 the "Declaration of the Clergy of France" proclaimed the French Church to possess higher ecclesiastical authority than the pope. The declaration has been synthesized into what are known as the Four Gallican Articles.

QUOTE

Gallican Article I in part reads: "St. Peter and the popes, his successors, and the Church itself have received dominion from God only over things spiritual and such as concern salvation and not over things temporal and civil. Hence kings and sovereigns are not by God's command subject to any ecclesiastical dominion in things temporal."

Gallicanism (Febronianism in Germany, Josephinism in Austria) gained significant adherents into the eighteenth century. The rise of secular monarchical power at the expense of the pope was indicative of a general slide away from the ecclesiastical authority to one more politically and nationally based. It would not be until the mid-nineteenth century that the church recovered sufficiently to adequately respond by reasserting its authority.

The French Revolution

Historians agree that the French Revolution was a watershed event that led society into the modern age; it brought significant change to the face of Europe. The French Revolution transformed society. It was waged as a response to France's economic woes of the latter eighteenth century, which brought famine and disease and placed the nation on the brink of bankruptcy, as well as political and social factors, such as the Enlightenment's rejection of royal absolutism and the rejection of privileges held by the nobility and clergy. Monarchies throughout the continent fell and were replaced by more democratic and representative national governments.

ESSENTIAL

The Civil Constitution of the Clergy created a schism between those priests who pledged loyalty to the revolutionary government (jurors) and those who remained loyal to Rome (nonjurors). Pope Pius VI never accepted the Civil Constitution, leading to his imprisonment and death and the massacre of many priests in France.

This situation transformed the church as well. The drive for national autonomy within church structures was enhanced greatly by the ideas of the revolution. The church was seen from a national perspective; the local secular ruler, not the pope, was perceived to be the defender of the faith. As a consequence, the church became an agency of the state. In France a massive shifting of power occurred. Under the *ancien régime* the church held power in many different ways, including functioning as the largest landowner in the country. However, shortly after the revolution began, legislation removed church authority to levy taxes; much church property was simply confiscated. Clerical privilege was removed, and by the Civil Constitution of the Clergy, enacted on July 12, 1790, priests and religious were subject to the state, including the need for them to take a loyalty oath. Ultimately, the church was basically proscribed. Sacraments were performed as civil ceremonies; clergy were hunted down as criminals, and people practiced worship of the "Supreme Being," a form of Deism created by Maximilian Robespierre, rather than God.

Napoleon and the Restoration

The political and religious chaos in France was a major factor in the rise of Napoleon Bonaparte as self-proclaimed First Consul in 1799. Bonaparte believed that religion was necessary, but it needed to be controlled by the state. This form of compromise allowed Napoleon to be successful. He was not a man of faith, but he understood the need for the church to support state efforts.

The Concordat of 1801

Napoleon parlayed his more conciliatory position toward the church into creating an advantageous agreement with the papacy. Between November 1800 and July 1801, Bonaparte and papal officials negotiated an agreement, or concordat, between France and the Holy See. This document, signed on July 15, 1801, became a model for the relationship between church and state in many European countries. Its conditions allowed the church to operate, but the state held a tight leash, only allowing the church to operate in a way beneficial to Napoleon and his future plans for conquest. The agreement stated that Catholicism was maintained as the religion of the majority but was not a state religion, as the pope had desired. The church would be allowed to be free and public, but it was still subservient to the state. Along with the general concept of Gallicanism, new diocesan boundaries would be drawn and a totally new hierarchy named by state officials. Lastly, clergy were to swear allegiance to the state and would be paid clerical salaries.

Restoration of the Church

Napoleon's defeat at the hands of the Duke of Wellington at Waterloo on June 18, 1815, allowed peace to come to Europe through the Congress of Vienna (1815). The powers that had defeated Napoleon sent representatives to the congress to realign the European map in order to prevent future political domination that existed during the Napoleonic Wars. The pope was represented by Cardinal Ercole Consalvi. His task was to preserve the Papal States and return them to the church.

Napoleon's defeat also allowed the papacy to re-emerge with greater strength and authority. Pope Pius VII, released from his confinement in

1814, established the Congregation for Extraordinary Affairs, which made suggestions to reorganize the church in the wake of the French dictator. Pius death in April 1823 brought Leo XII to the papacy. On May 5, 1824, Leo issued *Ubi Primum*, an encyclical letter that reasserted that religion must be restored; the church had the duty and the authority to fight against all errors that threatened the faith. Specifically, the document called for religious renewal under the control of the clergy, direct negotiation with national states toward the formation of concordats, and direct association between the papacy and bishops. It moved to root out Gallicanism and similar national church ideologies. Lastly, the encyclical insisted that the Faith must be defended at all costs; the authority of Church officials, subjugated for generations, must now be restored.

The Challenge of the Nineteenth Century

Although the church in the early nineteenth century sought to restore its position and authority, at the same time various forces proclaiming ideologies inconsistent with Roman Catholicism gained strength in Europe. The period of restoration (1815–1830) saw the ascent of the bourgeoise and with it the rise of economic and political liberalism. Politically this meant the doctrine of the "happy mean," a middle ground between the despotism of the *ancien régime* and rule by the masses. The rights of the individual were considered supreme. The philosophy of natural law, which called for the emancipation of each citizen, was used by liberals to justify the political supremacy of the bourgeoise.

Risorgimento and Revolutions

In Italy, political liberalism was experienced through the *Risorgimento*, or national unification drive. At the time of Napoleon's defeat in 1815, the Italian peninsula was a galaxy of city states, including the Papal States that were geographically located in the middle of the "country." Italian patriots held political ideas in line with the emerging bourgeoise attitude in Europe. Thus, a series of uprisings, including skirmishes in Naples and Piedmont in 1821, vaulted the Italian national unification drive onto the international scene.

The *Risorgimento* movement initially had two possible directions, but it settled on a revolutionary path. The chief architect for the movement was Vincenzo Gioberti, who called for a federation of Italian states under the presidency of the pope. However, two revolutionary figures, Giuseppe Garibaldi and Giuseppe Mazzini, who both rejected the church, called for an Italian Republic. Garibaldi was anticlerical but intelligent enough to realize he needed to win the people and the clergy in order to achieve his goal. Mazzini believed in a personal God; he counted on moral forces to attain his ends. It was Camillo di Cavour, however, who was the true architect of national unification. He called for a free church in a free state; the church could claim no privilege but rather must be subject to the law of the land. On May 31, 1871, the Law of Guarantees was passed, depriving the pope of all sovereign lands save the Vatican, the Basilica of St. John Lateran, and Castel Gandolfo, his summer residence. The pope, Pius IX, rejected this legislation completely.

Age of Revolutions

In 1848 the combination of economic crises and political discontent led to a series of revolutions in Europe. Agricultural failures, especially potatoes and grains between 1846 and 1847, created a severe shortage of food. Unemployment caused by competition between domestic industries and automation added to the general woes of people. These economic problems, occurring at a time of political discontent and for many the absence of liberty, caused people to take up arms. Absolute governments in France, Italy, Prussia, and Austria angered people and forced them to action. Thus, in these countries and in the Netherlands, major political revolts occurred.

The Ideological Challenge

Europe in the nineteenth century was a hotbed for liberal and progressive thinking on many fronts. The devastation wrought by the French Revolution and the Napoleonic Wars was the catalyst that generated various responses to the dilemma of society. Liberalism and the rise of the individual, championed by promoters of the French Revolution, was one solution. Karl Marx, through his publication of the *Communist Manifesto* in 1848, offered socialism to right the economic ship and Communism as a political structure to guide nations. Enlightenment thinkers, fostering reason over faith, offered religious indifferentism as a solution to what they perceived to be a church stranglehold over society.

Church insiders also played their role in the ideological challenge to Roman Catholicism. Félix Dupanloup was a champion of the Gallican cause. In 1852, working with three Sulpician priests, Dupanloup drafted a special *Memoire* that synthesized the Gallican position. It rejected the Vatican's use of the Roman Index of Forbidden Books to exclude the works of Gallican authors. In short, the document understood Roman decrees in their historical context, not as infallible statements. When informed of the document, Pope Pius IX placed it on the Index. The concept of Gallican liberties, that dioceses were autonomous and decisions and documents from the Vatican were purely advisory, was unacceptable to the pope.

The Roman Response

The Roman response to Gallicanism and the ideological wars of the nineteenth century was its promotion of ultramontanism, the philosophy that the universal church, headed by the pope, not the local church, held ultimate authority. Beginning with the pontificate of Leo XII (1823–1829), the Vatican promoted the ultramontane position through encyclicals, other papal documents, and use of writers and theologians to highlight its position.

Pope Pius IX

Ultramontanism and the Roman response to the challenge of the nineteenth century found its greatest champion in Pope Pius IX. Initially, Pius was viewed as a champion of reform, moving away from the more staid policy of his predecessor Gregory XVI. He proclaimed a general amnesty for political prisoners in the Papal States, appeared to be more open to a liberal press, and valued the opinions and ideas of common people.

However, by 1850, after returning from two years of exile in Gaeta, the pope had reversed his general thinking, rejecting the ideas of the *Risorgimento* movement and other liberal forces active in Europe at the time. He decided to assert his religious authority as a response to the progressivism present in European politics and economics. Pius's action was highlighted by his definition of the dogma of the Immaculate Conception (the belief that the Virgin Mary was conceived without original sin) presented in *Inef-fabilis Deus* of December 8, 1854.

FACT

While Pius was open to more liberal ideas, he firmly rejected some aspects of this perspective from the outset. In his encyclical *Qui pluribus* (November 1846), he condemned rationalism, religious indifferentism, and the theory of progressive revelation. He told Catholic sovereigns of their duty to show deference to the church as well as their subjects.

Ten years later Pope Pius again asserted his authority through his publication of the *Syllabus of Errors*, an addendum to his encyclical *Quanta Cura*. The *Syllabus* presented eighty propositions that the pope considered to be errors. The document rejected religious liberalism, the growing secularism and materialism of the age, religious indifferentism, and pantheism. It reasserted the rights of the church and criticized governments for their usurping power at the expense of the papacy. Its last proposition (number eighty) specifically addressed those who believed the pope did not hold universal authority. It maintains as an error: "The Roman Pontiff can, and ought to, reconcile himself, and come to terms with progress, liberalism and modern civilization."

Vatican I

Publication of the *Syllabus of Errors* prompted Pius IX to entertain the question of calling a council to meet the extraordinary needs of the day. The last council, Trent, met (as explained in Chapter 2) to address abuses in the church and the ideas of the Protestant reformers. Viewing the present situation of the nineteenth century, the pope, in April 1865, wrote to thirty-four bishops asking their opinions on what issues a council might address. The general response was the need to condemn the erroneous "isms" (liberalism, pantheism, socialism, communism, religious indifferentism) of the day, call religious orders to a renewal of their common life, generate an official

catechism, and reform canon law. On June 29, 1867, after considerable consultation, Pius publicly announced the council.

Vatican I met in four general sessions between December 8, 1869, and September 1, 1870. The council produced two documents, but the one history remembers is *Pastor Aeternus*, for its definition of papal primacy and infallibility. In Chapter 4 the document states that the pope, when speaking *ex cathedra* "possesses, by the Divine assistance promised to him in blessed Peter, that infallibility which the divine Redeemer willed his Church to enjoy in defining doctrine concerning faith or morals." While some bishops asserted the timing of the proclaimed dogma was inappropriate and other bishops left Rome in order not to participate in the council's action, the definition passed with only two dissenting votes.

The Church of the Twentieth Century

Roman Catholicism in the twentieth century faced an initial theological challenge, followed by a half century of relative peace, that culminated in Vatican II (see Chapter 4), which in many ways transformed the landscape of the church. The truly universal (that is, Catholic) nature of the Faith became evident through international extension of the church to all continents and lands. Additionally, through the miracles of modern transportation and communication, a sense of globalization began to appear.

Theological Modernism

The latter decades of the nineteenth and the first years of the twentieth centuries found Catholic theologians in conflict with each other and the Vatican. New academic tools for the study of the Scriptures prompted some to question long-held assumptions concerning authorship of Biblical texts. For example, it had long been assumed that Moses was the author of the Pentateuch, the first five books of the Old Testament (see Chapter 5). However, using what became known as the historical-critical method, some Biblical scholars questioned this conclusion. At the same time, using similar intellectual analysis, some suggested that church doctrine developed over time.

These two concepts, the use of the historical-critical method and the development of doctrine, became the twin pillars of theological modernism.

Theologians such as George Tyrrell, Alfred Loisy, and Baron Friedrich von Hügel found themselves in between two opposed poles. As intellectuals they sought to advance scholarship using the contemporary techniques and academic tools available to them. On the other hand, they wished to be loyal to church teaching. The Vatican viewed this conflict, which was waged in high-level theological circles, as a continuation of the earlier nineteenth-century attacks on church authority. In 1907, believing it necessary to remove such thoughts from the church, Pope Pius X acted by issuing two important statements, *Lamentabili sane exitu* and *Pascendi dominici gregis*, the latter describing theological modernism as the "synthesis of all heresies."

The Church at Peace

The condemnation of theological modernism in some ways silenced high-level theological thought, but it also ushered in a period of peace after the trauma generated in the wake of the French Revolution. The first half of the twentieth century saw the Church re-extend itself in missionary efforts, especially in Africa, Asia, and Latin America. One especially noteworthy new contributor to this missionary outreach was the United States. The efforts of new groups such as the Catholic Foreign Mission Society of America (Maryknoll), established in 1911, and the Missionary Society of St. James the Apostle (Archdiocese of Boston), founded in 1958, helped to spread and strengthen Catholicism worldwide. In a different, but nonetheless important vein, Pope Pius X's promotion of devotion and frequent reception of the Eucharist was significant for its outreach to ordinary (and especially young) Roman Catholics. Politically, the relationship between the papacy and the Italian state, which had been the cause of such unrest in the nineteenth century, was brought to a peaceful end through the Lateran Treaty of 1929, which gave political recognition to the Holy See and established a concordat between the church and the Italian government.

CHAPTER 4

The Church of Vatican II (1962–Present)

The Second Vatican Council (1962–1965) provided the blueprint for the church of the twenty-first century. Pope John XXIII's call for the council was a surprise to all, and the sixteen documents it produced, looking at all major areas of the church, propelled Roman Catholicism into a period rather unique in history. While seeking to engage the contemporary world more than had previously been seen, the council and the events of the last half century since its completion have vaulted the church into a time of experimentation, confusion, and dissent that persists today.

The 1960s: A Time of Challenge

The Second Vatican Council (Vatican II) was held during a time when significant world events had great impact on all aspects of society. The 1960s was a time of great upheaval. The counterculture of the hippies, drugs, and communes attracted many. Protests, strikes, and other forms of civil unrest dotted the landscape and were reported each evening on network news programs. College campuses became hotbeds for student unrest. Rejection of typical authoritarian structures on campus, anger over the United States' activity in Vietnam, and the desire for more student authority and freedom brought unrest to colleges across the country. The Berkeley free speech movement of 1964–1965 and the action of Ohio National Guard troops at Kent State in May 1970 became almost national cause célèbres. The most significant protest of the decade was the civil rights movement. Initially peaceful under the watchful eye of Martin Luther King Jr., who advocated the nonviolent resistance philosophy of the Indian freedom fighter Mohandas Gandhi, the movement became more violent when Malcolm X and Stokely Carmichael advocated Black Power.

Internationally, but with strong impact in the United States, the Cold War and military action in Vietnam also colored the 1960s. The nuclear age saw the Soviet Union and the United States locked in a titanic struggle for control and influence in the world. The space race for peace was coupled with an arms race for war. The Cuban missile crisis of October 1962 was the critical showdown that nearly brought nuclear holocaust. In Vietnam, as United States military activity increased steadily during the decade, so too protests against the war became more common and vocal. The loss of over 58,000 troops on the United States side alone forced people to question the cost and sacrifice.

The Church and Pope John XXIII

As a large and worldwide institution, Roman Catholicism could not be unaffected by the events of the 1960s. As mentioned in Chapter 3, the church found itself in relatively calm waters during the days after World War II. In the United States this sense of calm was illustrated in two different ways. First, popular religiosity, as exemplified in various devotions to saints, Eucharistic adoration (Forty Hours Devotions), and Marian devotion (such as the rosary), was widespread. Catholics, who freely chose to center their activities about their local parish, were very happy to "pay, pray, and obey."

ESSENTIAL

Historians suggest John XXIII was elected by the conclave as an interim pope. Elected at age seventy-six, the cardinals saw him as a safe noncontroversial man who would maintain the basic policies of his predecessor. It seems, however, that John's previous international experience as nuncio in various countries prompted him to see the need to consider updates of church policy.

The tranquility of the church, along with the rest of the society, was broken by the 1960s. On October 9, 1958, Pope Pius XII died and was succeeded by Angelo Roncalli, Cardinal Archbishop of Venice, who took the name John XXIII. The contrast between the two men typified the movement of society and ultimately the church at this time. Pius XII was perceived as a rather stern and staid man who held the church together during World War II and the Holocaust. Change or a belief in openness was not consistent with his personality. John XXIII, on the other hand, possessed a bubbly and gregarious personality that was attractive to many and seemingly open to new ideas. Nonetheless, it was a shock to all when on January 25, 1959, at the Basilica of St. Paul's Outside-the-Walls, Pope John announced his desire to call an ecumenical council. Believing that the postwar church needed new solutions to contemporary issues, John believed the answers could be determined by the council rather than by edicts from the Vatican.

Vatican II

Historically, ecumenical councils have been called for two basic reasons. Some, such as Nicaea and Trent, were summoned to address significant issues within the church that required adjudication. Others, such as Vatican I, were called to respond to external forces that were in some ways problematic or harmful to the church. The uniqueness of Vatican II is that it was called to address neither of these traditional concerns but rather to see where the church was in relation to contemporary society.

Preparations for the Council

The pope's call for a council caught many off guard, including Cardinal Alfredo Ottaviani, Prefect of the Holy Office (today called the Congregation for the Doctrine of the Faith), who was given the task of organizing the council. Twelve preparatory commissions generated seventy schema for possible debate. These drafts were neoscholastic, juridical, and moralistic in their tone and content. When the council was formally convoked on December 25, 1961, Pope John reversed a long-standing edict published at Lateran V (1512–1517), which had said, "Men must be changed by religion," to "Religion must be changed by men."

FACT

When John XXIII called the council on January 25, 1959, he gave three purposes: First, to promote ecumenism; second, to bring the church into the modern world through *aggiornamento* (meaning "updating"); and third, the council was to be pastoral in nature and work, seeking to strengthen the church's mission to all peoples.

The Council Sessions

Vatican II formally opened on October 11, 1962, with some 2,700 bishops, ninety superiors of religious communities, fifteen women, 400 *periti* (theological experts), and thirty-nine Protestant representative observers present. In his opening address, the pope strongly emphasized certain ideas concerning how he hoped the council would proceed. First, the council was to celebrate Christian faith. Secondly, the council was to express optimism by emphasizing the presence of the Holy Spirit in the world. Lastly, the pope reiterated his desire that the council be pastoral and forward thinking.

Vatican II met in four sessions during the fall months between 1962 and 1965. From the outset of Session I, held between October 11 and December 8, 1962, the course was determined of what would become one of the most significant ecumenical councils in church history. One of the first tasks of the bishops was to establish ten conciliar commissions to replace those that had prepared the preliminary schema. One group of more traditional or conservative bishops, led by Cardinal Ottaviani, who perceived little if any need for change in the church, sought to control membership on these commissions. However, a majority of bishops led by the more progressive Cardinal Augustin Bea, who sought greater shared responsibility and *aggiornamento,* was able to gain control in this process. In the end, national alignments of bishops made suggestions for memberships on the commissions, a move that allowed a more progressive view to proceed forward.

QUESTION

Why did such wide variance in understanding of the council's purpose exist at the outset?
Many believed that a generally healthy, vibrant, and active church needed no reform. Others, however, in line with the prevailing thinking of the creative 1960s, fully supported Pope John XXIII's call for *aggiornamento*. There was a need to examine the church in light of the contemporary world.

Session I was also instrumental for the progress of debate on contentious issues. Referencing the ancient church dictum *lex orandi, lex credendi* (the law of prayer is the law of belief), Pope John suggested the council begin its deliberations with the liturgy, since the Mass lay at the heart of Catholic belief and practice. Could modifications in liturgical practice, including use of the vernacular language, be instituted? In the end, the bishops would give their assent to this idea; a stream of new ideas had begun to flow. Session I also experienced a significant debate on Revelation, an issue that had ties to the Protestant Reformation and the Council of Trent.

The council continued despite the loss of its initial guiding light when John XXIII died on June 3, 1963. His successor, Cardinal Giovanni Montini, Archbishop of Milan, who took the name Paul VI, decided the council must go forward. Paul simplified some procedures, but like his predecessor he allowed the bishops a free hand to debate issues, save for a few instances of papal intervention. Sessions II (September 29 to December 4, 1963), III (September 14 to November 21, 1964), and IV (September 14 to December

8, 1965) were highlighted by significant debates on numerous issues, most of which were settled in favor of the more progressive position.

Several significant debates with important consequences for the future direction of the church were conducted during the latter three sessions. One significant issue asked whether episcopal authority should be vested in individual dioceses or in national conferences of bishops. Another issue was Revelation: was there one source of Revelation with two component parts, Scripture and Tradition, or were there two sources? A significant debate arose over religious liberty. Were people free by conscience to choose and thus be liberated from human coercion in the choice of religion? The relationship of Roman Catholicism to Protestantism, the issue of ecumenism, was matched with the similar question of the church's affiliation with non-Christian faiths. The latter issue involved the deeper question of the status of Jews, including the question debated over centuries about their involvement with the crucifixion of Jesus. Lastly, the bishops spent significant time discussing the relationship of the church to the modern world. Was the church to engage the world or stand aloof?

The Documents

Vatican II produced sixteen documents, which are divided into three separate categories: four constitutions, nine decrees, and three declarations. Theoretically these categories are in descending order of significance, but both the debates at the council and the past fifty years of history suggest that this precedence is not always followed. Viewing the documents after nearly fifty years of debate and study shows what has been most significant for the progress of the church.

"The Constitution on the Sacred Liturgy" was the document that initiated changes that Catholics experience in the celebration of the sacraments, but most especially the Eucharist. "The Pastoral Constitution of the Church in the Modern World" provides insight into contemporary issues and the Church's response. "The Dogmatic Constitution on Revelation" was instrumental in the promotion of Biblical scholarship. "The Decree on Ecumenism" and "The Declaration on the Relations of the Church to Non-Christian Religions" provided the base for religious dialogue among peoples of faith. "The Decree on the Apostolate of Lay People" helped the laity to understand their responsibility as members of the church. Lastly, "The Declaration on Religious Liberty," the only document with any significant input from American bishops, verified the trend in modern governments to remove coercive means with respect to religion in the governance of their nations.

Key Texts and Practical Effects

The sixteen documents of Vatican II were wide-ranging in their orientation, but specific texts and ideas brought about noticeable and practical effects in the life of everyday Roman Catholics. The breadth of topics addressed by the council was significant. The documents speak of the church as the "People of God," emphasize the centrality of the Eucharist, uphold the primacy of Scripture, promote ecclesial and theological pluralism, encourage the practice of ecumenism, and demonstrate concern for secular human values such as justice and peace.

QUESTION

Why was the exodus of priests and religious so precipitous at this time?
First, a more accepting society that no longer viewed priesthood and religious life as "better" or "special" made such a departure easier. Second, the fact that people could choose ministry but simultaneously choose marriage and family made the vocation of priesthood and/or religious life less attractive.

This wide range of topics is supported by a series of important ideas that allow the church to engage the modern world. Collegiality—the idea that the bishops and pope work as a collective episcopal college—was endorsed and was a concept of fundamental importance at the Council of Constance. It is noteworthy that the documents say that the unique Church of Christ "subsists in" rather than "is" the Roman Catholic Church. Religious freedom, autonomy of national churches and their rites, condemnation of anti-Semitism and war, and the endorsement of dual responsibilities of marriage, namely children and love, are other significant ideas in the documents that supported the council's broad orientation.

The council documents, or those generated as a result of them, brought about many practical effects that are daily visible. Today, Roman Catholics experience the sacraments, especially Mass, celebrated in the vernacular language. Mass is often concelebrated, with more than one priest present; the Eucharist is often received under both species of bread and wine. The return of a married diaconate (see Chapter 17) is a direct result of Vatican II. Rules associated with the practice of intercommunion (see Chapter 11), establishment of national episcopal conferences, and fostering of social justice were promoted by the council.

The Rise of the Lay Apostolate

Vatican II and the general trauma of the 1960s were two significant catalysts behind a shift in church life that saw the diminution of the roles of clerics and religious (members of a religious order) and a simultaneous rise in participation by the laity. The confused state of the church in the wake of the council left many priests and religious with significant questions about their vocations and futures. Long-held structures in religious life, including use of the habit, relationships between members and superiors, and theological understandings of the vows, began to crumble. The desire for autonomy, so much a part of the 1960s, was planted in the minds of many religious and priests. Others, viewing the rise of lay participation, began to question their identities and the reason for ministry. The result of this situation was a significant loss of priests and religious. Many took off their habits and left their convents, communities, and rectories; religious vocations began a steady and rather precipitous drop that has only recently been arrested at a new lower steady-state level.

Encouraged by "The Decree on the Apostolate of Lay People," and with diminishing numbers of priests and religious, laymen and -women found great opportunities for ministry in the church. These advances were manifested in two separate areas: those of a more volunteer nature that were associated with local parishes, and those more professional in nature, requiring specialized education. Laymen and -women, through the encouragement of clerics and religious, actively engaged liturgical ministries such as lector and extraordinary Eucharistic minister. Religious education programs were soon dominated by the laity. Numerous other ministries, such as assistance with the Rite of Christian Initiation for Adults (RCIA), became very popular, while popular precouncil ministries, such as the Society of St. Vincent de Paul, gained even more admiration. On a more professional level, laymen and -women took many positions within diocesan structures. Many women with degrees in theology or pastoral ministry became members of local parish teams as pastoral associates, often serving, save sacramental ministry, in roles previously held by priest curates.

Popes John Paul II (1978–2005) and Benedict XVI (2005–present)

The transition of Roman Catholicism into the twenty-first century is best illustrated by the two men most associated with that time period, Popes John Paul II and Benedict XVI. The unsettled state of the church in the wake of Vatican II created significant dissension and divisions in Catholicism. Believing in the need to return a sense of authority and respect to the papacy, John Paul sought to eliminate experimentation and calm stormy waters that threatened church unity.

QUOTE

At his papal consecration Mass, John Paul II stated: "Do not be afraid! Open wide the doors for Christ. To his saving power open the boundaries of states, economic and political systems, the vast fields of culture, civilization and development. Do not be afraid!" This statement became a hallmark of his papacy.

Pope John Paul II

On October 16, 1978, Karol Wojtyla, Cardinal Archbishop of Krakow, Poland, was elected to the Chair of Peter. He took the name John Paul II, succeeding John Paul I, who reigned only thirty-three days after the death of Paul VI on August 6, 1978. A vibrant and active Polish outdoorsman who loved to ski and climb mountains, John Paul II was the first non-Italian pope in over 500 years; at age fifty-eight he was the youngest since Pope Pius IX, elected in 1846 at age fifty-four. He brought his youth and energy to the papacy for almost twenty-seven years, dying on April 2, 2005.

John Paul's long pontificate was marked by several important contributions. His pastoral visits across the globe made him the most traveled church official in history. During 104 pastoral visits he visited 129 countries and logged more than 1.1 million miles. Wherever he went he attracted huge crowds. He was the first pope to visit Jerusalem and pray at the Western Wall; he was the first pontiff to visit and pray in an Islamic mosque. Included in his travels were several trips for World Youth Day, which he established in 1984. He made great strides in relationships with non-Catholics. Many suggest he was integrally important in the fall of Communism through his support of the Polish Solidarity movement. During his pontificate he wrote fourteen encyclical letters that provided instruction in areas such as faith and reason, the dependence of humanity on God, the promotion of the Gospel of life, and continuation of a long series of Catholic social teachings inaugurated by Pope Leo XIII through *Rerum Novarum*.

Pope Benedict XVI

Cardinal Joseph Ratzinger, who took the name Benedict XVI, was elected to succeed John Paul II on April 16, 2005. A German theologian and former college professor, Pope Benedict was possibly the best known and most well-versed cardinal in Vatican affairs from his long tenure as Prefect for the Congregation of the Doctrine of the Faith (1981–2005). Elected at the age of seventy-eight, he, nonetheless, has shown great energy by continuing John Paul II's policy of pastoral visits and World Youth Day. Theologically conservative, in his tenure as pontiff he has sought to reverse efforts toward de-Christianization and secularization by emphasizing a return to Christian doctrine and values, especially in Europe. Like John Paul II, he has sought to continue dialogue with non-Catholics.

The American Catholic Experience

Roman Catholicism in the United States today stands in a relatively good state of health and acceptance, although this present situation was only obtained over a long struggle in a difficult environment. The American

Catholic Experience is rather unique in Catholic history. The United States is the first country where Catholicism came to maturity and gained prominence under a democratic system of government. The concept of the separation of church and state, while being a hallmark to American democracy, was a unique environment for Catholicism where, especially in Europe, church and state had been one or at least completely supportive of each other. Starting as a mere 1 percent of the population in 1785, by 1850 Catholicism, principally as a result of immigration, became the single largest religious denomination in the United States, a status that continues today.

While Catholicism became the single largest religious denomination, it continued to be a minority against the Protestant majority. As a result of this situation and the enduring fallout from the Reformation, Catholics throughout the nineteenth and early part of the twentieth centuries were forced to endure anti-Catholic rhetoric on many fronts. Politically Catholics were shunned and their loyalty questioned due to their allegiance to the pope. During the mid-nineteenth century, books and newspapers told lurid tales of Catholic clergy and religious that were wildly popular and widely circulated. For example, in 1832, Samuel F.B. Morse attacked Catholics politically in *Foreign Conspiracy Against the Liberties of the United States.* Published four years later, *The Awful Disclosures of the Hotel Dieu Nunnery* in Montreal, by Maria Monk (supposedly a nun who "escaped" from the convent), told of sexual encounters between priests and nuns in the confessional. It took the election of John F. Kennedy in 1960, the first Catholic president, to break the back of anti-Catholicism, although as recent authors have stated, it remains the last acceptable prejudice in the minds of many.

American Catholicism today, while generally having weathered its past storms of rejection, is still hampered by the fallout from Vatican II, especially a shortage of clergy, and a splintered unity. Yet, American Catholics are more vibrant and faithful in their practice than those in many other lands. Challenges continue to exist, but systems and people are in place for the church to continue to lead others to Christ in the future.

PART II

Revelation in Roman Catholicism

CHAPTER 5

The Bible and Sacred Tradition

The study of Christianity begins with Revelation, how God is revealed. Vatican II's "Dogmatic Constitution on Divine Revelation" teaches that there is one source of Revelation that has two complementary parts: Sacred Scripture and Sacred Tradition. All teaching associated with Roman Catholicism begins with Revelation. Thus, it is essential to begin by examining Scripture, the Bible, and its sometimes mysterious complement Tradition. Understanding these foundational concepts helps to build the house of Roman Catholic teaching.

Ancient Writings

Why did ancient peoples find it necessary to provide a written record of their religious tradition? The answers to this basic question help us to understand why religions in general and Roman Catholic Christianity specifically possess scripture, namely a written record of their history and teachings. One important reason for such a written record was to preserve the tradition of the community. All communities, large and small, have certain traditions, including routines, celebrations, and rules. These traditions have been passed down from generation to generation. In order to preserve the tradition accurately, ancient peoples came to value writing down these traditions for posterity.

QUESTION

If ancient peoples wished to accurately pass on laws and traditions, why would the texts they wrote be different and open to interpretation?
We must realize that all people write from a particular perspective and bias. They desire to present information in a way to convince others that their ideas are correct. Therefore, one can understand how peoples, writing at different times and from different points of view, can create documents that seem in conflict.

A second reason for the development of ancient scripture texts was the need for law. Contemporary peoples assume the need for some codified set of laws to govern our everyday activities. Without some systematic set of laws societies would live in chaos, whether it be laws that govern highways, operations of government and business, or how families function in society. Similarly, ancient peoples recognized the need for law in their religious traditions and realized that a written record was essential.

Two additional reasons exist for the generation of ancient scriptural writings. One is the need for a permanent record. People today keep permanent records of important events and transactions, such as weddings or baptisms, business deals, or testimony in courts. Ancient peoples, especially in the foundational years of a religious tradition, also realized the need for a permanent record to accurately inform future generations concerning events, teachings, and other significant ideas. Lastly, ancient peoples, through the generation of scripture, better defined the beliefs of the community of faith, thus identifying and differentiating this group from others.

It is important to understand, therefore, that ancient writings are documents of faith, written by people of faith, for people of faith. They are not intended as an historically accurate record of the community but rather serve the essential functions previously described. While, as outlined at the end of this chapter, various academic and intellectual tools can be applied to the study of Scripture, understanding that at its heart Scripture is defined by faith helps one to realize why varied interpretations of the Bible are so common today.

Categories of Ancient Writings

There are three basic categories of ancient writings associated with the Bible: pseudepigrapha, Apocrypha, and canon. Pseudepigrapha, false texts written between approximately 200 B.C.E. and 100 C.E., are writings that have not been accepted by Biblical scholars as part of canon (official) Bible. There are numerous texts, some complete and others fragments, written by Jews and early Christians that, for reasons described below, are not in the Bible. Nonetheless, these texts have teachings that have become part of accepted Christian and Roman Catholic Tradition. For example, why do Christians accept Saints Anne and Joachim as the parents of the Blessed Virgin Mary? There is no information about Mary's childhood in the New Testament. Yet in the Gospel of the Birth of Mary, a pseudepigraphal text, this information is provided. Thus, it is possible to see the usefulness of ancient texts, even when they are not an official book of the Bible. Some of the more popular pseudepigraphal texts are the Gospel of Thomas, the Apocryphon of John, the Secret Book of James, and the recently discovered Gospel of Judas.

A second category of ancient writings is the Apocrypha. These documents, referred to as "hidden texts," were written at the same basic time as the pseudepigrapha. They were often used by Jews but have not been accepted as part of the Torah or Old Testament. Similarly, these texts are not accepted by Protestants, a fact that makes a sharp division in Christianity over the basic issue of Revelation. The "Catholic" Bible contains seven additional books in the Old Testament—Tobit, Judith, I and II Maccabees, Wisdom, Sirach (Ecclesiasticus), and Baruch—that are considered apocryphal by Protestants.

The canon of Scripture refers to the thirty-nine books of the Old Testament (for Roman Catholics the additional above seven books must be added) and the twenty-seven books of the New Testament. The canon was developed over time but only came into its present formulation after the Council of Trent (1545–1563). The accepted canon is used as the primary element of Revelation, and is thus used in all liturgical services.

Criteria for Canonicity

Why were certain ancient texts accepted as part of the Bible, others rejected, and others still accepted by Catholics but not by Protestants? The answers lie in what criteria were used to determine which texts became canon or official and which did not. The first criterion used was the origin of the text. Was the author of the text known by people of the time as authoritative, someone who was a leader and, therefore, knowledgeable of the faith? The audience to whom the document was addressed was a second criterion. Again, was this community of faith a known entity during the period when the text was written? Thirdly, and possibly most importantly, do the teachings contained in the text conform to the "rule of faith" of the community? Does the text contain ideas or teachings that contradict the basic wisdom or experience of the community? Fourth, was the text in public use when it was composed? Lastly, and not unimportantly, is the concept of chance. Sometimes texts, such as the letters of St. Ignatius of Antioch, satisfy the above criteria but still are not part of the canon. One can only say it is by chance that this is so.

Hebrew Bible (Old Testament) Structure

The Hebrew Bible, commonly known by Roman Catholics as the Old Testament, contains three major sections: the Pentateuch, Prophets, and Wisdom (often referred to as The Writings) Literature.

The Pentateuch

The Pentateuch, also known as the Torah, or the Law, comprises the first five books of the Old Testament: Genesis, Exodus, Leviticus, Numbers, and Deuteronomy. Biblical scholars believe these books were written between approximately 950 and 400 B.C.E., a period spanning the division of the Kingdoms of Israel and Judah to the time after the Babylonian exile (587–537 B.C.E.). These books contain the stories of creation and the great flood. They also describe the development of the patriarchs, beginning with Abraham, and the structure of the Hebrew community, including the twelve tribes of Israel. The book of Exodus describes the bondage of the people in Egypt, their rescue by the hand of God, and the creation of the Law. The latter three books of the Pentateuch describe the forty-year wandering of the Jews in the desert, the greater development of the Law, and the eventual arrival of the Jews in the Promised Land of Israel.

The Prophets

The Prophets, the second major portion of the Old Testament, has several major and minor subdivisions. The first portion of this section, called the Former Prophets, is better known as the Historical Books, comprising Joshua through II Kings. These books describe the conquering of the land, establishment of the monarchy, the kingships of David and Solomon, the division of the land into two kingdoms, and eventually the destruction of the Northern Kingdom of Israel at the hands of the Assyrians (722 B.C.E.) and the exile of the Southern Kingdom of Judah to Babylon (587 B.C.E.).

FACT

When Solomon, son of the great King David, died in 931 B.C.E., a dispute arose between his sons, Jeroboam and Rehoboam, leading to the creation of two kingdoms: Israel (North) and Judah (South). I and II Kings relate the events in these two kingdoms, which existed in parallel for approximately 200 years. Judah survived for another 200 years after the loss of Israel.

The Latter Prophets are the fifteen books of prophecy with names familiar to many, including Isaiah, Jeremiah, and Amos. These books are further subdivided in two ways. The so-called Major Prophets, designated solely because of their physical length, are Isaiah, Jeremiah, and Ezekiel. The Minor Prophets, which have messages as significant as the Major Prophets, if not more so, are the twelve other books of prophecy that are physically much shorter than the three aforementioned.

ESSENTIAL

While future events were part of the prophetic message, the most important idea presented was God's dissatisfaction with the ongoing actions and decisions of many religious and secular rulers in Israel and Judah. Amos, for example, warned the ruling elite that their failure to serve the poor, while attending to their own needs, was inconsistent with God's plan.

The prophetic books are also divided with respect to the audience of the writers and the time they were written. Some prophets, such as Amos and Hosea, proclaimed their message in Israel; Isaiah, Jeremiah, Micah, and others prophesied in Judah. Equally important as the audience is the time frame when the books were written. There are three divisions: books written prior to the Babylonian exile, during the exile, and prophecy in the restored land of Israel after the exile. Since prophets proclaimed God's word at various times and to two different communities, the messages presented were vastly different. A message of impending doom presented by Amos to Israel prior to its destruction in 722 B.C.E. can be contrasted with the words of hope to the Hebrews in exile found in Ezekiel and the new day proclaimed to the Jews after the exile by Isaiah (Chapters 56–65). The prophetic books, completed by 400 B.C.E. but not compiled until approximately 200 years later, are arranged by size and chronological order, as understood when the canon was finalized. The faithlessness of the Hebrew people to God's law is the central theme of the prophetic books.

Wisdom Literature

Wisdom Literature is the third major section of the Hebrew Bible. Some of the more prominent books of this section are Psalms, Proverbs, Job, Song of Songs, and Ecclesiastes. These texts, which are neither historical nor prophetic, form a separate section of the Old Testament. Their order in the canon of scripture is rather haphazard.

Authors of the Hebrew Bible

Who wrote the books of the Old Testament? Prior to modern scholarship, which began in the mid-twentieth century, the most prominent and accepted answer was Moses, the named prophets, and possibly one or two of the famous kings of Judah, such as David and Solomon. However, today we understand that the composition of the Old Testament was much more complex than understood in earlier generations. Most suggest the Pentateuch is a compilation of various literary traditions that over time were written and then brought together through a process known as redaction. The Yahwist (Southern Kingdom) and Elohist (Northern Kingdom) traditions were written at different times and from diverse perspectives, explaining events from the viewpoint of each particular community of faith. These two were brought together with a third tradition, the Priestly, which emphasized the Law, into what we know today as the Pentateuch.

The books of prophecy were most likely written forms of oral proclamations made by those prophets sent by God to present a specific message. The actual authors may have been the prophet, a scribe for the prophet, or a group of people who heard the proclamation and, inspired by God, wrote down the prophet's message for posterity.

FACT

The book of Isaiah is actually three books in one. Chapters 1–39 were written to Judah prior to the exile; Chapters 40–55 were written during the exile. The latter chapters, 56–65, were written after the Hebrews had returned to Judah. Isaiah is the only prophetic book with such a scope and consequently broad themes addressing varied circumstances.

Historically, Wisdom Literature has been closely associated with King Solomon, with many of the books attributed directly to his hand. Research shows, however, that this genre of writing is quite similar to literature prominent in Egypt during the same historical period. This cross-fertilization leads scholars to conclude that while Wisdom Literature is certainly a direct product of a definite and educated class of people, a popular version of this same genre was familiar to the peasant class and certainly became part of the books we read in the Bible today.

FACT

St. John's Gospel is very unique. It has no parables, contains no information about Jesus youth, presents his public ministry as a period of three years' vice one, as recounted by the Synoptic gospels, and makes no mention of the institution of the Eucharist at the Last Supper. John's Gospel is highly symbolic as well.

Compilation of the Old Testament took place during an approximate 500-year period. The texts themselves were composed between 1200 and 100 B.C.E. with their compilation achieved between 400 B.C.E. and 90 C.E.

New Testament Structure

The New Testament tells the story of Jesus Christ and the early days of the religion that bears his name as told by his first followers. Like the Hebrew Bible, the New Testament, which understands itself as the completion of Old Testament prophecy, is divided into at least three and possibly four sections: the Gospels, the writings of St. Paul, and the epistles of other apostles. Some scholars classify Revelation, the last book of the Bible, separately.

The Gospels

The first and primary part of the New Testament is the Gospels. Three Gospels, those of Matthew, Mark, and Luke, are grouped together due to their similarities in style, content, and theology. Labeled the Synoptic Gospels, these texts along with the Gospel of John, which is quite unique compared with the other three, provide an overview to the life and mission of Jesus of Nazareth. The Gospels are not short biographies of Jesus but, as stated in the *Dogmatic Constitution on Revelation* (paragraph 19), the evangelists "selected certain of the many elements which had been handed on, either orally or already in written form, others they synthesized or explained with an eye to the situation of the churches," in an effort to communicate to particular audiences the mission and message of Jesus. Matthew wrote to Jewish converts; the message of Mark and Luke was broadcast to Gentile Christians. The Gospel of John, unique in many ways, was written after the Synoptics and assumes its readers are familiar with the events and ideas presented in the Synoptic tradition. The Acts of the Apostles, written by the author of Luke, is often called the fifth Gospel in its presentation of the life of the nascent church and the travels of St. Paul.

The Writings of St. Paul

The corpus of St. Paul, the second major section of the New Testament, comprises thirteen letters, written to fledgling Christian communities of the first-century Mediterranean world. In most cases Paul addressed communities that he personally founded, as described in the Acts of the Apostles. Originally all thirteen letters were attributed to St. Paul, but scholars today suggest that in view of language used and theological perspective, it is highly unlikely that Paul wrote all of them. Rather, they have been broken into three groups: authoritative letters (Romans, I Corinthians, II Corinthians, Galatians, Philippians, I Thessalonians, and Philemon); pseudo-authoritative letters (II Thessalonians, Colossians, and Ephesians); and non-Pauline, or Pastoral Epistles (I Timothy, II Timothy, and Titus). St. Paul was the first and thus primary Christian theologian. He is still considered to be so today. The teachings and theology contained in his letters provide the foundation for many contemporary Roman Catholic teachings. The Letter to the Hebrews, attributed to St. Paul in earlier generations, is now viewed as non-Pauline due in large measure to language, theological content, and its form, which is completely foreign to the other thirteen letters.

Why did St. Paul write his letters? In a day when communication was not instantaneous and transportation was slow, Paul had only one vehicle to address concerns raised in the communities he founded and for which he felt responsibility. Thus, when he heard that contentious issues or questions were causing problems and dissension in distant nascent communities, he wrote letters and in the process presented his theology, which has become standard in Roman Catholicism today.

Epistles of Other Apostles

The last major section of the New Testament is a compilation of assorted epistles (letters) written by the apostles of Jesus. These include I and II Peter; I, II, and III John; James; and Jude. Although not as well known and used less in private and public prayer, these letters provide important insights concerning how the teachings of Jesus initially began to be broadcast throughout the world. The book of Revelation, ascribed to John, is often placed in a separate fourth division of New Testament writings. The book uses grand images in its apocalyptic presentation of the author's vision of the end times.

QUESTION

Which two letters of St. Paul are not addressed to communities he established?
The Letter to Philemon is the only surviving personal letter in the Pauline corpus. Romans, written by Paul to introduce himself to a Christian community he hoped to visit, contains his best presentation of systematic theology. The letter does not address specific questions or resolve problems but rather presents Paul's ideas as an overture for his future arrival.

Authors of the New Testament

Unlike the Hebrew Bible, especially the Pentateuch, where authorship is today understood to be a compilation of traditions or unknown authors who presented the messages of the prophets, information concerning the New Testament's authors is more certain. Matthew and John were apostles of Jesus; Mark is mentioned in the Acts of the Apostles. Luke is mentioned by Paul in Colossians and II Timothy. Names ascribed to the other New Testament texts are also apostles. Did these apostles actually write these texts? Today we must understand that ideas of authorship have changed. It is quite possible that Matthew wrote his Gospel, but it is equally likely that a disciple or team of disciples wrote under Matthew's guidance. The same is true for the other texts.

Disagreements are present with authorship of the five texts ascribed to St. John. An examination of these texts, like that conducted on the writings of Paul, shows major differences in structure and word usage in the original Greek texts of these documents. This analysis leads experts to conclude that most probably the Gospel and three letters of John, written in language more sophisticated than Revelation, were penned by some disciple of John. Revelation, composed in a more crude form of Greek, seems more consistent with the perceived lesser education of a Galilean fisherman like John.

Why Are There Differences in Bibles?

When browsing the shelves of a religious bookstore, there are several different Bibles. If there is one source of Revelation, why should there be so many versions of the Bible? Part of the answer to the question has already been addressed, namely the inclusion in Catholic Bibles of the seven apocryphal texts in the Old Testament. The other major reason is translation and the accompanying concern for the book's audience. The original languages of the Bible were Hebrew for the Old Testament and Greek for the New Testament. The first universally accepted translation was the work of St. Jerome, whose fourth-century Latin translation, the Vulgate, was standard for centuries. After the Protestant Reformation, numerous other translations from the original Hebrew and Greek appeared, including the often-cited King James Version. More recently the Revised Standard and Oxford Annotated Versions are considered more academically sound because of their close adherence to the original texts. There are at least two widely used Catholic Bibles (those that include the Apocrypha): the New American Bible, which is used in Catholic liturgical services, and the Jerusalem Bible. Other versions, aimed toward children, use more of a paraphrase than direct translation from the original text.

Sacred Tradition as Revelation

Sacred Tradition is Roman Catholicism's ongoing journey in seeking divine truth. As described earlier, the scrutiny of many criteria and the passage of significant time were necessary in order to generate what today is known as the canon of Scripture or the Bible. During this long gestation period, Christians, and more specifically Roman Catholics, especially in the early centuries after Jesus, lived lives of faith without the benefit of the Bible. How did they know the revelation of Christ? How did they understand church teaching? The basic answer is they followed the tradition of their ancestors. This tradition, found in sources other than the Bible, was integral to the life of the community. Most of these traditions were based on texts that became part of the canon, but others are derived from apocryphal or even pseudepigraphal texts. Yet these teachings, as research and history show, were part of church teaching from the outset.

Two dogmas associated with the Blessed Virgin Mary are good examples of the application of Sacred Tradition. Neither the Immaculate Conception (belief that Mary was conceived without original sin) nor the Assumption (teaching that Mary, at the point of death, was assumed body and soul into heaven) are found in the Bible, yet they are basic Roman Catholic dogmas. These teachings did not arise at the time of their proclamation, namely 1854 and 1950 respectively, but rather had been part of Catholic teaching for centuries. They were, in other words, part of Sacred Tradition.

Biblical Criticism

Biblical scholarship today uses various academic tools in order to explore more deeply the meaning and understanding of Sacred Scripture. The historical-critical method uses the discipline of history to help place in context the events of a particular time and the teachings that evolved from that epoch of history. It is extremely helpful, for example, to understand the relationship between Jews and Samaritans in order to appreciate Luke's popular and famous parable of the Good Samaritan (Luke 10:25–37).

Literary and form criticism use the academic tools associated with literature to analyze Biblical texts. What writing forms and patterns are evident in a particular text? What do forms, such as poetry, prose, or prayers, say about the literature under examination? It was through such analysis and similar questions that experts came to the conclusion that the Pentateuch was not the work of Moses but rather a compilation of three different literary traditions from different periods of Jewish history.

Redaction criticism seeks to find the original text and, therefore, the original intent of the author(s) in Sacred Scripture. Over the centuries, through copying errors, misinterpretations, and other human fault, intentional or unintentional, the text that exists today could easily have been distorted from the original. Like peeling away the layers of an onion until you reach the core, so redaction criticism seeks to get to the core or original thought of the writer. This could open a completely new vista of meaning for a particular passage or a whole book of the Bible.

CHAPTER 6

The Magisterium

Roman Catholicism teaches that Revelation is one deposit of faith, Scripture, and Sacred Tradition. There is nothing added to or deleted from Revelation, but how Catholics know and understand that deposit of faith receives regular input through the teaching office of the church, referred to as the magisterium. Somewhat mysterious to many, including some Roman Catholics, the teachings of popes, local bishops, and national episcopal conferences comprise the magisterium. While teachings fall into different categories and have various levels of significance, they all assist Catholics in their daily exercise of faith.

Historical Questions and Issues

One of the most significant questions raised in the history of Roman Catholicism, as described in Chapters 1 through 4, is authority. In some cases the issue has been authority between popes and secular rulers; in other cases it has been authority between popes and other bishops. The question of authority is critical in our understanding of the role of the magisterium in the life of the church. When speaking of Revelation (that is, how we know of God), it is vitally important to know who speaks with absolute authority on issues of great importance to the progress of the faith. A brief review of the events and personalities that brought Catholicism to the nineteenth and twentieth centuries, when the magisterium as it is known today was clearly defined, will help to understand this critically important aspect of Roman Catholic teaching.

The question of whether the secular or religious official held ultimate authority was the first debate to come to the forefront. In 800, Charlemagne, King of the Franks, was crowned the first Holy Roman Emperor. He believed his role as leader of the state was to fight for the church, while that of the pope was to pray for the church. As the church's protector he rejuvenated Catholicism through his reintroduction of the Gregorian sacramentary (used for liturgical rites) and his insistence on the need of renewal in religious life. In the eleventh century, Pope Gregory VII gained control over the Holy Roman Emperor, Henry IV, in determining who would invest (give symbols of office) to local bishops. Gregory's initial victory was made more permanent at the Diet of Worms in 1122 when it was declared that the church alone had the right to elect bishops, including their investiture with crozier (Episcopal staff) and ring, the two principal symbols of a bishop. The First Council of the Lateran (1123) formalized this decision. The publication of *Unam Sanctam* (1302) by Boniface VIII solidified the pope's authority in state and church matters.

Conciliarism

The Avignon papacy, leading to the Western Schism, raised the question of authority within the church. In order to resolve the situation with the bishops, the document *Sacrosancta* declared that the council had direct authority from God and thus was able to make decisions that even the pope must follow. This was the birth of the concept of collegiality, the pope and bishops working together as a teaching body. Collegiality has experienced a rollercoaster ride of highs and lows, greater and lesser acceptance within the church in the ensuing centuries. Constance and Vatican II, where the actions and decisions of the College of Bishops gained greater authority, were the periods of greater acceptance; Vatican I, with the declaration of the dogma of papal infallibility, was a point of less acceptance.

QUESTION

Why does it seem that the lines of church authority vary with time?
There are at least two significant reasons. First, while Catholics believe Matthew 16:18 gives clear authority to Peter (and by extension to future popes), historical situations, such as the Western Schism, require action. Secondly, clear and consistent definitions of roles within the magisterium only came at Vatican I and Vatican II.

Ordinary Magisterium

The magisterium is exercised on two different fronts. The ordinary magisterium, defined and applied regularly, is the proclamation of noninfallible teaching on both local and universal levels. The extraordinary magisterium (described later in this chapter), very clearly defined and rarely utilized, can issue declarations of infallible teachings on a universal level. Such dogmas may be formulated by the pope or the College of Bishops working with the pope.

Defining Ordinary Magisterium

The need to clearly define the authority of the College of Bishops arose in December 1863 during the reign of Pope Pius IX. In an apostolic letter, *Tuas libenter*, Pius wrote to the Archbishop of Munich-Freising to counteract the ideas of the German theologian, Ignaz Dollinger, who claimed that Catholic theologians were bound to hold only those teachings solemnly defined by the pope. In the letter Pius said that Catholic teachers and writers must abide by all teachings that have been divinely revealed, including those that emanate from the College of Bishops dispersed throughout the world.

Vatican I solidified this idea in *Dei Filius*, the first document discussed and passed at the council. In the document the bishops state that all contained in the "word of God, written or handed down," whether that be by solemn judgment or through the "ordinary and universal magisterium," is considered to be divinely revealed. Thus, the document places significant weight behind all teachings, not only those considered dogmas. The concept of ordinary universal magisterium was not clear, but it seemed to refer to the teaching of the whole College of Bishops with the pope, not the pope alone.

FACT

It is important to understand the difference between doctrine (that is, teachings) and dogma. While all teachings are significant and part of the deposit of faith, dogmas are teachings that must be accepted to be considered a Roman Catholic. Examples of dogmas are: Jesus Christ is human and divine, God is Trinity, and the Assumption and Immaculate Conception of the Blessed Virgin Mary.

Applying the Ordinary Magisterium

While the ordinary magisterium can be exercised on a universal level, it is more commonly seen in nonuniversal applications. Individual bishops in specific dioceses can often present teachings that apply only to Catholics in their jurisdictions. These teachings may be catechetical, pastoral, or doctrinal in their application. For example, church teaching says that on Fridays during the season of Lent, Catholics are to refrain from eating meat. If St. Patrick's Day, March 17, falls on a Friday, a local bishop may allow Catholics in his diocese to eat meat in order to celebrate this holiday according to popular custom. Local bishops often use the ordinary nonuniversal magisterium to set the age for children to receive their first communion or youth to receive confirmation. The nonuniversal ordinary magisterium may also be exercised by groups of bishops, such as a national conference of bishops or an international gathering of bishops, such as a synod. Again, teachings from such groups of bishops would apply only to those Catholics under their authority. Lastly, the pope, who also holds the title Bishop of Rome, may in his secondary capacity provide a teaching that is not applicable to the universal church but only his diocese.

Extraordinary Magisterium

The extraordinary magisterium refers to those teachings that have been declared infallible and, therefore, irreformable. As described in Chapter 3, Vatican Council I (1869–1870) generated the first official definition of extraordinary magisterium. In *Pastor Aeternus* the primacy of the pope and his privilege as pope to declare infallible statements, under tightly prescribed conditions, were formally defined. The nature of any infallible statement would, by definition, be universal in scope; there could be no concept of a nonuniversal infallible proclamation.

QUOTE

Lumen Gentium, paragraph 25 reads: "Although the bishops, taken individually, do not enjoy the privilege of infallibility, they do, however, proclaim infallibly the doctrine of Christ on the following conditions: namely, when, even though dispersed throughout the world, but preserving for all that amongst themselves and with Peter's successor the bond of communion, in their authoritative teaching concerning matters of faith and morals, they are in agreement that a particular teaching is to be held definitely and absolutely."

The conditions for an infallible definition make any such statement very rare. In fact, since the time of its definition, papal infallibility has only been invoked once: the definition of the Assumption of Mary into heaven in 1950. An infallible statement from the pope must be presented *ex cathedra*, that is, the pope speaking as pope, on the subject of faith and morals, to the universal church. It is also important to note that the pope must explicitly state that his teachings are binding to the entire church.

The basic principle of the extraordinary magisterium, defined as papal infallibility at Vatican I, was expanded at Vatican II through *Lumen Gentium* ("The Constitution on the Church"). Paragraphs 22 and 25 in this document extend the power of extraordinary magisterium to the College of Bishops in union with the pope. The council first wished to show that the College of Bishops could act while dispersed, not solely at an ecumenical council. More importantly, however, is the collegial idea that acting in a "bond of communion" they can proclaim a teaching to be infallible. The concept of extraordinary magisterium being found in the College of Bishops has to date never been exercised.

The critical term used in this definition is "bond of communion." This formal condition, necessary to exercise authority, must be fulfilled for the decisions of the bishops to be invested with supreme authority. This term does not mean that every bishop would agree with a particular teaching, but rather that no bishops are living in schism or reflecting heresy in their teaching.

Canon Law and Infallibility

The Code of Canon Law, the collection of laws that govern Roman Catholicism, revised most recently in 1983, provides added insight into the subject of infallibility. Canon 749, paragraphs 2 and 3, addresses the subject of infallibility through the College of Bishops. What the bishops can define, when exercising universal magisterium, is limited to the deposit of faith (Revelation's two-pronged source, Sacred Scripture and Sacred Tradition), and whatever is necessary to protect and explain that deposit. This must be divinely revealed and it must be a teaching that is held definitively. Canon 750 goes one step further. It suggests that for a doctrine to be so taught it must be manifested in the common adherence of the faithful to that doctrine. In other words, the *consensus fidelium* (the general consensus of Catholics) must be upheld.

Synod of Bishops

The Second Vatican Council, as described in Chapter 4, was an event of great magnitude in the history of Roman Catholicism. One of the more important ideas that was strongly promoted at the council was the re-emergence of the concept of collegiality, the pope and the bishops working together toward a common understanding of the faith. This concept, which was so integral to the Council of Constance in the fifteenth century, became somewhat lost through the events of the nineteenth century, especially the proclamation of papal infallibility at Vatican I. Thus, when Vatican II manifested a greater openness to the views of the College of Bishops, the door was opened for a renewed path of greater collegiality in the church.

Background to the Concept of the Synod

While Vatican II was a worldwide event that brought the concept of collegiality to the forefront, the basic idea of having the bishops serve in some consultative capacity was actually raised at the same time Pope John XXIII called the council. In early November 1959, Silvio Oddi, at the time Archbishop and Apostolic Pro-Nuncio in the United Arab Republic (later cardinal), suggested that some worldwide representative episcopal body be formed to discuss significant issues in the church and their possible solutions. In his comments he referenced the Latin American Episcopal Council (CELAM) as one example of what he was proposing on an international level. Similarly, in late December 1959, Cardinal Bernardus Alfrink, Archbishop of Utrecht, called for a periodic assembly of bishops to work with the pontiff and the Roman Curia in some legislative capacity. This would allow greater representation in the magisterium.

QUOTE

Lumen Gentium, paragraph 12 states, "This characteristic is shown in the supernatural appreciation of faith of the whole people, when, 'from the bishops to the last of the faithful' they manifest universal consent in matters of faith and morals." These constraints clearly demonstrate the limitations of the extraordinary magisterium.

Pope Paul VI, while still Archbishop of Milan, struck a similar chord seeking greater collaboration within the episcopate. After his election as pope he continued to make reference to a consultative body of bishops as a permanent structure within the church. On September 14, 1965, the first day of the fourth and final session of the council, Pope Paul publicly stated his intention to establish a Synod of Bishops. The next day the document *Apostolica Sollicitudo* was published, officially establishing the Synod of Bishops.

The Synod in Action

Since its formation in 1965, the Synod of Bishops has been called into session twenty-three times. The first assembly was held between September 29 and October 29, 1967. Its objectives were, "the preservation and strengthening of the Catholic faith, its integrity, its force, its development, and its doctrinal and historical coherence." Of these assemblies, thirteen were considered "ordinary general assemblies," and ten were called for "special" or "extraordinary" purposes. Some of the important topics covered in these synod meetings were: priesthood and justice, evangelization, family life, reconciliation, a review of Vatican II, the vocation and mission of the laity, and the word of God in the life and mission of the church.

ESSENTIAL

The Synod of Bishops is not limited in its competence, as are the congregations associated with the Roman Curia. Rather, the synod has full authority to deal with any subject that the pope presents for its discussions in his letter of convocation. The synod is not dependent on the Roman Curia; it receives its status and charter for operation directly from the pope, who calls the synod into session.

The United States Catholic Conference of Bishops (USCCB)

From the outset of its establishment in 1789, the Roman Catholic hierarchy in the United States has sought to be a source of significant teaching, thus exercising the ordinary, nonuniversal magisterium. Throughout the nineteenth century the United States Catholic bishops met regularly to discuss numerous issues pertinent to the situation of Roman Catholics in the country. The expansion of the nation through the concept of manifest destiny, significant anti-Catholic rhetoric, immigration, and Catholic education were just some of many issues that required decisions from the bishops. Although the bishops were not organized in any canonical way, their meetings and decisions were important in keeping unity within the American church.

Formation of the USCCB

Due in large part to the fallout from Americanism and theological Modernism, the Catholic bishops in the United States did not meet as a formal body between 1884 and 1917. During World War I, however, the bishops again met and formed the National Catholic War Council, an episcopal organization that sought to bring a united Catholic response to the effects of the war. In 1919, after the war ended, the bishops decided to continue their organization as the National Catholic Welfare Council (Conference after 1922) (NCWC). The bishops organized themselves with an Administrative Committee for oversight and five subcommittees of press, social service, mission, Catholic societies, and education. The NCWC became the official voice of the Catholic bishops in the United States, speaking on assorted issues such as immigration restriction, the Great Depression, war and peace, secularism, the Christian family, and federal aid for education.

Post–Vatican II USCCB

In 1966, following Vatican II, the NCWC was reorganized into two complementary organizations, the National Conference of Catholic Bishops (NCCB) and the United States Catholic Conference (USCC). The NCCB dealt with canonical issues and the USCC with matters of a civil and secular nature. During the 1980s the NCCB published two highly significant documents: "The Challenge of Peace: God's Promise and Our Response," (1983) and "Economic Justice for All" (1986). The first dealt with the question of nuclear war and the concept of nuclear deterrence. The latter document addressed how the United States' economy impacts the world and, therefore, the responsibility of America toward other countries in our era of globalization. During the 1980s, the bishops also wrote several drafts of a pastoral letter on women, but a final version was never published.

In July 2001 these two parallel groups, the NCCB and USCC, were formed into the United States Catholic Conference of Bishops. Today the bishops' conference continues to act as an important organization that exercises magisterial teaching in the church. It meets twice annually and continues to tackle difficult issues, including in 2003 a response to the revelations of sexual abuse of minors by clergy and religious.

CHAPTER 7

The Creed

The Creed, or Profession of Faith, is proclaimed by Roman Catholics at each Sunday Mass and other solemnities (see Chapter 19). This prayer succinctly, yet powerfully, encapsulates the core beliefs of Roman Catholics. Developed through an evolutionary process and finalized at the second ecumenical council, held at Constantinople in 381, the Creed is a radical statement of faith that exemplifies the countercultural nature of Roman Catholicism in the twenty-first century. For those who profess its teachings, it stands as a testimony to a system of belief often not fully appreciated today.

Roots of the Creed

The Creed, as with many Christian ideas, has its roots in Judaism. There is a natural progression of the development of the Creed from Judaism's *Shema Israel*. Deuteronomy 6:4 professes this ancient belief: "Hear O Israel the Lord Our God is one Lord. And you shall love the Lord our God with all your heart and all your soul and all your might." Three important ideas arise from this highly significant prayer. First, this is a call to communal commitment. The Jewish people always saw themselves as a community of faith, called by God to fidelity to the Law as articulated in the Pentateuch. Secondly, this commitment was exclusive; Yahweh made a covenant, beginning with Abraham, with a particular people at a specific time. From this the Jewish community always saw itself as the chosen people. Thirdly, the commitment, while that of the whole, is also highly personal. It is the individual's requirement to adhere to the requirements of God's law, lived within the context of a particular faith community.

Early Christian Roots

The *Shema* served the Jewish people well as a succinct profession of faith, but the early disciples of Jesus faced specific challenges that necessitated a more detailed and complete creedal statement. Early Christians needed to define their experience of Jesus. How did Jesus satisfy the long-held prophetic belief of a messianic figure that would save Israel?

Jesus' first followers also needed to clarify their complex understanding of God, namely the concept of the Trinity. Lastly, in order to maintain orthodoxy, Christians needed to correct misunderstandings that had crept into the narrative of those following the teachings of Christ.

ESSENTIAL

Initially, due to St. Paul's belief in the rapid return of Christ, his Second Coming, described in I Thessalonians 4:13–18, Christians saw no need for a formal creed. However, as time passed and Christ had not returned, the need to formally present and document the complex theology of what became Christianity became a necessity. Thus, various written creeds evolved.

The Christian Creed takes its origins from the same need to express a people's experience in story, as seen in the Jewish *Shema*, and to distinguish a specific allegiance within the context of competing claims of orthodoxy. Thus, the Creed evolved from the event of Christ's resurrection, not the physical experience, but the everyday experience of the risen Christ that permeated the hearts of those in the Christian community. Yet what Christians professed separated them from their Jewish ancestors. Proclaiming Jesus as the Messiah was not against Judaism; the prophecy of the Messiah was a hallmark of the Jewish tradition. However, to profess Jesus as the Messiah because of the resurrection was a significant problem. In order to believe Jesus to be the Messiah because of the resurrection required the establishment of a new order with Israel as political victor. Such, however, was not the case. Additionally, Jesus broke the Mosaic Law. Thus, Christians were attributing to Jesus, a failed Messiah and cursed criminal, a status reserved exclusively for God. Calling Jesus Lord could only refer to his divine status, a belief that would lead to the unpardonable sin of polytheism. Christians were, from the Jewish perspective, violating the *Shema*.

Latin Church Roots

Several early patristic apologists in the Latin or Western Church produced theological treatises that contained many basic teachings of the Creed. In the second century, Justin Martyr's *First Apology* gives the Christian baptism formula while expanding on the roles of the Father, Son, and Holy Spirit. Hippolytus' short treatise against the heresy of Noetus (circa 225) made the distinction between Father and Son clearer. Tertullian (145–220) in his "Rule of Faith" suggests his teaching was derived directly from the Apostles. One version reads, "Believing in one and only one God, omnipotent, the creator of the universe, and His Son Jesus Christ, born of the Virgin Mary crucified under Pontius Pilate, raised again the third day from the dead, received in the heavens, sitting now at the right hand of the Father, destined to come to judge the living and the dead through the resurrection of the flesh as well as of the spirit."

These efforts to define the person and work of Jesus led eventually to the generation of the Apostles Creed. This formula of twelve specific creedal statements is first found in the *Apostolic Tradition* of Hippolytus (circa 215). This became known as the Roman Symbol and is found in the writings of such distinguished theologians as Ambrose, Augustine, and Peter Chrysologus. Rufinius of Aquileia (circa 404) is the first in the Tradition to call this formula "The Apostles Creed."

Eastern Church Roots

While significant theologians in the Eastern Church, such as Eusebius of Caesarea, Cyril of Jerusalem, and Theodore of Mopsuetia, offered versions of the Creed in their writings (like those in the Latin Church), it was the formula produced at the Council of Nicaea (325) that was critical for the future of Christian orthodoxy. The first ecumenical council, held at Nicaea (present-day Turkey) was called by the Emperor Constantine I in 325 to denounce the heresy of Arius (see Chapter 1). In the process of validating the divinity of Christ, which Arius challenged, it was prudent to construct a Creed, not unlike the Apostles Creed, that clearly taught that Jesus was the divine Son of God. Thus, the most significant document produced by the council was the Nicene Creed.

The Importance of the Creed

The Nicene Creed was important for several reasons. First, since the emperor called the council, the influence of the state was brought into cooperation with the church. This was important, for prior to Constantine's conversion and Edict of Milan, church and state in the Roman Empire were at odds. Additionally, church and state cooperation became the basic norm, with a few exceptions, until the period of the Reformation. The Creed was also important for it imposed a universal profession of faith over local variations. Such a uniform document was critical for the promotion of orthodoxy. Lastly, the Nicene Creed purposefully uses philosophical language. This was done to respond to philosophical attacks against the church. Catholicism thus defended its own turf using the language of the "enemy."

The Creed and the First Council of Constantinople

The Council of Nicaea and the creed it produced did not settle the Arian controversy, which only grew in scope and virility over the next half century. In an effort to finally squelch the heresy of Arius and to enhance the basic formula of Nicaea, a second ecumenical council was held at Constantinople in 381. In an effort to combat the Arians, three important scholars, Basil, Bishop of Caesarea; his brother Gregory, Bishop of Nyssa; and Gregory Nazianzus, Patriarch of Constantinople, collectively known as the Cappadocian Fathers, contributed significantly to the creation of a new creed. Issued at the Council of 381, the Nicene-Constantinopolitan Creed differed from the formula at Nicaea in two important ways. First, it elaborated the dignity and role of the Holy Spirit. Second, the formula was written in a more narrative style.

The Creed as professed at Roman Catholic Masses today has one additional and historically highly controversial phrase added to the formula of Constantinople I. In 589 at the Council of Toledo, the word *filioque* (and the Son) was added (adopted by the Latin Church in 1014), making the Creed read "the Holy Spirit descends from the Father *and the Son*." This addition was very significant in the events that eventually led to the split between the Roman Catholic and Orthodox traditions. See Appendix B to read the Nicene-Constantinopolitan Creed and the Apostles' Creed.

What the Creed Is and What It Is Not

Like all creeds, the Nicene-Constantinopolitan Creed is a litany of beliefs. While it contains several significant dogmas of Catholicism, it is not inclusive. As explained in Chapters 11 and 12, Roman Catholicism is a sacramental religion. The Creed contains no information about this basic foundational characteristic of the faith. Additionally, the Creed says very little about the concept of salvation and nothing about church structure including the office of the pope. Thus, while the Creed is a rule of faith, it is not intended as a complete catechism in one formula. It is important, therefore, to see what the Creed is and what it is not.

Profession of Faith

First and foremost the Creed is a profession of faith that provides a statement of personal and communal commitment. Faith is always personal and subjective; the language of faith is rooted in confession, profession, and bearing witness. Confession is a risky term, for one can never be sure that a particular perspective is absolutely correct. Yet in the Creed, Roman Catholics confess their belief in the ideas and teachings contained in the formula. Catholics profess through their action of bearing witness as well. When we bear witness to the reality we believe, there is a risk of appearing foolish in the eyes of the sophisticated. In bearing witness, one risks body as well as mind. One can reduce the Creed to a document with little impact, but to truly bear witness requires a profession and confession of faith, as an individual, but within the communal whole.

Rule of Faith

The Creed is also a rule of faith. It provides a norm for Christian identity, how Christians should read and understand the Sacred Scriptures and apply them to their lives. St. Irenaeus used the concept of a creed as a rule of faith in his refutation of the Gnostics and other radical groups. The Rule of Faith guides our understanding of Scripture. It sees the Hebrew Bible and New Testament as one continuity; it provides a norm for Christian life.

Definition of Faith

As a definition of faith, the Creed provides boundaries of Christian belief and, therefore, Christian community. While establishing the standards, however, the Creed does not exhaust the meaning of Christian life and practice. As previously described, the Creed contains many important teachings that are integral to Roman Catholic faith, but its purpose, nature, and brevity do not allow it to incorporate all aspects of this complex religious tradition. It does, however, have some important defining moments. When the Creed describes Jesus as "Messiah and Lord," it denies these titles to all other people. When it speaks of God in some unity of three "persons" it sets a rule for how the Divine must be understood. In outlining both human salvation and the belief in the Second Coming of Christ, certain parameters and goals for Christian life are fixed. In general the Creed defines specific ideas about Christianity, which make Christians themselves more clearly identifiable.

FACT

It is critical to understand from a religious perspective the concept of myth. Myth does not in any way mean fiction. Rather, from the perspective of religion, a myth is a story that represents a truth for that particular religious community. For example, did Jesus actually calm the storm as described in Mark 4:35–41? Whether or not this story is historically accurate does not detract from its ability to present the author's contention that Jesus is divine.

The Creed as a Symbol of Faith

As a symbol of faith, the Creed provides a sign of reception and membership for Christians. To profess the teachings and beliefs of the Creed affirms the common Christian story. The Creed is a baseline or common denominator by which Roman Catholics can publicly proclaim what they hold as sacred. When recited in common, the Creed becomes a great symbol of that shared faith. As a symbol, the Creed allows us to speak through analogy about God, truly but inadequately. The formula presents teachings that provide the logic for the basic Christian way of life. From the Creed, the concept of symbol has been expanded over the centuries. This is most evident in the sacraments, seven special signs that have been raised to the highest level of dogma and used as the basic tools for participation in the faith.

Functions of the Creed

The Creed serves several important functions for Roman Catholics. First, it narrates the basic Christian myth. The Creed tells the story of God's interface with the world. It claims that Christian belief is embedded in the story of the world. Therefore, the Christian commitment to our world is central. The Creed also interprets Scripture. It does not dictate how Scripture is to be read but provides a guide and direction to the proper reading of Scripture. This is because most all of the language of the Creed is derived from the New Testament. Thus, it frames how one reads the Scriptures.

The Creed provides three other important functions. First, it constructs a worldview for Roman Catholics. When reciting the Creed, the Catholic constructs a world built on the Christian myth and Scripture. This world is countercultural to contemporary life. The radical nature of the Creed becomes readily apparent from its teachings that contradict today's society. Secondly, the Creed guides the actions of Roman Catholics. Since Christianity preaches values and affirms a belief system contradictory to the world in which we live, the Creed guides Catholics' lives in this radical new world. It does not provide answers for every question or specific direction for every crossroad in life, but it does establish right belief (orthodoxy) that helps believers to recognize right practice (orthopraxy). Lastly, the Creed serves as a preparation for worship. As described in Chapter 18, the Creed serves to transition between the two major portions of the Roman Catholic Mass—the liturgy of the word and the liturgy of the Eucharist.

PART III

God

CHAPTER 8

The Trinity

Christianity understands God in a distinctive way compared with other Western monotheistic religions. The Trinity, the belief that God can only exist as a unique union of the Creator (Father), Redeemer (Son), and Sanctifier (Holy Spirit), like many Roman Catholic teachings, emerged from an evolutionary process that only became fixed in the sixth century. The ability of the church to work through heresies to achieve orthodoxy solidified the Trinity's place as central to all Christian belief.

The Concept of the Trinity

The Jewish concept of monotheism was brought directly into Christianity, but in a unique way. The Jews claimed Yahweh to be God of the universe. But Christians, and therefore Roman Catholics, using the New Testament and the evolution of theological thought and teaching, have claimed from the outset as a basic premise of their faith that God, while always existing as one, is actually three "persons": the Father, Son, and Holy Spirit. English uses the word *person* to designate the Father, Son, and Spirit, yet this word is inadequate, as it conjures in the minds of all three separate individuals. However, the word is derived from the Greek *prosopon*, meaning *mask*, as in an actor's role. The difficulty lies in finding an explanation that satisfies the human desire for knowing but at the same time maintains the theological absolutes that God is one, three persons, and equal in person. From Scripture and the products of theology over time, Christianity has developed the dogma of the Trinity as a foundational belief of the faith.

Old Testament Ideas of the Trinity

Although the Hebrew Bible (Old Testament) predates Jesus and Christianity, and, therefore, has no concept of the Trinity, nevertheless its understanding of God is not inconsistent with that of Christianity. Along with the Law, the central feature of the Torah is belief in monotheism. The Jews were the first great world religion to hold this belief; it is fundamental to Jewish theology. The God of the Old Testament, sometimes referred to as Yahweh or Elohim, is a living God who is intimately involved in the history of the people of Israel. God called the Jews into existence through Abraham; God was present for the great Exodus event when the Jews left Egypt, wandered in the desert for forty years, and eventually reached the promised land of Israel. God sent judges and later prophets as leaders and proclaimers of God's word. God as seen in the Torah is a very personal God, with many references to God as Father.

It is theologically unsound to say that the Torah contains passages that foreshadow the Christian concept of the Trinity, but God is referred to in various ways, a reality that again gives some opening to the future Christian dogma of the Trinity. The Hebrew Bible speaks of God in a plural sense. For example, Genesis 1:26 reads: "Then God said, 'Let us make humankind in our image, according to our likeness.'" Again, in Genesis 3:22 a similar idea is proclaimed: "Then the Lord God said, 'See, the man has become like one of us, knowing good and evil.'" In a different context, Isaiah 6:8 reads, "Then I heard the voice of the Lord saying, 'Whom shall I send, and who will go for us?'"

ESSENTIAL

Genesis Chapter 18 speaks of a visible manifestation of God to Abraham. Verse 2 reads: "He looked up and saw three men standing near him." While Biblical scholars interpret this passage in various ways, it is interesting to see the author refer to these guests, often interpreted as God, in a pluralistic way. This passage provides a different perspective on God.

The Old Testament's use of Word, Wisdom, and Spirit with respect to God also provides a certain prelude to the Christian belief in the Trinity. Proverbs Chapter 8 speaks of a personal nature of divine wisdom. This wisdom is related to God but distinct from the divine. The divine word is also seen as an expression of God. Psalm 147:15 reads: "He sent out his command to the earth; his word runs swiftly." The divine spirit is personal, confers divine power, and is associated with the Messiah. Evidence for the latter claim is found in Isaiah 11:1–2a: "A shoot shall come from the stump of Jesse, and a branch shall grow out of his roots. The Spirit of the Lord shall rest upon him."

New Testament Ideas of the Trinity

Without investigation it might be concluded that the New Testament, as the premiere primary text of Christianity, would present explicit theology concerning the complexities of the Trinity. However, this is not the case. Rather, while the Father, Son, and Holy Spirit are mentioned in the New Testament, official Church teaching on the Trinity developed through an evolutionary process that found its final proclamation in 1442.

First, it is important to understand the various roles assigned to Jesus in the New Testament. For example, Jesus is seen as Savior (Matthew 1:21, Philippians 3:20, Ephesians 5:23), judge (Matthew 25:31–46, II Corinthians 5:10), bridegroom (Mark 2:19–20, II Corinthians 11:2), and creator (Colossians 1:16, Hebrews 1:2). The various roles of Jesus provide an example of the multiple functions of God, a view that helps to see the varied ways God's power has been manifested in the world.

QUOTE

Wisdom 7:27 reads, "Although she is but one, she can do all things, and while remaining in herself, she renews all things; in every generation she passes into holy souls and makes them friends of God and prophets." The passage is a clear indication that she (Wisdom) is distinct from God. This is more evidence for the Christian understanding of God.

As one might expect, the New Testament provides many passages that illustrate the presence of the three "persons" of the Trinity and numerous other passages that describe this reality. The most obvious example, described by all three Synoptic evangelists (Matthew, Mark, and Luke) is the baptism of Jesus. In all of these accounts the three persons of the Trinity are present: the Father speaks from the heavens, the Son, Jesus, is the one baptized, and the Holy Spirit is present in the form of a dove. In Matthew's Gospel (28:19), Jesus tells his disciples to baptize "in the name of the Father and of the Son and of the Holy Spirit." In his corpus of letters, St. Paul makes numerous references to the Trinity. Possibly the most familiar to Roman Catholics is found in II Corinthians 13:13: "The grace of the Lord Jesus Christ, the love of God, and the communion of the Holy Spirit be with all of you." In John's Gospel there are numerous references to the Spirit of God, beginning in the famous prologue (1:1–18), but found as well in several other passages.

Economic Versus Immanent Trinity

While the New Testament provides several references to the presence of the three persons of the Trinity and even more evidence about the specific work of the Father, Son, and Holy Spirit, the theology of the Trinity has an evolutionary history that required significant time before becoming the dogma that Roman Catholics profess today. This doctrine developed in ways that were chronologically consistent but theologically different in the Eastern and Western churches.

FACT

Later, St. Thomas Aquinas used the Augustinian idea of self-knowledge to create a similar Trinitarian analogy. He spoke of the unitary person as knower, known, and knowledge, as God is Father, Son, and Holy Spirit. Using natural reason, he used this analogy as a virtual proof of the Trinity.

Greeks in the Eastern Church concentrated on the Economic Trinity, the concept of how Father, Son, and Holy Spirit are experienced in the history of salvation. The Father is seen as the source and origin of all; he is the one to whom especially the name God belongs. The Son proceeds from the Father in an eternal generation (eternally begotten). Thus, the Son, too, is rightly called God. The Spirit proceeds from the Father through the Son. From the Greek perspective God has a nature that is dependent on the individual as any three humans have different natures and personalities that are dependent on the individual. The Eastern Church saw the Son as the image of the Father and the Spirit as the image of the Son. For the Greeks, God comes to humanity through the actions of the Son and Spirit. The Father is revealed through the Son; through the Son he reaches out to humanity in the actions of the Holy Spirit. Thus, God's contact with humanity is historically definite, through the actions of the Son, and immediate, through the actions of the Spirit.

The Latin Church developed the concept of the Immanent Trinity, meaning how the Father, Son, and Holy Spirit exist within the inner life of God. St. Augustine was a famous proponent of the Latin view. Starting with the concept of one divine nature, rather than three persons, he argued that the life of God was by its very nature necessarily Trinitarian. For him the divine nature precedes any concept of individual personalities as articulated in the East. Similarly, Augustine claimed that every action of God was an action of the Trinity; no individual action can be attributed to any one of the persons.

In order to explain his idea he used the mind as an analogy and metaphor. He said the mind was composed of memory, cognition, and thinking. All three of these ideas are endemic and vitally important to the brain as a whole. Augustine argued that the three members of the Trinity were also of equal importance and, therefore, shared equally divine being.

Heresies Associated with the Doctrine of the Trinity

Christians, like all peoples of faith, seek to understand the belief they profess and hold sacred. In efforts to try to explain that which is basically inexplicable concerning the Trinity, at least from the perspective of Enlightenment reason, several prominent and at times infamous heresies arose in the patristic period of church history. One major heresy was the concept of subordinationism. In an effort to differentiate how the manifestations of God were found in the world, some placed the work of God in a hierarchical order. The Creator, or Father, was first on the scene and, therefore, had precedence in authority and power. Jesus, the Son, was next in the hierarchy. The Holy Spirit, sent into the world by Jesus after his return to heaven, was viewed in third rank. On the surface it seemed a plausible way to understand how God was manifested in the world, but it violated the basic contention that the persons of the Trinity were all equal. Additionally, such a hierarchy might lead one to see God as three instead of one.

ESSENTIAL

The need to maintain a consistent orthodox theology was the principal catalyst for patristic scholars to continually root out heresy and maintain the equal balance of three persons of equal nature in one God. This delicate balance was often challenged but generally done so to better understand a mystery rather than cause a schism.

Sabellianism (after Sabellius circa 200), commonly known as Modalism, was another Trinitarian heresy. Some suggested if God manifested different qualities at different chronological times in human history, it could be concluded that God acted in various modes. God first began as Creator, but when creation was finished and humanity required salvation, God shifted into the mode of Redeemer. After Jesus' salvific death and return to heaven, God could again shift modes and become the Sanctifier, the role of the Holy Spirit. Such a theology explains the three persons while keeping sacred and inviolate the monotheistic principle.

FACT

More than 200 years later at Florence (1442), the last official proclamation made by the church professes, "One true God, Father, Son and Holy Spirit, one substance, one essence, three persons in one God." Since belief in the Trinity has not been seriously challenged, no further proclamations have been deemed necessary.

The orthodox position was to maintain a balance of three basic qualities, namely that God is one, three persons, and equal in person. If one emphasizes the monotheism of God and the concept of God as three persons to the detriment of the equality of persons, the heresy created is subordinationism. If one emphasizes too strongly the monotheistic principle and the equality of God to the detriment of three persons, the result is Sabellianism (Modalism). In an effort to maintain the equality of God and the belief that God can only exist in the three persons of the Father, Son, and Holy Spirit, it is natural to conclude that God is actually three gods and not one. This is the third heresy of tritheism.

Official Church Teachings on the Trinity

Over its 2,000-year history, Roman Catholicism has made several official proclamations concerning the Trinity. It is important to understand, however, that the Trinity is an absolute mystery of faith. Even after its revelation, it will remain forever a mystery, for its reality is inexplicable from a perspective of reason. Nonetheless, the Nicene Creed (325) and later the Nicene-Constantinopolitan Creed (381) make significant theological statements about the Trinity. Most especially the formulae speak of the consubstantial nature (of one substance) of God and the relationship of the Son and the Holy Spirit to the Father. At the Fourth Lateran Council in 1215, in reaction to the heretical Albigenses, who regarded all matter as evil and thus denied the Incarnation, the bishops declared, "There is only one true God . . . Father, Son and Holy Spirit: three persons indeed but one essence, substance, or wholly simple nature."

God as a Community

The dogma of the Trinity presupposes a theology of human existence and revelation. It is theologically impossible to reflect on the mystery of God from the perspective of Christian faith without reflecting at the same time on the mystery of the Trinity. God's oneness is singular but also, at the same time, one of diversity and community. The view that God exists as a community has great importance for people of faith today.

QUESTION

How can the communal nature of the Trinity be understood?
One way that several theologians have suggested is to say the Son is eternally begotten by the Father with the Holy Spirit proceeding from the Father and the Son as the love between them.

Unfortunately, this view of community is not well appreciated by contemporary society. In the twenty-first century, individualism runs rampant in almost every aspect of society. While sports teams often win championships, individual athletes are those who are exalted. In business, politics, and the arts, especially popular music and films, the individual is once again placed on an iconic pedestal. The political system, corporation, or work of art plays at best "second fiddle" to the individual. People, especially in the Western world, are schooled from youth to achieve as much in material possession and as high a rank in the eyes of the world as possible to measure their progress and value in society.

This perspective, however, is totally inconsistent with a Trinitarian God who, from the Christian perspective, can only exist and function as a community of love. The members of the Trinity are not in competition and do not seek recognition. Rather, the members of the Trinity have specific functions that have been manifested over the course of Salvation history. All of these functions, however, have one ultimate goal: to bring salvation to God's greatest creation, the human race. Humanity today would be well served to learn a lesson from the life of the Trinity and seek to live as a community of faith and love. Such an attitude, with consistent actions, would move the world forward to greater harmony and peace.

Trinitarian Heresies Explained

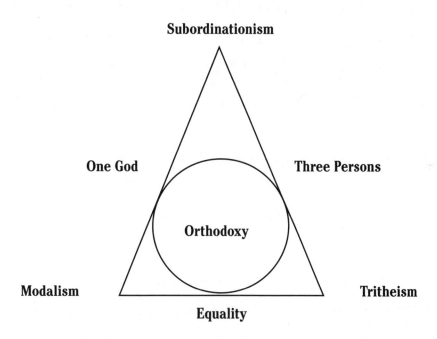

1. If one emphasizes that God is one and three persons, but fails to acknowledge God's equality, the heresy is subordinationism.
2. If one emphasizes that God is one and equal, but fails to acknowledge God is three persons, the heresy is modalism.
3. If one emphasizes that God is equal and three persons, but fails to acknowledge that God is one, the heresy is tritheism.
4. If one is able to balance all three basic concepts—that God is one, equal, and three persons—this is orthodox belief.

CHAPTER 9

Jesus Christ

Jesus Christ, understood by Christians to be the Son of God and the long-awaited Messiah proclaimed in the Hebrew Bible, is the central figure of Christianity. Like the Trinity, Jesus' existence as both God and man is a mystery of faith. It is essential to the study of Catholicism to be thoroughly grounded in the teachings associated with Christ and how these developed into the dogmas that are so fundamental to Catholicism today.

Jesus the Messiah

One of the central themes of the exilic and post-exilic prophets of the Hebrew Bible is the belief that God would send a Messiah to Israel. The prophecy, as understood by the Jews, foretold that this person would be a great king, a ruler who would restore the greatness of Israel as enjoyed during the reign of David and his son Solomon.

One of the best illustrations of this Jewish belief is found in Jeremiah 23:5–6: "The days are surely coming, says the Lord, when I will raise up for David a righteous Branch, and he shall reign as King and deal wisely, and shall execute justice and righteousness in the land. In his days Judah will be saved and Israel will live in safety. And this is the name by which he will be called: 'The Lord is our righteousness.'" This idea is reinforced by II Samuel 7:12–16. Here, the "messianic figure" is described as a virtuous person who will establish the Kingdom of God. He will bring judgment upon those who afflict Israel. This image of a powerful political ruler, sent by God, who would destroy Israel's enemies, was a foundational belief of the Jews. It was also assumed that this king would be a faithful Jew and completely observant of the Law, which was a basic premise of Orthodox Judaism.

ESSENTIAL

Another basic tenet to the concept of Messianism was the certainty that this king would be human. As the first monotheistic religion, Judaism could not even perceive that the Messiah would be divine. Any ruler sent by God must be human, or the basic premise of the oneness of Yahweh would be violated.

Jesus Christ, as described by the four Gospel evangelists, does not fulfill the requirements of the prophecy uttered hundreds of years earlier by Jeremiah and other prophets. The Gospels describe Jesus as a rather austere figure, who was born in a humble setting and lived his youth and young adulthood in almost total obscurity in a small town, Nazareth, well north of Jerusalem, the latter being the capital and center of Jewish government and religious faith. Although St. Matthew in his Gospel clearly draws a connection by ancestry between Jesus and King David, such knowledge was certainly disregarded if known at all by Christ's contemporaries. He neither lived like nor claimed to be a king from the human perspective, but rather preferred the life of an itinerant preacher who gained many disciples and appointed twelve apostles as his closest followers. Jesus often challenged the Jewish law, especially rules that govern the Sabbath, and the authority of the Jewish religious elite, often accusing them of hypocrisy. Such behavior was considered inconsistent for one who claimed to be the Messiah.

QUOTE

Matthew 27:11b–12 reads: "The governor [Pontius Pilate] asked him, 'Are you the King of the Jews?' Jesus said: 'You say so.' But when he was accused by the chief priests and elders, he did not answer." Jesus was intentionally vague when asked if he was a king. This was problematic for one who claimed to be the Messiah.

The Son of God

Clearly the most problematic claim made by Jesus and by many of his followers was that he was the Son of God. Jesus closely associated himself with God and often referred to his relationship with his Father. When he predicted his own death he often spoke of sending the Spirit into the world. The Gospels report not only his numerous miraculous healings of others and his ability to control the elements of nature (Mark 4:35–41, calming the storm on the Sea of Galilee, for example) but claim that he could forgive sins, a power reserved to God alone. This assertion was completely antithetical to both the concept of the Messiah and the premise of monotheism as presented in the Law. Judaism separated itself from all other religions by its insistence on the oneness of God. Yahweh is very clear in the first law of the Decalogue (Ten Commandments): "I am the Lord your God . . . you shall have no other gods before me." (Exodus 20:2–3)

Christian Understanding of Jesus as Messiah

Since Jesus did not seem to "fit the mold" of the messianic prophecy, why did Christians believe him to be the long-awaited Messiah? What was it about Jesus that justified others calling him the Christ, the Anointed One? The best answer seems to be that Jesus was executed for claiming that he was the Christ. While not outwardly claiming this title, he never denied it. Thus, his followers, believing him to be the Christ, were emboldened to proclaim their understanding to others.

Still, Christians had to adapt their understanding of Christ to include the fact that the Anointed One must die and rise. It was necessary for Christians to show how Jesus the Christ, the one who died and rose from the dead, could be found in Scripture. A prediction of his death is found in Psalm 2:1–2: "Why do the nations conspire and the peoples plot in vain? The kings of earth set themselves, and the rulers take counsel together, against the Lord and his anointed." Similarly, Psalm 118:22 reads, "The stone rejected by the builder has become the cornerstone." The resurrection of the Messiah is alluded to in Psalm 110:1: "The Lord says to my lord, 'Sit at my right hand until I make your enemies your footstool.'" The prophet Hosea (6:2) is even clearer on the resurrection: "After two days he will revive us; on the third day he will raise us up, that we may live before him."

Completing the Work of the Christ

Once Christians had found evidence in the Hebrew Bible that the Messiah must die and rise, it was necessary to show how Jesus had completed the work of the Christ. If Christ was to destroy the enemies of Israel, how did Jesus, an executed criminal, accomplish this task? Christians answered by saying that this task of the Christ would be accomplished in Jesus' Second Coming. Again, Christians went to the Scriptures for answers. In Mark 14:62 and Matthew 26:64 they found evidence that Jesus would come again.

A second Christian understanding of how Jesus completed the work of the Christ developed as a result of proclaiming the Gospel outside Palestine. When Jesus did not return immediately, as St. Paul firmly expected, peoples to whom he preached, namely Gentiles outside Palestine, proffered the idea that Jesus completed the work of the Christ by reigning in heaven. St. Paul, especially in Romans 5:12–6:11, which emphasizes sin and grace, provides an explanation of Jesus completing Christ's work in heaven.

QUOTE

Mark 14:62 reads, "Jesus said, . . . You will see the Son of Man seated at the right hand of the Power, and coming with the clouds of heaven." The powerful metaphor of Jesus coming to reclaim the world became a standard Roman Catholic teaching. It is best expressed in the writings of St. Paul in I Thessalonians 4:13–18.

A third explanation for how Jesus completed the work of Christ is seen in the Incarnation. The Gospels of Matthew and Luke, the two that have infancy narratives, both speak of Jesus' conception in the womb of Mary through the work of the Holy Spirit. This miraculous event is connected with the belief in Jesus' pre-existence, described especially well in the prologue of John's Gospel (1:1–18). This reality helped to form an alternative explanation of how Jesus did the work of the Christ. Jesus' words and deeds suggested to many that he was an emissary of Wisdom or possibly even Wisdom herself. If Jesus chose to come into the world as a human being (the concept of the Incarnation), then his life itself was the establishment of the Kingdom of God. From this perspective Jesus' pre-existence and Incarnation allow him to complete the work of the Christ.

Catholicism's Teachings about Jesus

As the central figure to all Christianity, the basic teachings associated with Jesus of Nazareth are common to all mainline Christian denominations. These teachings evolved during the patristic (0–600) period of church history, prior to the major divisions in Christianity (described in Chapter 2), namely the creation of the Orthodox traditions in the eleventh century and the Protestant Reformation of the sixteenth century. Some of these teachings are found in the New Testament; others developed through theological discussion and church councils that sought to rein in heretical beliefs.

The Incarnation

The Incarnation, the belief that Jesus, the second person of the Trinity (see Chapter 8) took human flesh, is described in the Gospels of Luke and Matthew. Luke's version is more detailed, describing that Mary, a young woman engaged to a man named Joseph, received from the angel Gabriel a message that she had been chosen to be the mother of God's Son, Jesus. Mary questioned how this was possible since she was a virgin. The angel responded that the child of her womb would be conceived through the power of the Holy Spirit. Mary's positive response, "Here am I, a servant of the Lord; let it be with me according to your word," her *fiat*, placed into action a whole series of events. This famous visit of the angel, known by Catholics as the Annunciation (celebrated March 25), leads directly to the Incarnation, celebrated as Christmas each December 25.

QUESTION

What is the significance of the three gifts presented by the wise men?
Gold represented their understanding that Jesus was a king. Frankincense signified the belief that Jesus was God. Myrrh represented that this divine king was also human and would die to save his people.

While the two Gospel accounts differ on many details, the basic teachings of the Incarnation are consistent. Luke's more descriptive account says Mary and Joseph were from Nazareth. He describes the couple's journey to Bethlehem as fulfillment of an order from the Romans for men to travel to their ancestral home for a census. Luke also describes Jesus' birth, including its humble circumstances. Matthew describes none of these events but does add that after Jesus' birth, the Holy Family (Jesus, Mary, and Joseph) was visited by three "wise men" from the east who, upon arrival, gave Jesus special gifts of gold, frankincense, and myrrh. Additionally, Matthew informs us that the Jewish King Herod, fearful of a "newborn King," ordered the slaughter of all infants in the region two years of age or younger. This order forced Joseph to take his family to Egypt until Herod died. These differences aside, both accounts agree that Jesus was conceived by the power of the Holy Spirit and born in Bethlehem.

Jesus' Relationship with God the Father

The divinity and humanity of Jesus were a subject of theological debate for many centuries. At the Councils of Nicaea (325) and Constantinople I (381), the teaching of Arius was condemned and the divinity of Christ affirmed. What precisely, however, was the relationship between the Father and Son? The bishops at Nicaea used the Greek term *homoousios*, meaning of the same substance, to describe how the Father and Son were related. This was expanded by the Cappadocian Fathers at Constantinople I where the words *ousia* and *hypostases* were utilized to speak of the complete relationship of the three members of the Trinity. That which was common to all was their *ousia*, and that which was proper to each was their *hypostases*. Since the Father and Son were of the same substance, there could never be the problem of subordinationism, with the Son and Spirit subordinate to the Father.

Atonement

Atonement is the concept that sin can be forgiven by God if one follows certain rituals. This belief is found in both Judaism and Christianity. In ancient Israel, the pardoning of transgressions was generally the task of the high priest and usually conducted on the solemn day of Atonement, Yom Kippur. However, this more generic concept of atonement was understood more personally through the actions of an innocent victim being sacrificed for the sins of another, whether that be an individual or a group of people. Known as vicarious atonement, this concept is best seen in a series of four "Suffering Servant" passages in Isaiah (42:1–4; 49:1–6; 50:4–9; 52:13–53:12). In these passages the servant, most probably a metaphor for Israel itself, becomes an instrument of salvation through his ability to suffer, innocent though he be, for the transgressions of another.

The Christian concept of atonement centers on the person of Jesus. Christ's death is seen as a ransom that liberates all people from their slavery to sin; Jesus atones for the sin of Adam and all humankind that came after him. The history of Christianity has developed three different metaphors to understand how the concept of atonement functions to save humanity. The first idea, championed by the fourth-century theologian Gregory of Nyssa, is referred to as the ransom theory. Matthew 20:28 reads, "The Son of Man came not to be served but to serve, and to give his life as a ransom for many." This idea, repeated in Mark 10:45, expresses the idea that Jesus gave his life freely to liberate humanity from its slavery to sin and, as a consequence, the inability to achieve eternal life. God pays the debt to Satan by exchanging the sinless life of Jesus for the sinful reality of humanity.

QUOTE

An excellent example of the atonement theme in the Suffering Servant passages is Isaiah 53:3a, 5: "He was despised and rejected by others; a man of suffering and acquainted with infirmity; . . . But he was wounded for our transgressions, crushed for our iniquities; upon him was the punishment that made us whole, and by his bruises we are healed."

The second theory, supported by St. Anselm in the eleventh century, uses the concept of "satisfaction." In this case God is the one who receives the payment of debt. Anselm believed that God was grieved by the imperfections of humanity. Thus, only a perfect sacrifice, that of Jesus, the God-man, would satisfy God and pay the debt.

A third metaphor, based on the concept of love, has both ancient and current roots. Both Peter Abelard, a contemporary of Anselm, and the twentieth-century Swiss theologian Paul Tillich describe Jesus' personal sacrifice on the cross as an act of God's love for humanity. In turn, humanity, God's greatest creation, is transformed by this love, with the aid of the Holy Spirit, to lead lives more consistent with the message of Jesus.

Second Coming of Jesus (Parousia)

The New Testament has numerous references to the concept that Jesus will return in a triumphant apocalyptic event. Throughout Christian history numerous individuals have predicted this event and, in the process, gathered many disciples as a community to await the end of the world. Various

Protestant groups hold two theories, based on different interpretations of the books of Daniel and Revelation, which speak of a millennial period. One theory suggests Christ will come and inaugurate a 1,000-year period of peace; the other belief suggests there will be a 1,000-year period of preparation with Christ returning at the end.

Catholicism, on the other hand, suggests that the second coming of Christ will be sudden and immediate, but it will be preceded by a time of significant trial that will shake the faith of many who believe. The Church suggests that it is pointless to speculate when the second coming of Christ will occur. Rather, Catholics are told to focus their attention on living the Gospel's message daily and, thus, always being prepared should the end come. The immediacy of Christ's return is demonstrated in Matthew 24:27, "For as the lightning comes from the east and flashes as far as the west, so will be the coming of the Son of Man."

Jesus the God-Man

Certainly the most basic teaching associated with Jesus Christ, that he is both divine and human, is the most difficult to explain theologically and has created the greatest controversies and heresies over time. It is essential to understand how the present Christian (and specifically Roman Catholic) teaching that Jesus is both God and man in one person was developed.

Once the definition of the Trinity was established to the basic satisfaction of all at Constantinople I in 381, a shift in emphasis toward the person of Christ became evident in theological debates. Christological controversies dominated the fifth and sixth centuries, especially in the Eastern Church. Christians did not question that Jesus was both human and divine; rather the question was how were his humanity and divinity united in one person. How could this be explained?

The Alexandrian School

Two schools of Christological thought arose, both of which sought to answer this weighty and difficult question. The Alexandrian School, stressing the divinity of Christ, took its initial ideas from Appollinarius, who strongly opposed the position of Arius. Appollinarius argued that Jesus could not have a human soul and remain sinless; he concluded, therefore, that Jesus had no human passions or ideas. The great champion of the

Alexandrian School was Cyril. He believed that both before and after the Incarnation the divinity of Jesus was present. Borrowing from his predecessor, Appollinarius, Cyril suggested that Jesus was one nature that was incarnate of the divine word. He used the term *hypostatic* (natural) *union* to explain how the human and divine are united in Christ. He insisted that there was no confusion or mixture between Jesus' divinity and humanity; they remained separate identities.

The Antiochene School

The Antiochene School, while defending the divinity of Jesus, opposed Appollinarius, Cyril, and the general Alexandrian School by emphasizing the total humanity of Jesus. This led to a sharp distinction between Jesus Christ, Son of God, and Jesus Christ, Son of Mary. The chief champion of the Antiochene School, Theodore of Mopsuestia, concerned that the complete divinity and humanity of Jesus be maintained in one person, suggested that he possessed two natures. The term *indwelling* was used to explain how the two natures operated as one functional identity.

ESSENTIAL

It was imperative for Christians to maintain that Mary was the *Theotokos*. If Mary is not the Mother of God, then at some time after the human birth of Jesus, God in some way came upon or "adopted" Jesus. Such an idea directly contradicts Christ's pre-existence and the unity of his divinity and humanity.

Debates Between the Schools

These two Christological schools clashed during the fifth century, requiring two separate ecumenical councils to finally develop a teaching to explain how divinity and humanity were united in Christ. In 431, the Roman Emperor, Theodosius II, called the world's bishops to meet at Ephesus in order to address the controversy raised by Nestorius, Bishop of Constantinople. A member of the Antiochene School, Nestorius believed that God could neither be born nor suffer. Additionally, like others who opposed Appollinarius, he believed that the one who atoned for sin must be of the same race as the one who caused it. Thus, Nestorius saw Jesus as a second Adam who overcame human sinfulness. However, he separated the human Jesus from the divine and, therefore, concluded that Mary was not the Mother of God, *Theotokos*, but rather only the mother of the human Christ, *Christoto-kos*. Cyril, champion of the Alexandrian School, opened the council and secured the condemnation of Nestorius despite his absence. However, this was not the end of the story. While the principals active at Ephesus died, their disciples took their place and continued the fight.

It was not until 451, when the world's bishops met at Chalcedon, that the question concerning the divinity and humanity of Christ was finally resolved in a definition that has stood the test of time. Two years earlier, Pope Leo I produced his famous "Tome," a document to be read at the council. It became the basis for the definition that the bishops ultimately produced. In this document the pope stressed that Christ was two natures in one person. He emphasized the humanity of Jesus by saying that his flesh was a substantive reality derived from the body of Mary. Equally, his divinity was through the work of the Holy Spirit. At Chalcedon, in words that have become central to the Catholic Tradition, the bishops defined Jesus as, "one and the same Christ, Son, Lord, Only-begotten, recognized in two natures, without confusion, without change, without division, without separation; the distinction of natures being in no way annulled by the union, but rather the characteristics of each nature being preserved and coming together to form one person and one subsistence, not as parted or separated into two persons, but one and the same Son and Only-begotten God the Word, Lord Jesus Christ."

Understanding Jesus Today

The theological debates of past centuries that eventually led to the definition of Jesus as two natures, human and divine, in one person, articulated at Chalcedon are not prominent today, but new and important contemporary questions, nonetheless, capture the attention of inquisitive Catholic minds. One of the basic issues arises from how one perceives Jesus Christ. For some, Jesus is seen as an exalted divine figure, so far beyond human conception and understanding that there is seemingly little connection between Christ and the human person. This perception, known as "high Christology," while not as common today, is still found in the thinking of many. The other basic image sees Jesus as one who is very approachable, close, and friendly. This idea, known as "low Christology," is more common today for it classifies Jesus as a friend and not one to be feared.

Jesus of History and Faith

The question of the historical Jesus has captivated scholars since the late eighteenth century; it continues to be a question today. What precisely can we know about Jesus from a historical perspective? The Gospels were not written to be historical biographies of Jesus of Nazareth, but rather are documents of faith that seek to present to various communities in antiquity the life and mission of Jesus. This question of the historical veracity of the extant sources that describe Jesus' life reached its apex in the work of Albert Schweitzer and his late-nineteenth-century monograph, *The Quest for the Historical Jesus*. Schweitzer said that, from an academic historical perspective, little can be verified historically about the actual events of Jesus' life save that he was born, lived and traveled in Palestine, was ordered executed, and was proclaimed by his followers to have risen from the dead.

The Christ of faith, in contrast, emphasizes the post-Resurrection Jesus described by the Gospels and revered through the Christian era as Son of God. The Christ of faith cannot be verified by extant historical documents but is rather marked by billions of believers over the centuries.

CHAPTER 10

The Holy Spirit

Pneumatolgy, the theology of the Holy Spirit, is possibly the least known and appreciated of Catholic subjects of study. Knowledge of the Holy Spirit, sent into the world at Pentecost, is often lost in the concentration on the Father and the Son. For some, however, the Spirit of God is integral to guide them toward Christ and eternal life. A study of Catholicism must include an overview of the theology of the Third Person of the Trinity and the special gifts the Spirit brings to humankind.

The Pentecost Event

Pentecost, celebrated fifty days after the Resurrection, is narrated in The Acts of the Apostles 2:1–13. The author, St. Luke, says that the apostles and other close disciples of Jesus were gathered together in one place when from heaven came a sound like the rush of the wind that filled the room where they were seated. Tongues of fire appeared to them and each, filled with the Holy Spirit, began to speak in languages "as the Spirit gave them ability." (2:4b) There were devout Jews from many regions in Jerusalem at the time. They were amazed to hear these unlearned men speak in their own native languages. They were perplexed and amazed and wondered what this great sign meant.

ESSENTIAL

During his life, Jesus prophesied that he would send the Spirit into the world. He said, "But the Advocate, the Holy Spirit, whom the Father will send in my name, will teach you everything, and remind you of all that I have said to you." (John 14:25–26) The Spirit's arrival was, thus, the fulfillment of Jesus' promise.

Inspired and enlightened by the Holy Spirit, the apostles went forward and fearlessly preached about Jesus to others. Peter experienced a spectacular conversion through the power of the Spirit. He cast timidity aside and with great zeal and without regard to personal risk became the great apostle to his brother and sister Jews. Tradition says that after the Roman Diaspora (A.D. 70), the apostles scattered to many lands and, inspired by the Holy Spirit, preached in many countries and to many people about Jesus.

The Holy Spirit in Scripture

The New Testament uses the word *Spirit* or *Spirit of God* to signify many different concepts. At times these words speak of the human spirit under the influence of God. St. Paul especially uses the concept of Spirit to signify God acting through humanity. However, the Scriptures also clearly demonstrate that the Holy Spirit is a divine person who is neither the Father nor the Son.

The distinctive nature of the Holy Spirit and that this person is synonymous with God is demonstrated in numerous Scripture passages. For Paul it is the Spirit of God who speaks through the prophet. While a prisoner in Rome, he stated, "The Holy Spirit was right in saying to your ancestors through the prophet Isaiah." (Acts 28:25) Similarly, in I Corinthians 3:16, Paul writes, "Do you not know that you are God's temple and that God's Spirit dwells in you?" The evangelists also attributed divine traits and power to the Holy Spirit. For example, baptism is conferred in the name of the Father, Son, and Holy Spirit. The Incarnation is accomplished when the angel Gabriel tells Mary that she is pregnant by the power of the Holy Spirit. In a post-Resurrection appearance, Jesus attributes the power to forgive sin to the Spirit: "Receive the Holy Spirit. If you forgive the sins of any, they are forgiven them; if you retain the sins of any, they are retained." The omniscience of the Holy Spirit is also addressed by Saint Paul: "These things God has revealed to us through the Spirit; for the Spirit searches everything, even the depths of God." (I Corinthians 2:10)

The Tradition and Theology of the Holy Spirit

St. Anselm's definition of theology, "faith seeking understanding," is no better illustrated than in the development of the theology of the Holy Spirit during the patristic period of church history. The early church fathers sought to understand the role and person of the Spirit and to explain the Spirit's relationship to the Father and Son. These early church scholars wanted to verify and expand the testimony of the New Testament concerning the Holy Spirit.

St. Clement of Rome, the fourth pope, in his "Epistle to the Corinthians" says that the Spirit was the inspiration and guide to the Evangelists; He was the voice of Jesus, as Paul had said earlier, who spoke through the prophets and other writers of the Hebrew Scriptures. The martyr, St. Polycarp (d. 155), expressed clear distinctions among the Father, Son, and Holy Spirit. In his great work, *Against Heresies*, St. Irenaeus (d. 202) spoke of the eternal nature of the Holy Spirit. Additionally, he attributed the value of the sacraments to the Spirit. Tertullian (160–220) seems to be the first church father to clearly affirm as an absolute reality the divinity of the Spirit by claiming that he was of the same substance of the Father and the same God with the Father and the Son. Moving chronologically closer to the Council of Nicaea, it was St. Athanasius who refuted the idea that the Holy Spirit was a creature but rather was clearly God. The church fathers' teaching on the Holy Spirit reached its apex with the Cappadocian fathers, at Constantinople I (381) (see Chapter 7).

Procession of the Spirit

Unquestionably, the most difficult and certainly most controversial theological teaching associated with the Holy Spirit is the concept of procession. In essence this term refers to the relationship between the divine persons in the Trinity. The Son proceeds from the Father and the Holy Spirit proceeds from the Father and the Son.

Belief that the Holy Spirit proceeds from the Father and the Son has been constantly held by the church fathers in their teachings. St. Athanasius claimed the Son was the source of the Spirit; Cyril of Alexandria wrote that the Holy Spirit draws its nature from the Son. A council held at Seleucia in 410 proclaimed faith in the "Holy Living Spirit, the Holy Living Paraclete, who proceeds from the Father and the Son." St. Augustine in his Tractate 99 synthesized the teaching of those who preceded him: "Just as there is only one Father, just as there is only one Lord or one Son, so there is only one Spirit, who is, consequently, the Spirit of both. . . . Why then should you refuse to believe that He [the Spirit] proceeds also from the Son, since He is also the Spirit of the Son?"

FACT

While the Latin West insisted that the Holy Spirit proceeded from the Father and the Son (*filioque*), the Greek East continued to insist that the Spirit proceeded from the Father through the Son. Historically the difference was extremely significant; theologically, however, both sides expressed the same reality in slightly different ways.

The Roman Tradition that the Holy Spirit proceeds from the Father and the Son must be slightly nuanced for a proper understanding. The Spirit proceeds from the Father and Son as from a single principle. Thus, the Spirit proceeds not from the distinctiveness of the two but from their one divine perfection. This teaching was verified at Lyons II (1274) and Florence (1431).

Is it appropriate to refer to God with the male pronoun He?
Limitations of the English language force one to choose he or she for God, since God is not an inanimate object. However, many theologians suggest that the Spirit, as love and charity, expresses the female element of God.

The means of procession of the Holy Spirit is different from that of the Son, who is eternally begotten of the Father. Theology uses the word *spiration* to describe the specialized procession of the Spirit from the Father and Son. The difference between these processions is difficult to describe. St. Thomas Aquinas suggested the Son proceeded through the Intellect and the Holy Spirit through the Will of God. Whereas the Son, using the words of Scripture, is the image of God, His Word, the holiness of the Spirit comes from His spiration. His holiness is found in the will of God. This theological perspective is the foundation that explains why in the writings of the Fathers the Spirit is often referred to as love and charity.

Gifts of the Holy Spirit

The unitive reality of God suggests that what is attributable to one person is found in all, yet each member of the Trinity possesses certain works and gifts that are especially associated with that person. The Father is most associated with creation; the Son, Jesus Christ, is the Redeemer of humanity. The Holy Spirit, the Sanctifier, has certain gifts that, while found in the Father and Son, are especially associated with the Spirit.

The spiritual gifts described by St. Paul in I Corinthians 12:4–11 are closely associated with the Holy Spirit. Paul says that there are a variety of gifts, services, and activities, but it is the same Spirit of God who is the source of all. The gifts are given to foster the common good. The traditional gifts of the Holy Spirit are wisdom, understanding, counsel/right judgment, fortitude/courage, knowledge, piety/reverence, and fear of the Lord. These gifts are given primarily to assist the person in achieving sanctification. These gifts help one to be attentive to the call of God and give the person who receives them the ability to obtain grace, making one more attuned to the common vocation of holiness to which all Christians are called.

QUOTE

St. Paul writes, "All these [gifts] are activated by one and the same Spirit, who allots to each one individually just as the Spirit chooses." (I Corinthians 12:11) It is clear from this passage that Paul understands the Spirit as the one who bestows gifts. Thus, the gifts are not earned but given freely at the discretion of God.

In addition to the spiritual gifts of the Holy Spirit, there is a second group, often referred to as charismata, which are also described by St. Paul in I Corinthians 12:28–31. Paul describes the gift of speaking with wisdom, knowledge, and faith. He also describes the gift of healing, the ability to perform miracles, and the gifts of prophecy, discerning spirits, speaking in tongues, and interpreting tongues. These special gifts, not required for the sanctification of a person, are nonetheless not bestowed indiscriminately. However, extant sources indicate that these gifts were relatively common during the apostolic age in larger Christian communities such as those in Rome and Jerusalem.

Fruits of the Holy Spirit

The popular expression "actions speak louder than words" can be aptly applied to the gifts of the Holy Spirit. St. James (2:14) reminds his readers, "What good is it, my brothers and sisters, if you say you have faith but do not have works? Can faith save you?" Individuals receive various gifts of the Spirit, but how these gifts are used and their manifestations in our society are critical. As they say, if we talk the talk, we must walk the walk.

These ideas, associated most strongly when speaking of the Third Person of the Blessed Trinity, are called the Fruits of the Holy Spirit. In Galatians 5:22–23, St. Paul lists several twelve specific actions through which the gifts of the Holy Spirit are manifested in our society. These fruits of the Spirit are not habits or permanent characteristics of an individual but rather specific acts performed through the use of the Spirit's gifts. The traditional fruits of the Holy Spirit are charity, joy, peace, patience, goodness, kindness, long-suffering, humility, faithfulness, modesty, continence, and chastity. In order to be fruits, these acts are to be performed without duress or mandate and through the exercise of one's free will. If any difficulty is incurred through these actions, the joy and satisfaction achieved through their accomplishment must always prevail. While such acts may bring hope, peace, and strength to others, they should bring an even greater sense of these virtues and others to the one performing them.

Charismatic Catholics

Catholic Charismatic Renewal, a relatively recent movement in Roman Catholicism, is characterized by active manifestations of the gifts of the Spirit in the faith community. This renewal movement originated in 1967 when students and faculty at Duquesne University in Pittsburgh claimed to have experienced a special presence of the Holy Spirit during a retreat. Several manifested specific gifts of the Spirit, especially speaking in tongues (glossolalia) and the ability to heal. The movement quickly expanded to the University of Notre Dame and the University of Michigan where similar retreats generated the same manifestations of the Spirit. Over the next thirty years, the movement expanded with groups of Charismatic Catholics gathering regularly in many locations across the world.

ESSENTIAL

Although initially cautious, the church universal has endorsed Charismatic Renewal. In March 1992, Pope John Paul II stated, "At this moment in the Church's history, Charismatic Renewal can play a significant role in promoting the much-needed defense of Christian life in societies where secularism and materialism have weakened many people's ability to respond to the Spirit and to discern God's loving call."

Worship by Charismatic Catholics is characterized by singing, personal sharing of faith and the spiritual journey, and often glossolalia. Those who regularly attend such prayer services and Masses believe that the ability to speak in tongues, one of the gifts specifically mentioned by St. Paul in I Corinthians, is given to some for the express purpose to praise God. The association of glossolalia with the Holy Spirit is clearly articulated in Acts 2:4: "All of them were filled with the Holy Spirit and began to speak in other languages, as the Spirit gave them the ability." Protestant churches, especially in the United States, collectively grouped as Pentecostal, see glossolalia as a definitive sign of one's baptism in the Spirit. This same idea is held by Charismatic Catholics.

Today the Charismatic movement is characterized by three common actions. Prayer services where people gather to sing, share their stories, and reflect on Scripture are held in many different parishes. Healing Masses are also part of the contemporary Catholic fabric of prayer. Believers attend with the hope that certain priests, possessed with the spiritual gift of healing, can bring relief and even cure various maladies of the body and/or mind. The traditional laying on of hands by the priest is often accompanied by individuals being "slain in the spirit," an effect experienced when people, overcome by the power of the Spirit, pass into a state which to an outside observer appears to be a fainting spell. A third common practice by Charismatic Catholics is participation in the "Life in the Spirit Seminar." A series of seven talks, often presented one per week, the seminar offers those who attend an opportunity to grow in the power of the Holy Spirit. The seminar's apex comes when those attending receive their baptism in the Spirit, the same gift received by the apostles on the day of Pentecost.

CHAPTER 11

The Sacraments of Initiation

Roman Catholicism, like all Christian denominations, holds Jesus Christ as its founder and principal teacher. The daily practice of Catholics, however, unlike their Protestant brothers and sisters, is centered about the seven sacraments, special signs that mark significant events in the life of Jesus and various rites of passage in the course of human life. It is essential to understand what sacraments are, their various categories, and how they developed, both historically and theologically. This study begins with the three sacraments of initiation: baptism, Eucharist, and confirmation.

The Concept of Sacraments

The seven sacraments of Roman Catholicism are the foundation for day-to-day practice of the faith. Why have people of faith throughout history found sacraments or signs to be so vital? There are some important reasons why communities of faith have used signs in their day-to-day practice of religion. From an anthropological perspective, communities of faith that endure need myth, ritual, and symbol. Myth, as explained in Chapter 5, provides stories that express religious truth to peoples of faith. Ritual and symbol help to provide identity for religion, which in turn helps bring order to society. From a theological perspective, signs are also extremely important. When trying to argue for the presence of God in the world, it is quite possible to move from created things to the creator. Additionally, finite things, as seen in ritual and symbol, help humanity to express an understanding of the infinite, in this case the divinity of God. Through ritual and symbol (that is, through signs), the supernatural can be found in the natural. Such signs have numerous meanings; they cannot be reduced to one particular idea. Therefore, these signs become symbols of an invisible reality.

ESSENTIAL

Religious symbols have two important functions. First, they represent some significant reality. When dealing with faith it is not always possible to have the reality present and, therefore, symbols represent such realities. Secondly, symbols affect that to which they refer. They draw members of the faith group closer, thus creating a community.

Ritual, which often accompanies symbol and sign, is the outward and repetitive action that communicates some religious teaching or reality. Such rituals communicate values, beliefs, and ideas that give both clarity and stability to religious communities, and help to transform individual members to a deeper sense of commitment to the teachings and ideas of the faith. These rituals are often expressed through rites of passage and sacrifice.

Definitions of Sacraments

Many famous theologians and significant documents of faith have, over the course of Christian history, provided definitions for sacraments. One of the most famous early definitions comes from St. Augustine. He wrote, "Sacraments are visible signs of invisible grace." The famous Baltimore catechism, produced initially at the end of the nineteenth century, gave this definition: "A sacrament is an outward sign instituted by Christ to give grace." In both of these definitions we see the concept of sign and the presence of grace from God. Additionally, we see that sacraments are a visible manifestation of an invisible reality. In other words, sacraments help us to visualize that which can only be known by faith. They help to place muscle and flesh on the skeleton of religious belief.

History of Sacraments and Sacramentality

While the New Testament seems to argue against noncultic practice in prayer, there is evidence as well that faith and possibly conversion can be ritualized. This is most evident in the post-resurrection account of Luke 24:13–25, the Road to Emmaus. In this story, Jesus encounters two disciples, one named Cleopas, who are walking from Jerusalem to Emmaus. Although disciples, these two men do not recognize Jesus until they arrive at their destination, and through ritual, in this case the breaking of bread, their eyes are opened and they realize they have been conversing with Jesus. The story, important in many ways, demonstrates the power and effect of ritual, a basic theological tenet of sacraments.

Early Development of the Sacraments

During the first few centuries of Roman Catholicism, development of the sacraments was not formal but rather an attempt to move away from mystery cults to the concept of sign and symbol. One important development during these early years was the concept of the sacramental seal. Certain sacraments, namely baptism, confirmation, and holy orders, impart on the recipient an indelible seal. These sacraments, therefore, can only be received once.

St. Augustine provided the first great theological insights to the development of sacraments. He first spoke of sacraments as rites that produce an effect. He taught that when one receives a sacrament, the individual always receives the *res* (effect) but not necessarily the *virtus* (grace).

ESSENTIAL

The New Testament provides direct evidence for some sacraments but only implies others. The Eucharist, first performed at the Last Supper, baptism, reported by the three Synoptic evangelists, forgiveness of sins (penance), addressed in the post-resurrection account of John 20:23, and the sacrament of the sick, referenced in James 5:13–15, are explicitly addressed. Marriage, confirmation, and holy orders are not directly addressed as sacraments, although their concepts are implied.

This significant teaching was developed as a result of Augustine's reaction to a heretical sect, the Donatists. This group arose in the wake of significant persecutions of the church in the third century. Those enforcing the pagan laws of Rome mandated that sacred books be burned and all were required to adopt the emperor's religion. Bishops that acceded to this edict were considered traitors by those who had held out against the persecution. When the persecution subsided, many of the bishops who had apostatized sought to re-enter the church and continue their ministry. However, many rejected this request, believing that apostasy could not be so easily forgiven. While this disagreement was ongoing, many of the offending bishops continued to perform their sacramental ministries. This raised the question of the efficacy of the sacraments. Was the effect of the sacrament received even if the minister was sinful and not in a proper position with God to perform such sacred rites? Augustine answered the question by postulating the concept *ex opere operato*, which means the sacraments are effective regardless of the worthiness of the minister performing them.

In the twelfth and thirteenth centuries, St. Thomas Aquinas advanced the theology of the sacraments in a few important ways. As described in his famous *Summa Theologica*, Aquinas expresses the idea that a sacrament is constituted by certain words and actions working in unison. He suggested that sacraments have three important yet different functions. First is their role in remembrance. The Eucharist (Holy Communion) is a celebration of the remembrance of the passion and death of Christ. Secondly, the sacraments are demonstrative—they make present and actualize grace in the life of the recipient. Thirdly, the sacraments are prognostic; they present a future eschatological function. Through the sacraments we are made ready for the future coming of Christ. For Aquinas, grace is the chief effect of the sacraments. God is the one who imparts grace and, therefore, the grace received in the sacraments is what makes us, the recipients, like God.

Aquinas went beyond Augustine's concept of *ex opere operato* and added *ex opere operantis*, meaning the proper disposition we hold when performing a pious act. Aquinas stated that God is the primary minister of all sacraments. While all the sacraments are efficacious regardless of the merit of the minister, he claimed that the minister must have the proper intention in his actions.

FACT

Non-Catholic Christians today hold various understandings of the number of sacraments. All accept baptism and Eucharist; the Orthodox Churches accept the other five. The Anglican community accepts the other five, but with a different theological understanding. This remains one of the major differences between Protestantism and Roman Catholicism.

St. Thomas must also be credited with ordering the sacraments in various categories. He suggested that five sacraments (baptism, confirmation, Eucharist, penance, and the sacrament of the sick) perform ecclesial activities; two (holy orders and marriage) are for ecclesial status. He also broke down the sacraments by social and legal purposes. Social convention was seen through baptism, confirmation, Eucharist, penance, and the sacrament of the sick. Baptism celebrated birth; confirmation gave credence to human growth and maturity. The Eucharist is part of human nutrition; penance provided healing. The sacrament of the sick brought a restoration of health. The communal aspect of sacraments is seen in marriage, performed for the propagation of humanity, and holy orders that addressed the question of leadership in the church.

Challenges During the Reformation

The seven sacraments of Roman Catholicism—baptism, Eucharist, confirmation, marriage, holy orders, penance, and the sacrament of the sick—were long-established and normative by the early years of the sixteenth century when the Protestant Reformation began. The greatest challenge to the theology of the sacraments was raised during this period of church history. Martin Luther's call for *sola scriptura* (Scripture only) led him and other reformers to reject Catholicism's claim of seven sacraments, reducing them to baptism and the Eucharist. The reformers claimed that Scripture does not support the idea that Jesus inaugurated all seven sacraments.

Baptism

What is baptism? Chapter I of the *General Introduction to Christian Initiation* provides three important responses. First, it says that this is a new life in Christ. Through baptism, Catholicism teaches that one becomes a formal member of the church and receives a new life that is shared by all who are members of the same religious family. Secondly, baptism is a sharing in the kingship of Christ. Jesus' kingship is not of the nature recognized by society, but rather is a formation of God's reign in our world. Through baptism one has the ability to share as a member of the Kingdom of God on earth. Thirdly, baptism washes away the stain of original sin and provides an indelible character upon the recipient.

Baptism and the Bible

The baptism of Jesus is one of only a few events in Christ's life that is narrated by all three Synoptic evangelists. While the accounts vary, they all speak of the presence of the Holy Spirit and the voice of God from the heavens. In the Scriptures, baptism has three important meanings. First, it is a source of enlightenment through the presence and the power of the Holy Spirit. The Spirit enlightens one to a new life. Secondly, baptism brings regeneration or new birth. The story of Jesus' encounter with Nicodemus,

John 3:1–21, speaks of the need to be born again in Christ. Baptism provides this new birth. Lastly, baptism is significant in the New Testament as a source of death and resurrection. St. Paul (Romans 6:3–11) speaks of baptism as death to sin and rising to new life.

The Practice of Baptism in Christian History

During the apostolic and early patristic periods of church history, baptism was a sacrament for adults. In his corpus of letters, St. Paul mentions the baptism of individuals and whole households. (See, for example Acts 16:15 or I Corinthians 1:16.) Since it was necessary to express one's faith in Christ in order to receive baptism, only those who had reached the age of reason could properly be baptized. Beyond the apostolic era, converts to Christianity were prepared for baptism through a process known as the *catechumenate*, a spiritual journey often "walked" by a group rather than individuals. Candidates for baptism were trained in the teachings of the faith over a period of time that varied with locale, opinions of those preparing candidates, and historical time period.

ESSENTIAL

Catholicism teaches that the disobedience of Adam and Eve, as described in Genesis 3:1–24, commonly known as the fall, generated for humanity a common or original sin to which all human beings are subject. Baptism cleanses the recipient's soul of the impurity caused by Adam's fall. Theologians today understand this "sin" in varied ways, many suggesting it is a condition that is common to all humans.

The concept of infant baptism, standard practice for Catholics today, was started by St. Augustine. He believed that it was very important for baptism to be conferred as early as possible for at least two significant reasons. First, what was the status of people who died before receiving baptism? Were such individuals, even if desirous to be Christians, eligible for salvation without removing original sin? Secondly, Augustine argued that baptism formally made one a child of God, a member of the church. There was no need to delay such a privilege. However, Augustine needed to negotiate the stumbling block of personal faith in Christ as a necessity for baptism. His solution was adult sponsors, commonly known today as Godparents, who as members of the church could speak on behalf of the child to be baptized. This same theological principle has been used for close to 1,600 years.

QUOTE

Romans 5:18 reads: "Therefore just as one man's trespass led to condemnation for all, so one man's act of righteousness leads to justification and life for all." While scholars argue the point, many suggest this passage refers to how Adam's sin was negated by Christ's salvific death and resurrection. Baptism is the symbolic act that brings Christ's saving act to the individual.

Contemporary Catholicism welcomes new members of the faith through baptism both as children and adults. In the traditional way inaugurated by St. Augustine, baptism of children is normative. Generally both parents and Godparents are asked to attend some catechesis in preparation for the baptism of their child. Additionally, the post–Vatican II Church reinstituted the catechumenate for adult converts. Known today as the Rite of Christian Initiation of Adults (RCIA), this program allows teenagers and those older to journey together in a program of faith formation and catechetical training. Candidates generally begin their training in early fall and conclude it with reception of Sacraments of Initiation (baptism, Eucharist, and confirmation) at the Easter Vigil Mass.

Confirmation

Confirmation celebrates the Christian's rite of passage from youth to adulthood by the Holy Spirit entering the person's life in a special way. The New Testament speaks of no separate rite of confirmation; rather the Holy Spirit is given in connection with baptism. During the patristic church, confirmation was part of the whole initiation process, beginning with baptism, moving to reception of the Eucharist, and culminating in confirmation. Originally, the sacrament was simply a laying on of hands as a public affirmation of baptism, which was done privately. This post-baptismal rite was reserved to a bishop as the minister of the sacrament.

Toward the end of the patristic period, the unitive initiation process began to separate with confirmation becoming a separate rite. This came about for two principal reasons. First, as described in the theology of St. Augustine, the urgency for infant baptism suggested that waiting for the whole process of initiation to be celebrated at one time was inappropriate. Additionally, bishops were not always available to celebrate post-baptismal rites, such as confirmation. This separation of confirmation from the initiation process led to much confusion concerning the sacrament's theology. However, separation of the two rites was seen by most as abnormal and certainly less than ideal. It was only in the thirteenth century that opposition against the separation of the sacraments began to relax. During the medieval period a new theology developed whereby confirmation provided certain grace and protection for the Christian. In essence, the sacrament made one a soldier for Christ.

Today, from a theological perspective, baptism and confirmation are in essence one sacrament. Confirmation is viewed as a ratification of baptism; the sacrament gives one the opportunity to freely enter and purposefully choose the faith that was given to the individual as a child through baptism.

The Eucharist

The Eucharist is the central sacramental sign of Roman Catholicism. Indeed, Vatican II's "Constitution on the Sacred Liturgy" (paragraph 10) reads: "The liturgy [Eucharist] is the summit toward which the activity of the Church is directed; it is also a font from which all her power flows." Roman Catholics believe that Eucharist is the real sacramental presence of Jesus Christ. Unlike Protestant faiths, which understand the Eucharist as Christ in some representational form, Catholicism stresses the real presence based on the accounts provided in the New Testament.

The Eucharist in the New Testament

Like the baptism of Jesus, the Eucharist is a central and critical subject in the New Testament. There are four accounts of the institution of the Eucharist, those provided by the Synoptic evangelists, Matthew (26:26–29), Mark (14:22–25), and Luke (22:14–23), and one provided by St. Paul in I Corinthians 11:23–26. Additionally, chapter 6 of John's Gospel, often referred to as the "Bread of Life Discourse," while not describing the institution of the Eucharist, is central for the theology it provides concerning the sacrament. Scholars suggest that these institution narratives were included in the Gospels for at least three reasons. First, they described what was happening liturgically in local Christian communities after the time of Jesus. Secondly, these accounts directly identify Jesus with the meal and his death and resurrection. Lastly, the accounts specifically say that Jesus told his apostles to continue this tradition in his memory.

The Theology of the Eucharist

As we have seen with many teachings in Roman Catholicism, the church's understanding of the Eucharist has developed over the course of Christian history. The first and most central question concerning the Eucharist is that of Jesus' real presence. Using the Gospel accounts as its base, the patristic church from the outset declared that the Eucharist was no longer common bread and wine, but rather Jesus present in the sacramental sign. In his Letter to the Ephesians, Ignatius of Antioch (A.D. 110) called the Eucharist the "medicine of immortality." At the same time the other central teaching concerning the Eucharist, that it is a sacrifice, was also established. St. Cyprian, the third-century bishop and martyr, stated that the Eucharist was a bloodless repetition of the sacrifice of Christ on Calvary. It was, therefore, a sacrifice of praise and thanksgiving.

The Eucharist and St. Thomas Aquinas

The theological developments concerning the Eucharist during the patristic church were given greater explanation and basically finalized through the work of St. Thomas Aquinas. In his *Summa Theologica*, Thomas first addressed the issue of the real presence. How was it possible that simple elements of bread and wine were transformed, through the action of the priest at Mass, into the real sacramental presence of Jesus Christ? Thomas responded by using the philosophy of Aristotle as a tool for explanation, a technique known to history as Scholasticism. Aquinas used Aristotle's treatise *The Categories* to explain philosophically the theological reality of Christ's real presence in the Eucharist. Aristotle's basic category was substance, the "stuff" of which anything is composed. This substance can exist in various forms or "accidents." Aquinas argued that what happened at the Last Supper, and what is recreated in every Mass, is that the substance, the bread and wine, are transformed into the real presence of Christ, although the accidents, the form of that substance, remain the same. The elements, bread and wine, look and taste like bread and wine both before and after the action of the priest, but their substance has changed. Aquinas used the term transubstantiation, a philosophical term, to explain this theological reality.

Aquinas' other great teaching concerning the Eucharist was that it is a sacrifice. The Mass is an image of Calvary, a representation of the passion of Christ. Since Christ is present in the Eucharist, it is the same Christ that is sacrificed.

The Council of Trent

The theology of the Eucharist was not seriously challenged from the time of Aquinas to the Reformation. However, Martin Luther, in his treatise *The Babylonian Captivity of the Church*, rejected the two basic teachings central to the Eucharist, real presence and sacrifice. Essentially, Luther argued that the philosophical concept of transubstantiation could not adequately explain how the elements of bread and wine became the real sacramental presence of Jesus Christ. Thus, Luther and other reformers, to various degrees, believed the Eucharist to be representational. Additionally, Luther rejected the concept of the Eucharist as sacrifice. As stated in Chapter 2, Luther championed the concept of *sola fide*, salvation by faith alone. If the Eucharist, the central action in the Mass, was a sacrifice, then it was a form of meritorious work that helped one to "earn" heaven. Such a belief was completely inconsistent with salvation by faith alone and, therefore, Luther rejected it. The council fathers at Trent (1545–1563), however, refuted the claims of the Protestant reformers and affirmed the two basic teachings of transubstantiation, thus affirming the real presence of Jesus in the Eucharist and the Mass as sacrifice.

Contemporary Questions Associated with the Eucharist

The contemporary post–Vatican II church continues the tradition of Trent in its theological understanding of the Eucharist, but new questions have arisen that must be addressed. The most significant question, referred to as inter-communion, concerns reception of Eucharist in other churches, both non-Catholics in Catholic churches and Catholics in Protestant and Orthodox churches.

FACT

Those churches in communion with Roman Catholicism basically comprise the community of Eastern Rite Catholics. These churches, while not well known, hold some ideas that differ from the Roman Catholic Church, such as married clergy and various liturgical rites. However, they proclaim loyalty to the Roman pontiff and are in communion with the Holy See.

This question is especially relevant when people attend weddings, funerals, or baptisms, or at other special times when peoples of various faiths may be simultaneously present for a celebration. Inter-communion, both for non-Catholics in a Catholic church and Catholics in a non-Catholic church, is possible only when the non-Catholic faith tradition is in communion with the Roman Church. This, by definition, excludes all Protestant churches, as they do not hold communion with the Roman pontiff.

CHAPTER 12

The Sacraments of Commitment and Healing

The seven sacraments, special signs provided by the church for the day-to-day living of the faith, begin with initiation but are celebrated throughout one's life, marking special rites of passage. Two sacraments of commitment, marriage and holy orders, celebrate an individual's choice for union with a spouse or a specialized vocation of service to God and the church. The two sacraments of healing, penance and the sacrament of the sick, assist Catholics to find spiritual and physical fullness throughout their lives.

Concept of Discipleship

Christianity is based on the concept of discipleship, the ideal of following Jesus. Discipleship requires a sense of commitment, but our contemporary twenty-first-century world seems to avoid commitment on many fronts. A couple of generations ago it would have been typical for a professional athlete in the United States to spend an entire career with one team. Today, however, the major factor that determines where an athlete will play is salary. The best athletes go to the highest bidder. It is very typical for business people, especially those in high-ranking positions, to move about frequently, again largely based on salary and benefits. While one cannot fault any individual for doing the best he can for himself and his family, this common experience is found in our personal commitments as well. Marriages, close friendships, business partnerships, and other more directly human-centered commitments are all affected by this basic propensity to forego loyalty and strike out on one's own. Even commitment to ideals, both secular and religious, is in jeopardy these days.

The discipleship that Jesus Christ asks of us is one of complete commitment. Jesus is the one who initiates the call. In the Gospels, Jesus calls the apostles to be members of his special family. He called Peter and Andrew, saying, "Follow me, and I will make you fish for people." (Matthew 4:18b) The invitation that Jesus extends to the apostles in a very specific way is made inclusive to all, but it demands a radical change of heart, what the Greeks call *metanoia*.

QUOTE

Jesus said, "If any want to become my followers, let them deny themselves and take up their cross and follow me. For those who want to save their life will lose it, and those who lose their life for my sake, and for the Gospel, will save it." (Mark 8:34) Jesus' call to discipleship requires total commitment.

Being a disciple of Jesus asks much of the individual. First, such a vocation means one must share in Jesus' ministry. Christ's basic message of peace, justice, and love as tools to build the kingdom of God on earth must be the way we, his disciples, live our lives. Our vocations vary greatly, not only in our day-to-day work but in our lifestyle, whether married, single, or celibate religious and clergy. However, regardless of our particular vocation, we have a shared task of participating in Jesus' ministry. Discipleship also calls us to love in a way that is sacrificial and without conditions or limits. Jesus' death on the cross was a voluntary action; he chose to demonstrate his love in a way that was instructive for all who would choose to follow and be his disciples. In this sense discipleship is often associated with martyrdom, for it is personal and can be costly.

The sacraments of commitment are in essence specialized signs of discipleship. Marriage and holy orders are the two sacraments that in some sense determine church status, as a married person or a celibate cleric. Both of these sacraments are living symbols rather than ceremonies. The sacrament is the married or priestly life, not the rite that bestows this status upon the individual.

Marriage

Marriage, the vocation to which most men and women are called, is clearly a sacrament of discipleship in living for others, but it is very specific. Marriage commits one man to one woman for the rest of their lives. This basic commitment to each other is often extended to family through the birth of children. While Catholics are certainly called upon to be committed in a generic way to their brothers and sisters, marriage is a specific contract of love that binds men and women together. This commitment is the highest priority, second to one's commitment to God alone. In a very real and concrete way marriage is a sacrament one becomes rather than one that is received.

FACT

Marriage is the only sacrament in which the one celebrating the sacrament is not a bishop, priest, or deacon. Rather, the ministers of marriage are the couple themselves. The bishop, priest, or deacon is rightly referred to as a witness to the marriage, along with the best man and maid or matron of honor.

Biblical Understanding of Marriage

The New Testament has numerous references to marriage, both in the Gospels and the writings of St. Paul. Jesus obviously approved of the institution of marriage for he performed his first miraculous sign at a wedding feast at Cana in Galilee (John 2:1–12). In I Corinthians Chapter 7, St. Paul provides important information with respect to marriage and divorce. His basic advice to the Corinthians is for them to remain celibate, but if their passion is so great one does no wrong through marriage. Since Paul believed that the parousia (second coming of Christ) would happen soon, even during his lifetime, there would be little reason to marry, save one's inability to remain celibate. He forbids divorce save in cases of marriage to nonbelievers. In Ephesians 5:22–33, Paul presents the image of marriage as analogous to the union between Christ and his church. Christian men and women represent Christ and the church as a sacred union/marriage that cannot be dissolved.

QUESTION

Why would St. Paul suggest, "It is well for a man not to touch a woman?" (I Corinthians 7:1)
St. Paul firmly believed that the second coming of Christ would happen during his lifetime. Thus, there would be no need for one to change status. He suggests (7:8–10) for those single to remain so and for those married to be faithful. The perceived imminent return of Christ predicated Paul's understanding of the indissolubility of marriage.

Paul's belief in the permanence of marriage is made crystal clear by all three of the Synoptic evangelists (Mark 10:1–12, Luke 16:18, Matthew 19:3–12). This basic tenet of the sacrament of marriage is central to Roman Catholicism's belief that marriage, once contracted, is permanent and cannot be dissolved, unless proven to be invalid.

The Theology of Marriage

The theology of marriage has evolved greatly over the course of church history, with a significant update of thinking as a result of the Second

Vatican Council (1962–1965). The patristic church understanding of marriage was dominated by the theology of St. Augustine. He taught that marriage as an institution was good, but sexual intercourse was basically a necessary evil. Marriage was thus seen as a remedy for concupiscence. This rather negative perspective on sex continued to be prominent for many centuries, mostly because of Augustine's towering status as a theologian. The scholastic theology of Thomas Aquinas saw marriage as a contract. Two things were essential to this agreement: consent and intercourse. Thus, a marriage was not considered valid unless both parties had consented to the union and consummation had occurred. The church taught that the basic reason for marriage was for the procreation and education of children.

The Second Vatican Council, while maintaining church teaching from the past, offered new language and understanding on the institution of marriage. *Gaudium et Spes* ("The Pastoral Constitution of the Church in the Modern World") uses language that is much less dogmatic and more open to new ideas and thought. The council speaks of the need of "irrevocable personal consent" and that the institution of marriage "finds its crowning glory" in the procreation and education of children. Yet, the council also states that by its nature this indissoluble compact between a man and woman "demand[s] that the mutual love of the partners be properly shown, that it should grow and mature." (*Gaudium et Spes*, paragraph 50).

Marriage Preparation

The lifetime commitment that marriage requires necessitates a period of discernment and preparation prior to marriage. Indeed, such preparation is critical to a good marriage and serves as the church's only leverage to assist couples to prepare themselves for their chosen vocation. Dioceses in the United States have various requirements, but generally speaking a six-month period of preparation that includes a pre-Cana weekend retreat (or similar) is required. Most parishes also offer some extended preparation program conducted by parishioners or members of the parish staff. While most sacramental marriages join two Catholics, interfaith marriages are commonplace as well. The latter, often celebrated outside the context of Mass, necessitate certain permissions to assure their validity. Additionally, certain impediments to marriage may exist depending on circumstances and the individuals concerned.

FACT

Impediments to marriage, such as lack of physical maturity, prior marriage bond, or coercion to marry, render a sacramental marriage invalid. It is essential that the canon law be followed to assure both the licitness (legal correctness) and validity of a marriage.

Annulments

Roman Catholics are no less susceptible to problems in marriages then peoples of other faiths. Divorce, from the church's perspective, is a legal procedure that allows couples to return to their former single status, divide assets, and to settle other issues created through marriage, most especially the custody of children. However, utilizing the aforementioned Gospel passages on the indissolubility of marriage, the church does not recognize divorce. Rather, arguing in a way analogous to the United States system of justice, where one is presumed innocent until proven guilty, the church argues that a marriage is valid unless it is proven invalid. Thus, since a prior bond of marriage is an impediment to a sacramental marriage, it is impossible for Roman Catholics to be married after a legal divorce unless the first marriage is ruled invalid.

The process of annulment, which is very complicated and often poorly understood, exists to review the validity of marriages. Any Roman Catholic who participated in a sacramental marriage but seeks after legal divorce to enter a sacramental marriage must secure an annulment of the first marriage. Grounds for an annulment, as alluded to above, are governed by canon law, which provides specific rules concerning the validity of a marriage. Utilizing the canons, local diocesan marriage tribunals, acting in a way similar to a civil court of law, adjudicate marriage cases, with the assumption that a marriage is valid. If after a careful examination the marriage tribunal court determines that the first marriage was invalid, then the petitioner is provided with the proper permission to contract a valid marriage.

ESSENTIAL

A decree of annulment, rendered by a diocesan tribunal, says that from the outset, the marriage in question was for some reason invalid as a sacrament. Reasons include lack of canonical form or some other impediment to marriage. Thus, annulments render no judgment against children born of an invalid union.

Holy Orders

Holy Orders, the sacrament conferred upon bishops, priests, and deacons, is the second sacrament of commitment. Chapter 17 presents an in-depth description of the development of the priesthood, especially religious clergy. Here, the concept of sacramental priesthood, a brief history of its development, and a couple of relevant contemporary questions will be addressed.

The Priesthood in Scripture

As understood and formulated today, the Roman Catholic priesthood is not directly addressed in the Bible. The Hebrew Scriptures (Old Testament) speak of the concept of priesthood at great length. In ancient Israel the tribe of Levi was specifically tasked with the responsibility of the priesthood, the ministry of providing religious services to the whole nation. Over time the Levitical priesthood became a center of political and economic power in Israel. Jewish priests were not linked to any specific charism. Rather, the one common denominator was they were ancestral descendents of the tribe of Levi. During the time of Jesus, priests continued their work in the Temple of Jerusalem. The New Testament does not speak of the Christian priesthood. However, Acts 6:1–6 describes how seven were chosen to assist widows. Roman Catholicism sees this as the inauguration of the diaconate.

During the apostolic period, especially after the Roman Diaspora of A.D. 70, the first Christians, including the apostles, whom Jesus had commissioned to go forth and baptize the nations (Matthew 28:19–20), scattered throughout the eastern Mediterranean world. The apostles and their successors served as leaders in these disparate communities, but with time and a burgeoning Christian population there came a need for additional ministers to serve God's people. Thus, the concept of the presbyter was born, evolving into the sacramental priesthood. Presbyters were leaders of individual congregations, generally meeting in people's homes. The church leader to whom various presbyters held loyalty was a bishop, a successor of the apostles. These presbyters presided over the weekly celebration of the Eucharist and aided their congregations as was necessary. These men were called forth to this ministry from the community. The ancient rite of "laying on of hands," used when calling the first deacons, was a sacramental sign of what became the Roman Catholic priesthood.

The advance of the church from a proscribed sect to the religion of the Roman state led to a more formalized priesthood. As the church became better organized, more formal methods for the selection and training of priests were used. However, standardization of education and requirements for ordination did not come until the Council of Trent mandated diocesan seminaries as an antidote to the various clerical abuses noted by both church members and the reformers.

Clerical celibacy, a distinctive mark of Roman Catholic priesthood, is not a dogma of the church but rather a practice invoked since the twelfth century as a result of the Lateran I (1123) and Lateran II (1139) Councils. This policy has both Biblical and historical roots. The aforementioned teaching of St. Paul in I Corinthians Chapter 7, where he claims his status as a single person to be the best option, is one source. Imitating the life of Jesus, who was single, celibate, and poor, is another source of inspiration. The practical element of not allowing church properties and assets to be passed on through inheritance to children of priests was another factor in this development.

Contemporary Issues

The post–Vatican II era has seen a significant reduction in the number of priests, especially in the Western world and other more developed countries. This reality, coupled with a continual increase in the number of Catholics worldwide, creates a challenge for the church and raises certain questions with respect to the sacramental priesthood. One main question is the need to maintain clerical celibacy. Some argue, pointing to ministers in Protestant faiths and even priests in Eastern Rite Catholicism who are free to marry, that allowing Roman Catholic priests to marry would remove a significant obstacle, which they suggest is a hindrance to many who might wish to become priests. The other significant question, that of women's ordination, will be addressed in detail in Chapter 22. At this point the Roman Catholic Church, as guided by the ideas of Popes John Paul II and Benedict XVI, has shown no inclination to change the long-standing traditions of clerical celibacy and an all-male clergy.

QUOTE

Jesus said, "Listen to me, all of you, and understand: there is nothing outside of a person that by going in can defile, but the things that come out are what defile." (Mark 6:14) Jesus here is teaching that sin is not externally received but rather is formulated in the human heart.

Concept of Sin

The two sacraments of healing, penance and the sacrament of the sick, are significant signs that combat the effects of sin in the lives of men and women. The concept of sin is well described throughout the Bible. The story of the fall of Adam and Eve (Genesis 3:1–24) and God's wrath against the wickedness of humanity, resulting in the great flood (Genesis 6:1–8:22), are two major manifestations of the presence of sin in the world. Even after God gave Moses the Ten Commandments on Mount Sinai (Exodus 20:1–17), with its very specific ethical norms and proscriptions, the Hebrew people continually moved into and out of a good relationship with God as a result of sin.

In the New Testament, sin was taken for granted. Jesus assumes this idea in teaching that sin comes from the human heart. The most systematic New Testament treatment of sin is the Letter to the Romans. Paul taught that sin brings forth a three-fold death: (1) Temporal disintegration of our relationships—sin alienates us from one another. (2) He attributes physical death to sin. (3) Sin alienates us from God.

QUESTION

How has social sin been understood over history?
Social and political structures such as institutions of slavery or apartheid or stereotypes concerning indigenous peoples (as examples) exemplified social sin. Today these ideas continue in different formats and manifestations such as religious bigotry, economic stranglehold of countries, and jingoism.

Roman Catholicism teaches that sin is partially explained by the sinful community to which we belong. There is solidarity toward sin as there is solidarity toward salvation. The Tradition teaches that all sin leads to death, but not all sin is deadly. Mortal sin destroys our relationship with God; venial sin damages this relationship without severing it. Mortal sin must be serious in matter and committed with full use of our freedom. Thomas Aquinas taught that mortal sin requires grave matter, sufficient reflection, and full consent of the will.

In the twentieth century the concept of sinful structures, commonly known as social sin, entered the vocabulary of moral theology. Only individuals are capable of moral decisions, but insofar as structures embody the decisions and reflect the interests of sinful humans, they can be moral or immoral. Laws, social and economic structures, and various systems can embody a narrow self-interest and consequently violate human rights. Social sin is, therefore, morally culpable irresponsible accommodation to a structural evil.

The Sacrament of Penance

The sacrament of penance and its three contemporary rites of reconciliation find roots in the New Testament. The clearest reference is in the post-resurrection account of John 20:21–23. Here Jesus addresses his apostles, telling them, "If you forgive the sins of any, they are forgiven them; if you retain the sins of any, they are retained." The passage is directly linked to the action of the priest in the sacrament today. John 8:2–11, the story of the woman caught in adultery, is also instructive for sacramental penance. In this passage Jesus forgives the woman her transgressions, but he calls her to conversion: "'Has no one condemned you?' She said, 'No one, sir.' And Jesus said, 'Neither do I condemn you. Go your way, and from now on do not sin again.'" (8:10b–11) Thus, the New Testament provides both evidence of the efficacy of the priest to act in Jesus' name for forgiveness of sin and the need on the part of the penitent for conversion of heart.

History of Penance

The sacrament of penance has developed from a highly structured communal exercise to a less formal and very private celebration between priest and penitent. By the late second and early third centuries, a penitential system similar to that of the catechumenate began to appear. Groups of people, who acknowledged their personal sinfulness, were granted the privilege of reconciliation with the church on one occasion. Thus many, including the Emperor Constantine, waited until death's door to seek reconciliation, fearful that transgressions committed after this one opportunity to receive the sacrament would not be forgiven. Penances given to penitents were often long and severe, especially from a contemporary perspective.

Beginning in the sixth century, the practice of communal penance became more private. Additionally, restrictions on celebration of the sacrament were removed; penance was celebrated at the discretion of the individual. In Ireland this more personal celebration of the sacrament led to the practice of Tariff Penance. Penitential books were created that specified what penance would be required for any combination of sins confessed. Throughout the medieval, Tridentine, and modern periods of church history, regular celebration of sacramental penance was common. At this time as well, people directly associated the sacrament of penance with reception of the Eucharist. The latter was not received without the celebration of the former.

Celebration of Penance Today

As an outgrowth from the "Constitution on the Sacred Liturgy" from Vatican II, changes were made in the celebration of the sacrament of penance. The 1973 Rite of Penance provides three separate rites of reconciliation: the first, individual confession and penance (the norm); the second, communal penance services with individual confession and absolution; and the third, general absolution. The latter, which is very rarely celebrated, requires the individual penitent to seek individual confession and absolution at the first opportunity.

FACT

In the Patristic era, it was not atypical for a group of penitents to be asked to stand for two hours per day for a month outside the Cathedral church, dressed in penitent clothing. In a very public way people acknowledged their sin and suffered the pain of public scorn for their actions.

Sacramental penance, while not practiced as frequently today as prior to Vatican II, is nonetheless a powerful experience of healing, conducted through a frank yet pastoral conversation between priest and penitent. After listening to what the penitent shares, the priest offers advice to assist the individual to avoid such sins in the future as well as gives direction to aid one's spiritual life. The priest then suggests a penance, some act or possibly set of prayers, to be done by the penitent as an act of reparation. Finally, the priest prays the words of absolution over the penitent. The priest, acting as a representative of the church, forgives the penitent's sins in the name of Jesus Christ.

The Seal of Confession

Confessing one's sins to a priest can for some people be a fearful experience. Penitents, especially those who might know a priest outside this forum, whether as a member of the parish or from some social contact, might feel inhibited in telling the confessor the reality of one's life, especially one's faults, believing that such knowledge will damage their relationship or cause other negative ramifications. However, it is imperative to understand that when a priest participates in sacramental confession he is under the seal, meaning that whatever is said in the conversation is completely and perpetually secret. This is the case whatever is said, even if sins revealed might be relevant to criminal prosecution or the information might prevent a future problem.

FACT

There have been several celebrated cases where priests have been incarcerated for their refusal to reveal information learned in a confession. The seal is inviolate. Many do not understand the significance of the seal as a bond between priest and penitent.

Additionally, a priest is not allowed to use information gained through confession in any way that might prejudice a decision that concerns the individual penitent or others discussed during the celebration of the sacrament. Without this absolute assurance of secrecy, penitents might not be completely honest when confessing their sins. If a priest breaks the seal of confession, under any circumstances, he receives the penalty of excommunication, meaning that he is not able to receive the sacraments until he is reconciled through appropriate church procedures.

Sacrament of the Sick

The sacrament of the sick has direct New Testament roots. James 5:14–15 reads: "Are any among you sick? They should call for the elders of the church and have them pray over them, anointing him with oil in the name of the Lord. The prayer of faith will save the sick, and the Lord will raise them up; and anyone who has committed sins will be forgiven." Besides anointing with oil, the concept of human touch is integral to the celebration of the sacrament. In his ministry of healing, Jesus reached out and physically touched many, even those who were considered unclean by Jewish laws of the day.

Historical Development of the Sacrament of the Sick

Evidence of the practice of anointing the sick, referred to as *extreme unction*, is sparse in the early Christian era. However, before Charlemagne (circa 800), it seems that any person could anoint another with oil that had been blessed by a bishop. The Carolingian Reform, however, provided more structure by the creation of books that provided a specific rite of penance and anointing for the sick. The addition of the added feature of penance moved the sacrament toward its present administration by a priest or bishop. At this time, anointing was seen as a preparation for death.

Celebration of the Sacrament Today

In the wake of Vatican II, celebration of the sacrament of the sick has changed greatly. The name of the sacrament, moving from *extreme unction* to the sacrament of the sick is itself a great indication of the change in theological perspective. Rather than a sacrament celebrated only at the time of one's expected death, today the sacrament is regularly administered to those who are preparing for surgery, those with an acute condition, people with chronic medical problems, such as cancer, heart disease, diabetes, and so on, as well as those near death. Often the sacrament is celebrated with a priest and an individual, especially if sacramental reconciliation is part of the rite. However, communal celebrations are common. In many cases the sacrament is celebrated with family and friends of the infirm present to pray for the individual. Additionally, communal celebration, where groups of people receive the sacrament, is common during or after Sunday Mass.

CHAPTER 13

Moral Theology

Roman Catholicism is centered in adherence to the Scriptures and the practice of the Sacraments. Yet, it is the daily lived experience that must govern the faith Catholics hold and cherish. Moral theology is the study of how Roman Catholics apply the teachings of the church through the light of Revelation to daily decisions. While various approaches to moral theology exist, and disagreements abound on proper moral action, Catholics have always upheld the authority of the natural law in its application to daily life.

Pre–Vatican II Understanding of Moral Theology

Catholic moral theology as a separate discipline came into existence at the end of the sixteenth and the outset of the seventeenth centuries. During this post-Reformation period, two separate strands of moral theology existed. First, many commentaries on the moral teaching of Thomas Aquinas, as found in his *Summa Theologica*, were produced. Two of the more famous commentaries were produced by Jesuit priests Gabriel Vasquez (d. 1609) and Thomas Suarez (d. 1617). Aquinas was used as the base from which Vasquez and Suarez, among others, produced treatises that were used by theologians and other learned people as a pattern for daily life and moral decision-making.

The second direction for this discipline during the Counter Reformation period was the production of manuals of moral theology. These manuals, which included a strong emphasis on the sacrament of penance, were primers used for the education of priests. Thus, moral theology became a discipline basically confined to the classrooms of seminaries. This particular format continued until the onset of the Second Vatican Council in 1962. During this entire period moral theology was removed from Sacred Scripture and dogmatics and became closely aligned with canon law. Judgment was strongly emphasized in these manuals; it was very clear where people stood based on adherence to or violation of the various laws that were articulated in these manuals. During the seventeenth and eighteenth centuries, significant controversy arose between laxists and rigorists in these manuals.

Post–Vatican II Understanding of Moral Theology

While Vatican II verified and continued certain trends in moral theology, seeking continuity, it also produced new trends that became part of this discipline in the contemporary church. One important new area was the introduction of Scripture into moral theology. In his 1943 encyclical letter, *Divino afflante spiritu*, Pope Pius XII emphasized the need to bring Scripture into all theological disciplines. In partial reaction to Martin Luther's cry *sola scriptura*, Roman Catholicism, from the time of the Counter Reformation forward, kept Biblical study within the control of the clergy and, for the most part, out of the hands of the laity, while always acknowledging the importance and centrality of Scripture. Tradition, as exemplified in the work of Thomas Aquinas, was the primary base for theological study, including moral theology. After Vatican II, moral theology itself became more integrated into the whole fabric of Catholic theological discourse. Additionally, the post–Vatican II period has shown how other disciplines, such as theological anthropology (grace), eschatology, and Christology, have influenced moral decision-making.

FACT

Divino afflante spiritu, issued on September 30, 1943, has been described by many Scripture scholars as the "Magna Carta of modern biblical scholarship." In this encyclical, Pope Pius XII opened the door to modern Biblical criticism, which in large measure had been closed since the condemnation of theological modernism in 1907.

Another significant post–Vatican II premise associated with moral theology is the new trend toward pluralism of philosophical foundations for moral theology. In 1879, Pope Leo XIII issued *Aeterni Patris*, an encyclical letter that mandated that Thomism, the teaching of St. Thomas Aquinas, be the exclusive philosophical base for theological study. After Vatican II it became common to go beyond the teaching of Thomas in philosophical and consequently theological dialogue. This movement away from an exclusive Thomistic perspective created a new emphasis on the individual over the community in theological studies. This led to a life-centered moral theology with greater emphasis on the person, yet not without criticism from many within the church.

A pluralistic understanding of philosophies essential to theological study leads directly to the concept of dialogue in moral theology, a contemporary norm that is probably the most significant shift in this discipline after Vatican II. This dialogue takes place on at least two important fronts. First, moral theology must be in dialogue with other sciences, religions, and philosophies. Second, in the minds of many contemporary scholars, there is no one way to approach moral theology; the discipline has become pluralistic in study and by extension in action, as revealed in the daily moral decisions Catholics make. Additionally, such pluralism has placed strains on magisterial teaching authority and accentuated the role of dissent on numerous contemporary issues, especially those associated with sexual morals.

Moral Theology's Modern Contexts

Analysis of the last thirty years of moral theology study in the United States shows that four basic contexts have arisen in the study of this discipline. The first, the ecclesial context, states that there was little need for change in the United States: the study of moral theology, undertaken traditionally for the training of priests, was not in question. In Europe, however, the post–Vatican II era saw a call for a new orientation and different methodology. Rather than determining what was sinful, this new methodology in orientation, one based on life, reflected the totality of the Christian. Most importantly, with respect to the ecclesial context, is the obvious split in theological perspectives concerning absolute moral norms and the proper response to noninfallible teachings. Most academics today are associated with the revisionist position that suggests the need to concentrate on the individual in matters of moral theology.

ESSENTIAL

The more "open door" policy, one that stresses individualism over community, has been found objectionable. In the minds of many, movement away from the common good to the individual leads directly to the creation of personal theologies. Such a belief, in large measure, rejects the traditional belief of absolute moral norms.

Society has also played an important role in recent developments concerning moral theology. War, poverty, various political scandals (Watergate and Iran-Contra as examples), and infamous business debacles (Enron, insider trading scams, and Ponzi schemes, as examples) have raised many questions. Additionally, contemporary society continually asks about the role of women, a subject with significant overtones for moral theology.

The ecumenical aspect of moral theology is the third context. This is manifested most clearly through Catholic participation in traditionally Protestant-dominated academic societies. Many contemporary Catholic theologians are now educated in Protestant and nonreligiously affiliated schools.

It seems that rapprochement between Catholic and Protestant theologians is growing, to the delight of some and the horror of others.

What is the basic content of American moral theology today?
First, social issues are dominant. The plight of the poor and other marginalized peoples is given great emphasis. The other main issue is the tension between revisionists and those with a more traditional perspective on moral theology. Various schools and ways of thinking suggest there is no one way to apply rules and standards.

The fourth context is associated with the academic community. Before 1960, mainly all Catholic theology was not viewed as an intellectual discipline. It was primarily associated with seminary education. Vatican II highlighted a growing interest in the academic study of theology, as opposed to a confessional perspective.

Moral Theology Today

Since Vatican II, a schism has arisen in moral theology between revisionists and those who hold a new natural law ethical theory, called the Basic Goods Theory (BGT). This division arose at least in part from the Vatican II document "Decree on the Training of Priests." Consistent with Pope Pius XII's call in *Divino afflante spiritu* to use Scripture more widely in theological study, the decree calls for moral theology to move away from the manuals produced in the wake of the Counter Reformation and put more emphasis on the Bible. Revisionists and BGT proponents agree on most ideas with respect to Scripture. However, these two groups disagree on the role, foundation, and authority of Sacred Tradition in ethical theory. The former sees a lesser role for Tradition; the latter holds strongly to the belief that Tradition is a contemporary teacher.

Natural Law

While there are at least four factors that help define the two basic perspectives on contemporary moral theology, the most significant is that associated with understanding of the natural law. Numerous definitions are found for the natural law, but one that captures its essence is a set of principles that govern human interactions and are built into the structure of the universe, as opposed to being imposed by human beings. These principles, with respect to moral theology, are referred to as *ethical norms*. Revisionists tend to question ethical norms where BGT supporters defend them. Both groups recognize that there is a universal moral truth, and that truth can be justified through reason and Revelation. Both recognize the sources of moral knowledge, namely reason, experience, Scripture, and Tradition. All of these are used to develop a normative method for moral decision-making. What distinguishes these two theories is their acceptance or rejection of absolute specific norms that dictate intrinsically evil acts. Both accept absolute norms, but they differ on what norms are absolute. Much of this debate rests on definitions.

QUOTE

The "Decree on the Training of Priests," paragraph 16, reads, "Special care should be given in the perfecting of moral theology. Its scientific presentation should draw more fully on the teaching of Holy Scripture and should throw light upon the exalted vocation of the faithful in Christ and their obligation to bring forth fruit in charity for the life of the world."

The Basic Goods Theory is rooted in reason and defense of the existence of specific absolute norms and, by extension, intrinsic evils. According to this theory, specific norms are either absolute or nonabsolute. It is through Revelation that certain norms are transformed into a specifically Christian ethic.

The revisionist approach seeks to reverse the traditional understanding of natural law in the light of contemporary philosophical, theological, and scientific developments grounded in human experience. Revisionism philosophically formulates a norm grounded in reason and experience for determining the objective rightness or wrongness of an act. This criterion is often called *proportionate reason* and designates the revisionist school as *proportionalism*. Revisionism provides a norm or criterion (proportionate reason) for resolving cases of conflict in moral judgments when two moral norms conflict. Proportionate reason analyzes the aspects of an act to determine whether it is right or wrong. Similarly, proportionate reason functions as a norm for moral judgment in determining whether or not a nonabsolute norm applies in a particular situation.

What is an intrinsically evil act?
The traditional answer suggests certain acts are evil by their very nature, regardless of any circumstances, situation, or time. For many, murder and incest would be two examples of intrinsically evil acts. However, not all ascribe to this definition.

Scripture

A second factor that defines the two basic contemporary theories on moral theology is Scripture. Does Scripture do more than serve as a source of proof text and affirmation of ethical assertions that are deduced largely from reason? What is the role of Scripture in these ethical theories? Catholic moral theologian William Spohn suggests three questions must be asked with respect to the use of Scripture in ethical theories: What text is selected, how is the text interpreted, and how is it applied to contemporary moral questions? Followers of BGT hold the perspective that it is the sole function and authority of the magisterium to determine the use of Scripture in moral theology. Revisionists, on the other hand, do not view Scripture as central in establishing moral norms. Rather, it is used to justify the claims of universal natural law.

Reason, Experience, and Method

The third factor that defines the two competing theories, reason, experience, and method, is based on different views of Catholic Tradition. One view, the classicist, asserts that natural law is static, necessary, fixed, and universal. A second perspective, historical consciousness, sees reality as dynamic, evolving, changing, and particular. Both the BGT and revisionist theories reject classicism per se, but they have different understandings of historical consciousness. Revisionists see historical consciousness as foundational to their theory; it is the basic premise of proportionalism. BGT proponents have a much more nuanced understanding of historical consciousness, viewing it as only one of many factors, but always remembering the fundamental reality of absolute norms and intrinsic evils.

FACT

> An example of conflicting moral norms that require resolution in order to make a proper moral decision is the prohibition against artificial birth control and the need to limit one's family size in order to practice responsible parenthood. The two sides differ on the application of these two perceived conflicting norms.

Experience is exhibited in the diverse views held between objective and subjective morality. The Basic Goods Theory suggests moral acts are objectively constituted by what people think they are doing. Subjective morality is the possibility of a person's confusion and/or error about the moral goodness or badness of an act. Revisionists, however, define objective and subjective morality quite differently. Revisionists are most concerned with defining those characteristics that determine an action's objective rightness or wrongness, not the subjective goodness or badness of a moral agent, motive, disposition, or character. Revisionists view experience as an important input to moral knowledge; it can transform perceptions and norms that are understood as immutable under the BGT. Experience is seen as a central fundamental component of moral truth. The Basic Goods Theory, on the other hand, while acknowledging experience as a moral teacher, does not consider it a factor that draws one away from absolute norms. Differences in method are found in how the two groups look at absolute norms. Revisionists formulate norms from the objective, subjective, and a combination of the two. The BGT, however, formulates norms from the objective realm only.

Tradition and Magisterium

The final factor that differentiates between BGT and revisionism is the relationship between Tradition and magisterium. What is the role of the theologian? Proponents of BGT believe theologians are advisers to the magisterium; the theory rejects the "cancer of dissenting theologians." In the end it ascribes to the ancient dictum, "Rome has spoken, there is nothing more to be said." Revisionists, on the other hand, understand theologians and the magisterium to be in dialogue. Revisionists hold a strong presumption of truth in magisterial teaching, but if there are serious reasons for questioning the teaching, one can knowingly and willingly act against such teachings on the authority of conscience.

FACT

Pope John Paul II, in his encyclical letter *Veritatis Splendor*, rejected the concept of consequential actions. In essence he was asserting that situation and experience have no direct impact on the moral correctness of certain acts, namely those held as absolute moral norms.

Different ecclesiologies and models of relationships between theologians and the magisterium lead to different hermeneutics on the criteria of determining whether or not a pronouncement of the ordinary universal magisterium (see Chapter 6) is infallible. Recall that canon law (750) says universal consensus is necessary for an infallible statement, yet it is not clear what precisely this means. Some say the consensus refers to the bishops; others say it is a theological consensus.

The division between BGT and proportionalism in Tradition and magisterium is found in those teachings not directly addressed in Divine Revelation. Both sides agree that infallible teachings from Scripture or Tradition are not to be questioned; disagreements arise concerning teachings not directly addressed in Divine Revelation. Are objective norms to be applied to these latter teachings? The BGT says norms are applicable; the revisionist school denies this claim.

Sin and Grace

The two competing schools of contemporary moral theology seek to provide guidance and answers to the faithful in their daily living of the faith. Actions that are judged consistent with God's law, as presented in Divine Revelation, are properly called righteous. Those, on the other hand, that are found in conflict with Scripture and Tradition are labeled sinful. At its core, moral theology, as understood in contemporary language, seeks to aid people to perform actions that are consistent with God's law. Yet over the course of church history, a theology to describe sin and its antidote, grace, has developed to aid Catholics in their daily lives of faith.

Augustine and Pelagius

In the early fifth century the church saw a titanic battle over sin and grace, a struggle that still has implications for moral theology today. St. Augustine (354–430), whose theology has been instrumental in the Catholic Tradition for 1,500 years, held the orthodox position in a battle with Pelagius, a British monk who in the late fourth and early fifth centuries was preaching his theology in Rome. Pelagius held an exalted view of the human person. He claimed that through reason we could distinguish between moral good and evil and, therefore, were endowed with the ability to always choose the good. Furthermore, he suggested that by the law of nature we will always follow God since nature is oriented toward God. He combined these two ideas with the gift of human free will. His conclusion was that humanity had the ability through its own free will to always choose God. It was, therefore, possible to live without sin. Such an idea meant that humanity could work out its own salvation; there was no absolute need for the redemptive and salvific death of Christ to attain salvation.

Augustine strongly rejected Pelagius' theology, offering as a counter what became the doctrine of grace. He reasoned that humans, at the outset, were given a command to obey and the ability to keep that obligation, but they rejected this opportunity, creating the fall. Grace, a gift from God, was, therefore, needed as a remedy to this "original sin." Furthermore, he said that grace proceeds and accompanies all human works on the way to salvation; grace is needed for final perseverance. Humanity is dependent on God and the redemption brought by Christ to gain eternal life.

The teaching of Augustine became a basic tenet in Roman Catholic theology. Jesus Christ's salvific death on the cross was absolutely necessary for the salvation of humanity. Augustine acknowledged human free will, but he realized that the sin of Adam had created a situation where all people (except the Virgin Mary) are flawed from the outset. Therefore, the salvific grace that only Christ could bring was absolutely necessary to achieve salvation.

CHAPTER 14

Salvation

Roman Catholicism teaches that all people have been called by God to attain eternal life. Jesus' salvific death, his atonement for our collective sin, made salvation and eternal life possible. Jesus' life, death, and resurrection are central to Christian salvation. While Catholicism shares this basic salvific belief with Protestantism, these two major divisions of Christianity understand the attainment, method, and ends of salvation quite differently. Catholic teaching on salvation is rooted in Scripture and Tradition, which has been advanced by the teachings of the magisterium through the centuries.

Salvation in the Bible

The Christian concept of salvation is not directly addressed in the Hebrew Bible, but the story of the Jewish people does prepare for the arrival of Christ. Several of the books of the Old Testament bear witness to the divine pedagogy of Christ's saving love. This is most evident in the four so-called "Suffering Servant" passages of Isaiah (42:1–4, 49:1–7, 50:4–11, and 52:13–53:12) described in Chapter 9. Collectively these passages speak of one who willingly suffers for others. The servant, understood by some Scripture scholars as a prefigurement of Christ, does not turn back from adversity but rather bravely endures whatever comes for the sake of the people.

ESSENTIAL

It is important to understand that God's desire for human salvation was a free gift, yet it required men and women to respond positively to the invitation of the Lord. The consistent message of the prophets, that God desired the people to be his own, was often rejected, leading to the destruction of Israel in the north, and the infamous Babylonian exile of Judah in the south.

The mystery of salvation is also presented in the Hebrew Bible in a hidden way. It is manifested most clearly in various demonstrations of God's care for his people. Salvation history is a litany of events where God comes to his people in overt ways. God created the world and gave humanity the ability to subdue it, but through the fall men and women turned away from God, choosing the enticements of evil. Yet even the overt sinfulness of the world could not keep God from saving Noah and his family. The call of Abram (later Abraham) to be the father of a great nation was a seemingly impossible proposition due to his and his wife Sarah's ages. However, God overcomes all obstacles to show care for his people. When the Israelites cried out in Egypt, God sent Moses to rescue the people and lead them through the desert to the Promised Land. God provided judges, kings, and numerous prophets, all as signs that God was ever present to his chosen people and desired them to be saved, both from the evils of the world and even the misdeeds of the people themselves.

The concept of salvation in the New Testament is centered on the person of Jesus. The Gospel evangelists provide significant evidence that while Jesus came to teach, inaugurate the Kingdom of God on earth, and, from the perspective of Catholicism, to initiate the church, the principal reason for the Incarnation was to bring salvation, the gift lost through the collective sin of Adam and Eve, to humanity. The centrality of Jesus as the source of salvation is made especially clear in John 14:6: "Jesus said to him [Thomas], 'I am the way, and the truth, and the life. No one comes to the Father except through me.'" John portrays his followers as lost without Jesus. John 6:68–69 reads, "Simon Peter answered him, 'Lord, to whom can we go? You have the words of eternal life. We have come to believe and know that you are the Holy One of God.'" Written at least one generation after the Synoptic Gospels, and assuming its readers are familiar with much of the basic story of Jesus, John's Gospel is more theological. The absolute need to make Jesus an integral part of one's life is made most explicit in this text.

QUOTE

Jesus said, "I am the living bread that came down from heaven. Whoever eats of this bread will live forever; and the bread that I will give for the life of the world is my flesh." (John 6:51) This highly theological verse associates the Eucharist with salvation.

Salvation in the Synoptic Gospels

The Synoptic Gospels also clearly portray Jesus as the central figure for human salvation. The baptism formula of Matthew 28:19, "Go therefore and make disciples of all nations, baptizing them in the name of the Father and of the Son and of the Holy Spirit," demonstrates that membership in the community of believers is found through the Trinity, including Jesus.

Jesus' claim that he has the power to forgive sin clearly associates his ministry among the people with salvation. An example is found in the story of Jesus' cure of a paralytic in Capernaum (Mark 2:1–12). The story concludes with Jesus saying, "But so that you may know that the Son of Man has authority on earth to forgive sins—he said to the paralytic—'I say to you, stand up, take up your mat and go to your home.'"

The principal concept of salvation found throughout the Gospels is atonement, the idea that Jesus' death was part of God's plan through salvation history as the only possible recompense for the sin of Adam. For the Synoptic writers the apex of Jesus' salvific action comes through the Resurrection. The Lord's conquest of physical death is the foretaste of Jesus' action to raise humanity to eternal life at the final judgment. John, on the other hand, uses the cross itself and Jesus' death as the event that brings salvation. For John, Jesus, in a very real way, reigns as king from the cross; this instrument of torture becomes for him a royal throne.

QUOTE

Romans 10:9–10 provides possibly Paul's best example of how Jesus is central to salvation: "If you confess with your lips that Jesus is Lord and believe in your heart that God raised him from the dead, you will be saved. For one believes with the heart and so is justified, and one confesses with the mouth, and so is saved."

Beyond the Gospel evangelists, St. Paul has the most significant understanding of Jesus as a central figure of salvation. As described in Chapter 12, Romans Chapter 5 is central to Paul's understanding of how Jesus was the antidote to the sin of Adam. Romans 5:18 reads, "Therefore just as one man's trespass led to condemnation for all, so one man's act of righteousness leads to justification and life for all." Paul also describes how the promise of Christ will be manifested in humanity's great victory and reward. In I Corinthians 2:9 he writes, "What no eye has seen, nor ear heard, nor the human heart conceived, what God has prepared for those who love him." Thus, Paul not only speaks of Jesus' central role in salvation, but also provides some insight into how that eternal life will be lived.

History of the Doctrine of Salvation

Roman Catholicism's belief in salvation through Jesus is a reflection of how the church understands human existence and the human condition.

If Christ chose to save us, then one can easily conclude that there must be something worthy of salvation in us. If we are totally without worth, what does this say about Christ's redemptive work on our behalf? If humanity was not worth saving or if there was no reason to be saved, then there would have been no need for God to send his son into the world, especially to suffer and die in such an ignominious way.

Nature and Grace

Catholicism's doctrine of salvation is integrally associated with the connection between nature and grace. Nature is understood as human existence apart from God's self-communication. Theologically this means that we are bodily creatures who are intelligible and open to full human growth apart from the divine. However, in Catholic theology, the human person has a radical capacity for the divinizing grace that only Christ can give. The Catholic Tradition teaches that the grace of God is given to us, not to make up for something lacking as human persons, but rather as a free gift that elevates us to a new and unmerited level of existence. Hypothetically it is possible to have a natural state alone, but since grace, the gift of God, permeates humanity, a state of "pure nature" does not exist. If grace presupposes nature, nature in its own way presupposes grace inasmuch as grace sustains us in our actual existence and orients us toward a supernatural end.

How is grace understood in the New Testament? First, it is understood that grace is *charis*, the gift or good will of God; it is the principle of Christian life, action, and mission. Grace is God's self-communication to humanity. Important especially for history, grace stands in opposition to the law. Paul in Galatians 5:4 makes this clear: "You who want to be justified by the law have cut yourself off from Christ; you have fallen away from grace." Additionally, grace stands in opposition to works. Again, St. Paul provides a good example. He writes, "So too at the present time there is a remnant, chosen by grace. But if it is by grace, it is no longer on the basis of works, otherwise grace would no longer be grace" (Romans 11:5–6). Grace refers to a divinely given capacity and, thus, to a future salvation event.

FACT

The association of grace with faith and its break with the law and works is synthesized in Ephesians 2:8–9: "For by grace you have been saved through faith, and this is not your own doing; it is the gift of God—not the result of works, so that no one may boast."

Catholic Church doctrine with respect to grace was drafted in response to two principal distortions. First, Pelagianism in the fifth century exalted and presented a far too highly optimistic idea of human freedom. On the other hand, Protestantism, as illustrated best by the theology of John Calvin, held a far too pessimistic view of human freedom. Thus, church doctrine seeks a middle ground between these two extremes. The Second Council of Orange (529), in opposition to Pelagius, spoke of the necessity of grace in one's life from beginning to end. In response to Calvinism, the Council of Trent (1545–1563) asserted that Christians are transformed internally by the grace of Christ.

The Problem of Nature and Grace

The centrality of the relationship between nature and grace with respect to the whole subject of salvation can be addressed by analyzing two basic questions. First, does grace change human nature, and if so, how is human freedom preserved? In other words, does God's grace in any way lessen or possibly obviate human freedom? Secondly, how is the human person able to accept freely the self-communication of God in grace? If grace is so pervasive in nature, can humans accept it freely and without coercion?

As suggested above, Catholicism answers these questions by traveling the path between Pelagianism, which emphasizes the superiority of nature over grace, and Protestantism, which places grace over nature and effectively submerges the dimension of human freedom and cooperation in salvation. Catholicism teaches that the intrinsic orientation of the human person is toward God. This is referred to as the *supernatural existential*. This is a permanent modification of the human person that transforms the individual from within and orients him toward the God of grace and glory. In this context sin is understood as an exercise of human freedom that seeks to destroy the supernatural existential. However, grace cannot be destroyed by sin. Thus salvation history is the story of how God's grace endures and conquers all challenges presented by sin.

Salvation Outside the Church

The Catholic teaching (since the patristic era) that outside the church there is no salvation (*extra ecclesiam nulla salus*) has been widely misunderstood and, thus, the source of much needless angst and ill will between Catholics and non-Catholics. While various proclamations of this doctrine have been made since the time of Pope St. Gregory the Great (590–604), some of the more cogent statements were made at the Fourth Lateran Council (1215), the papal bull *Unam Sanctam* (1302), and the profession of faith issued at the Council of Florence (1442).

QUOTE

The "Declaration on the Relation of the Church to Non-Christian Religions" (paragraph 2) reads in part: "[The] Catholic Church rejects nothing of what is true and holy in these religions. She has a high regard for the manner of life and conduct, the precepts and doctrines which, although differing in many ways from her own teaching, nevertheless often reflect a ray of that truth which enlightens all men."

This teaching, which appears to be very straightforward and clear, must, however, be understood in the light of more recent documents, especially Vatican II and the *Catechism of the Catholic Church*. Although the nineteenth century saw the church fighting against various heresies, including religious indifferentism, one document, *Singulari Quadam* (1854), acknowledged that individuals outside the church may simply be in ignorance of the truth through no fault of their own and, therefore, "are not subject to any guilt in this matter before the eyes of the Lord." Several important

Vatican II documents address the general topic of salvation outside Roman Catholicism. Vatican II in general emphasized what unites Christians rather than divides them. These documents state that the church denies nothing that is true from other religions; it holds inviolate the right of religious freedom based on conscience.

ESSENTIAL

It is important to note that while contemporary Catholicism acknowledges the possibility of salvation outside the church, its members still have the obligation to evangelize the world. While salvation comes from Christ, the fullness of Christ's truth subsists in Roman Catholicism.

Contemporary Catholicism understands the dictum "outside the church there is no salvation" to mean that salvation comes from Christ through the church, which is his body. This affirmation is not aimed at those who, through no fault of their own, do not know Christ and his church. *Lumen Gentium* ("The Dogmatic Constitution on the Church") paragraph 16 states: "Those who, through no fault of their own, do not know the Gospel of Christ or his Church, but who nevertheless seek God with a sincere heart, and, moved by grace, try in their actions to do his will as they know it to the dictates of their conscience—those too may achieve eternal salvation."

Judgment

Salvation is the attainment of eternal life with God. Scripture speaks of the need for justification as well as providing a snapshot into what eternal life with God means and how it might be manifested. But what criteria will be used to determine whether or not an individual has been found worthy of an eternal life with God? What is the process that must be endured in order for God to make the proper decision with respect to one's salvation? Catholicism answers these questions through the concept of judgment.

Biblical References

Judgment is understood in the Hebrew Bible in several ways. Isaiah speaks of judgment as both defense and vindication of Israel by Yahweh. The prophet writes (1:27–28), "Zion shall be redeemed by Justice, and those in her who repent, by righteousness. But rebels and sinners shall be destroyed together, and those who forsake the Lord shall be consumed." Judgment is also understood as punishment. Ezekiel 24:14 provides a good example: "I the Lord have spoken; the time is coming, I will act. I will not refrain, I will not spare, I will not relent. According to your ways and your doings I will judge you, says the Lord God." Yahweh is seen as Judge of the world. This theme is brought forth in the famous conversation between Abraham and God over the fate of Sodom. Abraham says to Yahweh (Genesis 18:25), "Far be it from you to do such a thing, to slay the righteous with the wicked, so that the righteous fare as the wicked! Far be that from you! Shall not the Judge of all the earth do what is just?" Generic judgment of all peoples and nations is characteristic of apocalyptic literature, such as presented in Joel 3:9–12 and Daniel 7:9–11.

The New Testament also has many references to judgment. For the Synoptic evangelists, judgment is often associated with condemnation of sinners. Jesus says, "But I say to you that if you are angry with a brother or sister, you will be liable to judgment; and if you insult a brother or sister you will be liable to the Council; and if you say, 'You fool,' you will be liable to the hellfire." (Matthew 5:22) In the Gospel of John, judgment is seen more in the present. John 3:18 reads, "Those who believe in him are not condemned; but those who do not believe are condemned already, because they have not believed in the name of the only Son of God." For St. Paul, judgment is found in the past, present, and future. Concerning future judgment, Paul writes in Romans 2:1–3: "Therefore you have no excuse, whoever you are, when you judge others; for in passing judgment on another you condemn yourself, because you, the judge, are doing the very same things. You say, 'We know that God's judgment on those who do such things is in accordance with truth.' Do you imagine, whoever you are, that when you judge those who do such things and yet do them yourself, you will escape the judgment of God?" In the Letter to the Hebrews (6:2), judgment is seen in the resurrection of the dead. In sum, Biblical judgment is the act by which evil is overcome by God once and for all.

Particular and General Judgment

The church has addressed particular judgment over the centuries, but no council has presented a formal definition, nor has the subject been addressed in the most recent *Catechism of the Catholic Church*. It is necessary, therefore, to piece together indirect references that describe this teaching. The doctrine refers to the idea that immediately after death judgment is rendered by God concerning the eternal destiny of each soul. Pope Eugene IV, in 1439, declared that souls that leave a body in a state of grace yet are in need of additional purification are rendered to purgatory; those souls in the state of perfect grace are brought immediately to the beatific vision, the opportunity to see and encounter God at every moment. The teaching is also addressed in various professions of faith, including those of Pope Gregory XIII (1572–1585) and Benedict XIV (1740–1758).

FACT

The book of Revelation, while highly metaphorical, does nonetheless present the best insight into the Biblical concept of judgment. For example, speaking of those who have not apostatized during the great trial, the author (possibly the apostle John) says that the judgment of those loyal to Christ "is the first resurrection." (Revelation 20:5b)

Particular judgment is indirectly addressed by both the New Testament and theologians. There is no particular Biblical text that affirms with any certainty the teaching of particular judgment; however, there are passages that certainly allude to this teaching. In the story of the rich man and Lazarus (Luke 16:19–31), Jesus seems to indicate that the fate of both men, Lazarus in the arms of Abraham (eternal life) and the rich man (traditionally known as Dives) in Hades (eternal damnation), had been determined at the moment of their deaths. Similarly, Jesus' promise to the "good thief" on the cross, "Truly I tell you, today you will be with me in Paradise," (Luke 23:43) suggests immediate or particular judgment.

Theologians generally view particular judgment as instantaneous, at the moment of death, but again evidence to support such an opinion is not completely clear. St. Augustine in his work *The City of God* (Chapter 20) and St. Thomas Aquinas in his *Summa Theologica* (Supplement) speak of particular judgment in this light. As evidence to support this belief they cite Romans 2:15–16. Here Paul speaks of "the day when, according to my gospel, God, through Jesus Christ, will judge the secret thoughts of all." Revelation 20:12 gives additional evidence: "And I saw the dead, great and small, standing before the throne, and books were opened. Also another book was opened, the book of life. And the dead were judged according to their works, as recorded in the books." In addition to the reality of particular judgment, the common opinion of theologians is that this event will occur at the individual's moment of death.

In contrast to particular judgment where Biblical evidence and theological opinion is indirect, the concept of general judgment is firmly established. The Hebrew Bible refers to the "Day of the Lord," (Ezekiel 13:5, Isaiah 2:12) when nations will be brought to judgment. The New Testament speaks of general judgment through reference to the parousia, or second coming of Christ (see Chapter 9). References to this teaching abound but are most prominent in the Gospels and the corpus of St. Paul, with I Thessalonians 4:13–18 being especially illustrative.

The Bible speaks of numerous signs that will precede general judgment. These include a general proclamation of the Christian faith, the conversion of the Jews, the onset of a great apostasy, the reigning of the Antichrist, extraordinary events of nature, and a universal conflagration, often referred to as Armageddon (see Revelation, Chapter 16). The advent of general judgment is not known, but it will be swift, like a lightning strike (Matthew 24:27) or a thief in the night (Matthew 24:42–44).

Resurrection of the Body

General judgment, coming at the end of created time, will be preceded by the resurrection of the body. This basic tenet of Roman Catholic faith, which teaches that the soul and body will be reunited at the end of time, finds its source in the New Testament. John 11:25–26, where Jesus proclaims the famous words, "I am the resurrection and the life. Those who believe in me, even though they die, will live, and everyone who lives and believes in me will never die," and Hebrews 6:2, which refers to the "resurrection of the dead," are indirect references. The best illustration of this teaching is found in John 5:28–29: "Do not be astonished at this; for the hour is coming when all who are in their graves will hear his voice and will come out—those who have done good, to the resurrection of life, and those who have done evil, to the resurrection of condemnation." The resurrection of the body is officially proclaimed in the Apostles and Nicene-Constantinopolitan Creeds, as well as proclamations from two church councils, Lateran IV (1215) and Lyons II (1274).

QUESTION

Why is there a need for general judgment if the eternal fate of individuals has been determined at death?
Catholicism teaches that an all-just and loving God would want both rewards and punishments to be awarded at a public and general judgment, both to reveal the wicked and to award the righteous.

Destiny of the Faithful

Judgment, both particular and general, determines the destiny of all souls. What is referred to by Christians as heaven is more accurately described as the Beatific Vision. Those found justified in the sight of God are rewarded with an eternal vision of divinity. The *Catechism of the Catholic Church* (#1023) teaches that those who die in God's grace and are thus purified will live with Christ forever. Referencing 1 John 3:2, the *Catechism* states that we will become like God and will see him as he is, face to face. The promise of this vision is also described by St. Matthew (5:8) and St. Paul (II Corinthians 3:12–18).

One teaching that separates Roman Catholicism from other Christians is the doctrine of purgatory. While there is no clear Biblical foundation for this teaching, the apocryphal text II Maccabees 12:38–46 does describe the efficacy of prayers for the dead. Western theology has always emphasized the penal character of purgatory, while the Eastern Church saw it more as a process of maturation and spiritual growth. While Protestant reformers questioned the efficacy of praying for the dead, the Catholic Tradition, as continued today in the *Catechism*, has always affirmed the reality of purgatory as a state of final purification of the elect. Pope St. Gregory the Great (590–604) stated, "As for certain lesser faults, we believe that, before Final

Judgment, there is a purifying fire." This teaching is affirmed by the Council of Florence (1439) and the Council of Trent (1545–1563).

FACT

The fact that condemnation, and consequently hell, is a free human choice is illustrated in the Gospel of John 3:18–19. In part this reads, "This is the judgment, that the light has come into the world, and people loved darkness rather than light because their deeds were evil."

Justification of an individual by God, resulting in the ultimate reward of the Beatific Vision, either immediately or after a temporal period in purgatory, is countered by the judgment of condemnation by God, resulting in an individual's consignment to hell. This is a state of definitive exclusion from God, a condition brought about by the actions of the individual. The church affirms the existence of hell and its eternity, a reality confirmed by Jesus himself. In his famous Sermon on the Mount, Jesus, in metaphorical language, says if our eye or hand causes us to sin it is better to remove it "than for your whole body to be thrown into hell." (Matthew 5:29c) Equally importantly, the church also teaches, rejecting Calvin's concept of predestination, that God does not predetermine the eternal fate of any individual. Mortal sin, which an individual can only commit by willful act, is the state that leads one to condemnation, and consequently to hell.

CHAPTER 15

Mariology

The Blessed Virgin Mary holds a significant role in salvation history. As the Mother of God, the *theotokos*, she gave Jesus Christ flesh and served to nurture him as he grew and matured. Over the Christian era Mary has been the subject of great devotion. Catholicism has encouraged this devotion through sacred art, prayer, Church-recognized apparitions, Mary's strong presence in various liturgical celebrations throughout the year, and especially the proclamations of four Marian dogmas that serve as the foundation to Mariology.

Church Teachings on Mary

Devotion to the Blessed Virgin Mary has been a hallmark of Roman Catholicism from the apostolic era forward. Mary's role in salvation history was essential; her great *fiat*, her yes to God as expressed in Luke 1:38: "Here am I, the servant of the Lord; let it be done with me according to your word," allowed God's master plan to unfold. Although at the moment she did not know all its consequences, Mary's *fiat* transformed her life and was a necessary building block in the formation of the Christian faith.

Biblical Roots

Mary holds an important place in the story of Jesus. This is expressed by three of the four Gospel evangelists. Matthew and Luke provide information about Mary's pregnancy, the birth of Jesus, her flight with her husband Joseph and her newborn son to Egypt, and some information about Jesus' childhood. John's Gospel provides information about Mary's role in prompting her son's first miracle at a marriage in Cana and Mary's presence at the time of Jesus' crucifixion at the hands of the Romans.

St. Luke's Accounts

St. Luke's Gospel provides the most detailed information about Mary, especially in his infancy narrative, Chapters 1 and 2. Luke 1:26–38 relates the story of the Annunciation. The evangelist tells us that the angel Gabriel was sent to a virgin, named Mary, living in the village of Nazareth. She was engaged to a man named Joseph of the house of David. The angel's startling message to Mary was that she was to conceive a son and name him Jesus. Confused by the angel's words, since she was a virgin, Mary was told this would happen through the power of the Holy Spirit. Thus, the child to be born would be the Son of God.

Immediately after her *fiat*, Mary leaves Nazareth and travels to the "hill country" to visit her elder cousin Elizabeth. The angel has told Elizabeth she is also pregnant. Referred to as the Visitation, Mary's three-month stay with Elizabeth ends with the birth of Elizabeth's son, John the Baptist, who would serve as the last prophet and the precursor of Christ. We next encounter Mary in Luke's Gospel as she and her husband Joseph travel to Bethlehem by the order of the Emperor Augustus to register for a worldwide census. Shortly after their arrival, Jesus is born and laid in a manger, a feeding trough for animals, for, as Luke says (2:7b), "There was no place for them in the inn."

QUOTE

Simeon's prophetic words about Mary's future are striking: "This child is destined for the falling and the rising of many in Israel, and to be a sign that will be opposed so that the thoughts of many will be revealed—and a sword will pierce your own soul too." (Luke 2:34b–35)

St. Luke relates two more important stories about Mary during the infancy of Jesus. In 2:22–38, we hear of the presentation of Jesus in the Temple. The prophet Simeon predicts a difficult future for Mary, one that she could never fully imagine. At the same time, Mary and Joseph encountered the prophetess Anna. She and Simeon praised God for the opportunity they were given to encounter the anointed of the Lord before they died. Luke closes his infancy narrative by relating a story of the Holy Family in Jerusalem. He tells us that when Jesus was twelve, during the annual pilgrimage to Jerusalem to celebrate Passover, Jesus remained behind in the city, unknown to his parents. Mary and Joseph, traveling with family and friends, began the trek northward to Nazareth. When they discover Jesus is missing, Mary and Joseph frantically return to Jerusalem and ultimately find Jesus in the temple, conversing with some teachers. Jesus tells them that he must be in his Father's house, a comment not fully understood by his parents at the time. In the end, Jesus returned to Nazareth, was obedient to his parents, and his wisdom increased over the years.

St. Matthew's Accounts

St. Matthew is the other Synoptic evangelist who provides information on the infancy of Jesus. Concerning the above events, he relates a similar story with a few differences, but he adds important information that is not provided by Luke. Matthew provides no details concerning the Annunciation, or birth, of Jesus, but he does emphasize that Mary's pregnancy came through the Holy Spirit. The evangelist adds two important stories, both of which involve Mary, that are not included in Luke's Gospel. First, he describes the arrival of three wise men from the east who have followed a star to Bethlehem to pay homage to the newborn King of the Jews (2:1–12).

Known as the Epiphany, the event says something fundamentally important about how those outside the Hebrew community understood Jesus. Matthew also narrates how the Holy Family fled to Egypt to escape the murderous King Herod who, in his efforts to kill Jesus (whom he perceived to be a rival), ordered the execution of all male children in the Bethlehem area two years of age or younger. Lastly, Matthew tells his readers that after Herod's death, Joseph led his wife and foster son back to Nazareth.

ESSENTIAL

Catholic Tradition, using John's Gospel as its reference, has maintained that after Jesus' ascension, Mary lived under the care of John, the apostle, possibly in Ephesus. From the cross, Jesus said to Mary: "Woman, here is your son." He continued to John, "Here is your mother." The evangelist concludes, "And from that hour the disciple took her into his own home." (John 19:26–27)

St. John's Accounts

St. John's Gospel relates two other important events at which Mary played a significant role. In Chapter 2:1–12, John describes Jesus' first public miracle when he transforms water into wine. Mary, Jesus, and his disciples were present at a wedding at Cana. When the wine for the celebration had been consumed, Mary asked Jesus to act. Initially he balked, telling her (2:4): "Woman, what concern is that to you and to me? My hour has not yet come." In the end, however, he responds, demonstrating his power, saving face for the couple, and responding positively to his mother's wishes. Lastly, John is the only evangelist who places Mary beneath the cross at Jesus' crucifixion.

Four Marian Dogmas

The Roman Catholic Church holds many teachings associated with the Blessed Virgin Mary. Four of these specific doctrines have been raised to the level of dogma, meaning in technical terms that they must be held by the faithful as essential to participation as Roman Catholics. Examples of dogmas detailed in other chapters of this book include beliefs in the Trinity, that Jesus is both divine and human, and in the real sacramental presence of Jesus in the Eucharist. Four Marian dogmas have been defined by the magisterium over the course of Christian history, using both Scripture and Sacred Tradition, the two elements of the one source of Revelation as evidence for these proclamations.

QUESTION

What differentiates a teaching from being a doctrine or dogma?
Mysterium Ecclesiae (June 24, 1973) provides an answer by defining dogma: "All those things are to be believed by divine and Catholic faith which are contained in the written or transmitted Word of God and which are proposed by the Church, either by a solemn judgment or by the ordinary and universal Magisterium, to be believed as having been divinely revealed."

Mary the Mother of God

The first dogma concerning the Blessed Virgin Mary is Catholicism's belief that she is the Mother of God. Celebrated liturgically annually on January 1, this dogma is rooted in the controversy associated with Nestorius in the early fifth century (see Chapter 9). Recall that Nestorius was a member of the Antiochene School of Christology that emphasized the humanity of Jesus. He refuted the idea that Mary was the *theokotos* (Mother of God), suggesting that she was only the mother of the human Jesus, *christotokos*. The ecumenical council at Ephesus in 431 condemned Nestorius's belief and declared Mary to be the *theotokos*.

Perpetual Virginity of Mary

The New Testament and church Tradition provide evidence to the second Marian dogma, her perpetual virginity. As introduced earlier, the two infancy narratives of Luke and Matthew declare that Mary was a virgin at the time she conceived Jesus through the power of the Holy Spirit. Additionally, Matthew (2:25) says that Joseph and Mary had no marital relations before Jesus' birth. More evidence comes from the Gospel of the Birth of Mary. Chapter 8:12 says, "Joseph . . . did not know her, but kept her in chastity."

This dogma is celebrated through the twin solemnities of the Annunciation, March 25, and Christmas (Incarnation), December 25. While many confirmed this dogma in the fifth century, its official proclamation was not made until the Lateran Synod of 649, under the direction of Pope Martin I.

ESSENTIAL

It is important to understand how Roman Catholicism responds to Matthew 13:55, which speaks of Jesus' brothers and sisters. The Catholic Tradition has always understood these "brothers" and "sisters" in a generic sense, viewing them as brethren or possibly distant relatives. They have never been understood as children of Joseph and Mary and, therefore, blood siblings of Jesus.

The Immaculate Conception

The third Marian dogma, the Immaculate Conception, was not proclaimed until 1854. This dogma teaches that Mary, as a preparation for her future role as the Mother of God, was preserved from the moment of her conception from the stain of original sin. The dogma, hotly debated through history, was solemnly defined by Pope Pius IX on December 8, 1854. In the papal constitution *Ineffabilis Deus*, the pontiff stated that the Blessed Virgin "in the first instance of her conception, by a singular privilege and grace granted by God, in view of the merits of Jesus Christ, the Savior of the human race, was preserved exempt from all stain of original sin."

This dogma is supported indirectly by Scripture and through the Tradition of the church. The two scriptural passages that serve as general reference, but not actual proof of the dogma, are Genesis 3:15 and Luke 1:28. In the Genesis text, God tells the serpent, "I will put enmity between you and the woman." As the new Eve, Mary's soul was placed in an exalted state that could not be touched by the evil of Satan. In Luke 1:28, the angel tells Mary, "The Lord is with you." Gabriel's words speak of grace, a supernatural grace that is bestowed upon Mary. The Tradition of the church supports this dogma through the work of many theologians. Among others, Justin Martyr, Irenaeus, Tertullian, and Cyril of Jerusalem view Mary as the new Eve who cannot be subject to original sin. Numerous church fathers and other theologians have also attested to Mary's absolute purity over the course of Christian history.

It must be noted that this dogma has been controversial. For example, Origen, St. Basil of Caesarea, and St. John Chrysostom during the patristic period, as well as two later giants of the theology, St. Bernard of Clairvaux and St. Thomas Aquinas, questioned the validity of this dogma.

The Assumption of Mary into Heaven

The fourth (and chronologically most recent) Marian dogma is the Assumption of Mary into heaven. This teaching comes exclusively from sacred Tradition, as there is no Biblical reference to Mary after John's description of the Blessed Mother beneath the cross. The apostolic

Tradition is consistent that Mary, at the time of her death (celebrated as the Dormitian), was granted the privilege of being assumed, body and soul, into heaven. Her role as Mother of God made it inappropriate for her to experience the corruption of the grave. Thus, certain texts, specifically *De Obitu S. Dominae* and *De Transitu Virginis*, describe the Assumption. By the seventh century, this feast was being celebrated in Rome at the Basilica of St. Mary Major. Over the centuries the date and specifics of the feast changed, but the basic tradition of Mary's Assumption was never questioned.

This feast was only officially sanctioned, however, in the middle of the twentieth century. On November 1, 1950, Pope Pius XII published *Munificentissimus Deus*, which proclaimed the Assumption as an infallible dogma. Today this feast is celebrated each August 15 and is commemorated as a holy day of obligation, meaning Catholics are obligated, as with Sunday, to attend Mass.

FACT

Possibly the most interesting idea behind the declaration of the Assumption is that it is the only time since Vatican I proclaimed papal infallibility that this particular privilege of the Roman pontiff has been exercised. Clearly papal infallibility is a privilege judiciously exercised.

Mary as Co-Redemptrix

The four Marian dogmas previously explained form the core of Mariology, but the twentieth century also saw a significant drive to establish a fifth and final Marian dogma, her title as Co-redemptrix. It is extremely important to understand what this proposed dogma means. This teaching does not provide Mary with divine powers, making her co-equal to her son, Jesus, in the act of human redemption. Rather, it means Mary uniquely participated in the redemption of the human family by Jesus Christ. She cooperated fully in her role as the Mother of God, giving Jesus flesh and thus participating in his act of redemption. Mary's role as Co-redemptrix, while unique and highly significant, is completely secondary and subordinate to the work of Christ.

Beginning with Pope Leo XIII in the latter nineteenth century, many popes have made statements favorable to defining Mary as Co-redemptrix. Pope Benedict XV in his Apostolic Letter *Inter Sodalica,* issued on March 22, 1918, stated, "One can say, she redeemed with Christ the human race." In the papal bull *Munificentissimus Deus* on dogma of the Assumption, Pope Pius XII described Mary as "the noble associate of the divine Redeemer." Pope John Paul II described Mary as Co-redemptrix on a few occasions. For example, in 1985 he was quoted, "May, Mary our Protectress, the *Co-Redemptrix*, [emphasis edded] to whom we offer our prayer with great outpouring, make our desire generously correspond to the desire of the Redeemer." Although the present pontiff, Benedict XVI, has also used this title for Mary in public prayers, it is uncertain whether the church will soon, if ever, define this dogma.

Additional Teachings on Mary

While the four Marian dogmas serve as the core of Roman Catholicism's teachings about the Blessed Virgin Mary, there are numerous other doctrines, most of which are celebrated by special feasts throughout the liturgical year. In the post–Vatican II church, February 2 is celebrated as the "Presentation of Jesus." However, prior to the council (and the liturgical changes that came from it), this feast was known as the Purification of Mary. It is celebrated forty days after Christmas, the birth date of Jesus, and represents a celebration of the ritual purity that Jewish women commemorated after the birth of a child. Mary, like all Jewish women of her time, would have been considered ritually impure until forty days after the birth of a child. Thus, this celebration, ancient in its roots, celebrated Mary's re-entry into the Jewish worshiping community.

Two additional liturgical celebrations commemorate events as narrated in the New Testament. The Visitation, commemorating Mary's three-month visit to her cousin Elizabeth (Luke 1:39–56) is celebrated annually on May 31. Mary's complete selflessness in immediately traveling away from her home, although pregnant herself, to be with her elder relative is the basic message of this liturgical celebration. Our Lady of Sorrows, celebrated on September 15, recalls the "spiritual martyrdom" of Mary. As previously stated, Catholic Tradition professes that Mary was assumed body and soul into heaven at the time of her death. Thus, she was not a physical martyr. However, the New Testament and Sacred Tradition describe several different events and incidents, all of which clearly demonstrate the psychological suffering she was forced to endure as a result of her role as the Mother of God.

QUESTION

What are the seven sorrows of Mary?
Four are specified in Scripture: the prophecy of Simeon (Luke 2:25–35), the flight into Egypt (Matthew 2:13–15), the loss of Jesus in the temple (Luke 2:41–52), and the crucifixion (John 19:25–27). The other three, meeting Jesus on the *Via Dolorosa*, taking Jesus down from the cross, and burial of Jesus come from Sacred Tradition.

There are several other doctrines associated with Mary that are found in the Sacred Tradition. The Immaculate Heart of Mary, celebrated on the second Saturday after Pentecost, is a twin celebration with a similar feast of the Sacred Heart of Jesus, observed the previous day. The Queenship of Mary, August 22, recognizes her distinct and unique role in salvation history and her special place within the heavenly host. The birth of Mary is celebrated on September 8, precisely nine months after the Immaculate Conception. The Presentation of Mary, November 21, described in the second-century text Book of James, commemorates the dedication in 543 of the church of St. Mary the New in Jerusalem.

Mary and Popular Devotion

Christianity as a whole celebrates the distinctive contribution of Mary in God's plan of salvation history, but Roman Catholicism has always honored Mary in unique ways. In addition to the four Marian dogmas and numerous other doctrines associated with her, Mary has always been the object of significant popular devotion within the church. These devotions have been manifested most especially in two genres: official proclamations of Marian apparitions and specialized prayers and devotions made in her honor.

Marian Apparitions

Throughout the Christian centuries, there have been numerous incidents where it has been claimed that the Blessed Virgin Mary appeared. The official church's response to such apparitions is highly guarded. The church has been cautious to approve, disapprove, or condemn any reported apparitions. In general, such apparitions are classified as "not worthy of belief," "not contrary to the Faith," or "worthy of belief." Some of the more famous and popular Marian apparitions that have received full approbation from the Holy See are Guadalupe in Mexico (1531), La Salette (1846) and Lourdes (1858) in France, and Fatima in Portugal (1917). These and numerous other sites throughout the world are centers for Marian devotion. Additionally, Our Lady of Lourdes (February 11) and our Lady of Guadalupe (December 12) are celebrated in the liturgical calendar.

ESSENTIAL

Many people today speak of the ongoing apparitions of Mary at Medjugorje in Bosnia-Herzegovina. Since 1981, a small group of seers have been receiving daily messages from Mary. At this point, since the apparitions are ongoing, the church has made no official proclamation on the validity of these visions.

Prayer Devotions to Mary

Faithful Catholics have always prayed to the saints, but certainly prayer and devotion to Mary has been primary in the minds of many. Individual prayers, such as the Hail Mary, derived from the Scriptures and Tradition, and the Memorare (see Appendix B) are often memorized from childhood and prayed regularly. There are, however, two specialized devotions to Mary that are popular today.

The rosary, a specialized series of prayers, has a long history in the church. While popular tradition suggests that the rosary was personally given to St. Dominic by Mary in the thirteenth century, it is more accurate to suggest that this prayer devotion developed over time from a series of penitential prayers to the now more familiar fixed prayer form, consisting of five decades of ten prayers (Hail Marys) each, preceded by recitation of the Our Father (Lord's Prayer, Matthew 6:9–13), and concluding with the doxology (Glory Be). An integral part to rosary devotion is the mysteries upon which people are asked to meditate when praying the rosary. Traditionally fifteen mysteries, five each of glorious, joyful, and sorrowful, were prayed throughout the week. However, in October 2002, Pope John Paul II announced the addition of five luminous mysteries.

FACT

The mysteries of the rosary are based on sacred Scripture and Tradition. They recall significant events of salvation history, all of which directly or indirectly involved Mary and/or Jesus. Traditionally the following schedule is followed during the majority of the liturgical year in praying the rosary: glorious mysteries—Sunday and Wednesday; sorrowful mysteries—Tuesday and Friday; joyful mysteries—Monday and Saturday; luminous mysteries—Thursday.

The second significant prayer devotion to Mary, popularized much more recently, is the Divine Chaplet of Mercy. This devotion, which only came into Catholic Tradition in the 1930s, is associated with the writings of St. Faustina Kowalska, a Polish nun who in obedience to her religious superior wrote a diary in which are presented various revelations concerning God's mercy. Even before her death in 1938, devotion to the Divine Mercy had spread. The basic message of St. Faustina is that God's mercy far surpasses any human sin. God's mercy will come to any individual by following the simple formula of: (1) asking for God's mercy, (2) being merciful to others, and (3) demonstrating complete trust in God. The chaplet, like the rosary, is a series of prayers offered in repetitive fashion. In the contemporary church, Divine Mercy Sunday is celebrated one week after Easter.

PART V

Study of the Church (Ecclesiology)

CHAPTER 16

The Church: One, Holy, Catholic, and Apostolic

The Nicene-Constantinopolitan Creed, professed by Roman Catholics each Sunday and solemnity, recognizes that the church is one, holy, Catholic, and apostolic. These significant terms, often referred to as the four marks of the church, not only describe fundamental qualities of Catholicism but also are foundational to how it has been understood over the Christian era and is organized today. It is important, therefore, to understand what these terms mean and signify in Roman Catholicism today.

Biblical Foundations and Development of the Church

The Roman Catholic Church as an institution looks to Revelation and more specifically sacred Scripture for its self-understanding. In turn the Bible provides both the origins and meaning to the church. The Hebrew Bible clearly articulates how the Jews were a special "chosen" people, marked out by God for a special relationship, a covenant, given by God to Abraham. However, this special relationship that God held with the Jews was constantly frayed. The disobedience of the Israelites in the desert, the refusal of the people to heed the warnings of the prophets, and the extreme self-interest and corruption evident in many of the kings of both Israel and Judah kept God's relationship with his chosen people constantly on edge. God's fidelity to the covenant was not always matched by a similar loyalty on the part of the people. From the Christian perspective, this fracture in the relationship reached its apex when the Jewish people refused to acknowledge Jesus as the Messiah. Because of this failure, St. Paul has told us, "The Gentiles have become fellow heirs, members of the same body, and sharers in the promise in Christ Jesus through the gospel." (Ephesians 3:6)

ESSENTIAL

Matthew 16:18 reads, "And I tell you, you are Peter, and on this rock I will build my church, and the gates of Hades will not prevail against it." Roman Catholicism teaches that Jesus' words to Peter inaugurated the concept of the papacy. Peter was designated by Jesus specifically to lead the church. Roman centrality came from the tradition of Peter's death in the Eternal City.

St. Paul's words are echoed in the Gospels. This is best seen in the famous dialogue between Jesus and Peter (Matthew 16:13–20). Jesus directly asks Peter, "Who do you say I am?" When Peter responds, "You are the Messiah, the Son of the living God," Jesus informs him that he is the rock upon which the church will be built. Roman Catholicism understands this conversation as clear evidence that Jesus desired to inaugurate a church that would continue his work after his earthly life had ended.

The Acts of the Apostles, especially chapters 1–12, is the basic primary source that tells the story of the nascent church. Buoyed by the arrival of the Holy Spirit at Pentecost (Acts 2:1–13), the apostles went forward courageously and with great enthusiasm preached that Jesus was raised from the dead. Transformed in many ways from their timid and fearful existence after Jesus' death, Acts describes how Peter and the other eleven went forward in Jesus' name, preaching, teaching, and in some cases performing miraculous healings. This second treatise penned by St. Luke provides much information about how this small band of Jesus' followers, initially existing as a sect within Judaism, gained many converts from their own Hebrew ranks. We are told that the community came together, sharing all things, while enduring severe persecution at the hands of zealous Pharisees such as Saul of Tarsus.

It is this same Saul who, after his conversion along the road to Damascus (Acts 9: 1–19a), became the great catalyst for the rapid development of the church within the eastern Mediterranean world. Paul, as historians sometimes speak of him, turned the world upside down through his three evangelistic journeys that led to the establishment of Christianity throughout the region. In his travels, Paul established numerous local churches in cities and communities with names familiar to us through his corpus of letters: Corinth, Ephesus, Galatia, Thessalonica, and Philippi.

As the church developed in local communities, certain distinct ministries and operations also arose. The Pastoral Epistles (I and II Timothy and Titus) speak of the ministries of bishop and presbyter. Acts 6:1–6 describes the appointment of seven men to assist the apostles in the work of ministry. This is seen as inaugurating the ministry of deacon. These ministers and others were granted specialized gifts to conduct their service of God's people in proper and appropriate ways. In I Corinthians 12:4–7, specialized gifts of the Holy Spirit are bestowed upon the faithful for purposes of building up the community of faith.

The Roman Church

Evidence indicates that Christianity was present in Rome in the first years after Jesus' death, approximately A.D. 40. Most of these "Christians," it seems, were Judaizers, zealous converts who strongly believed in the absolute necessity for one to become Jewish before converting to Christianity.

This was ritually symbolized for males through the act of circumcision. Judaizers clashed with a more lenient position, held by St. Paul and his disciples, over what was necessary to become Christian. In the end, the Council of Jerusalem (Chapter 1) decided that Gentiles did not need to be circumcised in order to join the ranks of Christianity. In other words, one did not need first to become Jewish in order to be Christian.

FACT

The polytheistic world of the Roman Empire had no regard for Christian worship; Sunday was simply another day of the week. Thus, Christians were forced to celebrate their commemoration of Jesus' passion, death, and resurrection at times and in places that did not ill-effect their position in society. Christians kept a low profile to reduce the possibility of persecution.

House Churches

The Roman Church comprised several local house churches. Paul mentions in Romans 16:3ff the names of several local people who played host to various small Christian communities. Rome's prominent position as capital of the empire made it the likely geographic locus for the church. Additionally, the tradition has always held that both Peter and Paul were martyred in Rome. Thus as Rome was the dominant city of the ruling empire and the burial place of the nascent church's earliest premier evangelists, it was natural for the city to assume a leadership role in Christianity. The Roman Church and Christianity in general evolved from a group of enthusiastic Jews to a community dominated by Gentiles. This process, though progressive, was also quite slow.

The church's development within the Roman Empire required a sense of accommodation to the prevailing political, religious, and social atmosphere. As a proscribed religion, Christianity could not be practiced in the open. Christians were forced to worship privately, without the benefit of public institutions. Local communities, whether in Rome, Corinth, or other cities and regions, met in the homes of prominent local Christians, both men and women. For example, in Romans 16:5, Paul speaks of the church in the house of Prisca and Aquila. In Colossians 4:15, Paul writes of the church in the house of Nympha.

QUESTION

If Christians met in the homes of prominent women, who presided at the Lord's Supper, what later became the Mass, in these earliest days of the church?
The answer to this question is not obvious, but it would seem highly plausible that the hostess or host of the community would play a significant role in the weekly celebration.

The Church Is One

Recall that it was the Council of Constantinople in 381 that professed the church to be one, holy, Catholic, and apostolic. These are often referred to as the four marks of the church. Why were these four specific qualities considered so vital that they were placed in the Creed? In order to answer, an exploration of the rationale for these four specific marks is necessary.

Why was oneness, meaning the concept of unity, so important for the patristic church? Initially, especially prior to the Edict of Milan in 311, the concept of the church being one was vitally important to justify its existence against its many enemies. First, Christianity had to demonstrate a united front against the Romans. It was imperative that the basic belief, as articulated in the Creed, as well as Church practice be uniform. From the Christian perspective it was very important for Rome to know that it faced one united religious minority, not a series of fringe groups with various ideas, practices, and beliefs. Secondly, after the collapse of the empire, the concept of the church as one served to justify Catholicism against rival heretical groups that arose throughout Christian history. Catholics could always point to the church being one as a clear message that other competing theologies were simply aberrations of the true faith.

More contemporary theology sees the unity of the church in two different senses: as a way of drawing uniqueness and as a statement of its ideal unity. These concepts are found in seeing the church as a witness. This ideal unity is expressed in the Acts of the Apostles 2:44: "All who believed were together and had all things in common." Similarly, Acts 4:32 reads: "Now the whole group of those who believed were of one heart and soul, and no one claimed private ownership of any possessions, but everything he owned was held in common." It's important to note, however, that unity has always allowed diversity. In other words, unity is not uniformity. The church moves together, united as one body, but within that body often exists varied ideas, opinions, and perspectives, including theological perspectives.

QUOTE

St. Paul expressed the concept of the Church as one in this way: "There is one body and one Spirit, just as you were called to the one hope of your calling, one Lord, one faith, one baptism, one God and Father of all, who is above all and through all and in all." (Ephesians 4:4–6)

What doctrines and ideas associated with Catholicism bring unity to the Roman Church? One important concept is the unity of God. Since God can only exist as a united Trinity, three persons in one God, the church must share this oneness. Belief in Jesus also brings unity to the church. The idea that God sent his own Son into our world to be one with us in every aspect, save sin, and to suffer, die, and rise to bring us the possibility of eternal life, is a strong unifying factor to the church. Baptism is the third significant unifying symbol for the church. Lastly, the unity of the church is solidified by the power and presence of the Holy Spirit. The Pentecost event reversed the destruction wrought by God who scattered the nations due to human arrogance in building a tower to the heavens at Babel (Genesis 11:1–9).

One might rightly ask today how the Christian Church and Roman Catholicism more specifically can claim to be one when divisions seem so prominent. On one level brokenness and factionalism have characterized the church throughout its history. This is true even during the apostolic era when St. Paul, among others, was fighting against rival groups such as the Judaizers and "Super Apostles." Schism and heresy have often been present leading to various factions. Additionally, nationalism, economic and social conditions, plus disagreements concerning church discipline and practice have created other factions. However, through it all the church has always managed to maintain a united front and persevere through many raging storms.

The Church Is Holy

The church's claim to be holy is highly significant since God alone is holy. This is a call, therefore, for the Church, the people of God, to be different, to be renewed and transformed. Through its association with God, who made all things, the created world is itself holy, for it bears the mark of the Creator. The church can also claim to be holy from its initial foundation, as described earlier, by Jesus himself.

ESSENTIAL

While Roman Catholics follow many vocations, the one common calling for all is to seek holiness. Catholics are married, single, or possibly celibate priests and/or religious; they may be teachers, engineers, medical professionals, store clerks, or construction workers. All, however, are called to lives of holiness as members of the Body of Christ, the church.

Many people, Catholics and non-Catholics alike, look to history and ask with some skepticism how the church can be holy when events such as the Crusades, Inquisition, and in recent memory the sex abuse crisis appear to contradict such a claim. Some have answered this challenging question by stating that the church is not without sinners but is without sin itself. Clearly sin is present in the world, and all people in some way find themselves under its grasp. Thus individual acts perceived to be sinful in the minds of many often bring scandal and much heartache to the church, both locally and universally. Others, however, understand the church to be sinful, yet there is always holiness in the midst of sin. Catholicism understands the church should be a divinely inspired and instituted community, but it also understands that its membership is human and, therefore, incomplete and imperfect. The presence of sin does not in any way obviate the power and reality of the church's holiness.

The Church Is Catholic

It took some time before the word "Catholic" was used to describe those first followers of Jesus. The Acts of the Apostles 11:26 tells us that the nascent church was first called Christian in Antioch. The first time the word "Catholic" is found in association with the church is in St. Ignatius of Antioch's Letter to Smyrna, Chapter 8: "Wherever the bishop shall appear, there let the multitude [of the people] also be; even as, wherever Jesus Christ is, there is the Catholic Church."

During the patristic era the concept of Catholic to indicate universal became more prominent. For Augustine, Catholic meant the church spread throughout the world. Later, during the medieval period, the word "Catholic" was used to distinguish the Western Church from Eastern Orthodoxy. Later still, during the Reformation, Catholic was used to specify the Roman Church as the one true church, seeing itself in opposition to the multitude of Protestant denominations arising from Luther, the Reformed Tradition of Calvin, radical reformers, and the Church of England under King Henry VIII.

FACT

"The Dogmatic Constitution on the Church," paragraph 8, states while the fullness of truth is found in Catholicism, elements of truth are found in other religious traditions: "This Church constituted and organized in the world as a society, subsists in the Catholic Church, . . . although many elements of sanctification and of truth are found outside of its visible structure."

The contemporary church understands "Catholic" to truly apply in a universal way. The church is not simply a local community or a sum of local communities throughout the world. Rather, Catholic means universality of extent and inclusiveness that embraces differences within a larger unity. When St. Paul wrote to the Ephesians (3:6) telling them "The Gentiles have become fellow heirs, members of the same body, and sharers in the promise in Christ Jesus through the gospel," he was describing the church as a place where differences can be reconciled. If the church fails to be a community of reconciliation, it has fallen short in one of its essential missions. If the church is Catholic, she must do what is possible, as suggested by Vatican II, to promote Christian unity. Openness and the desire to learn from other traditions is essential.

QUESTION

What was Jesus' attitude toward Christian unity?
While the question is difficult and the answer uncertain, some have offered Jesus' own words as the best answer: "That they may all be one. As you, Father, are in me and I am in you, may they also be in us, so that the world may believe that you have sent me."

The Church Is Apostolic

The fourth mark of the church, apostolic, refers to an unbroken continuity in the church. This succession means much more than unbroken authority, as in the office of the pope; it also means continuity in faith, proclamation, and interpretation of the Gospel. To be an apostolic church means one that teaches the truth. A very energetic and at times complex theological debate continues in contemporary Catholicism, especially in the post–Vatican II era, concerning continuity versus discontinuity of church teaching over the centuries.

Continuity in succession of church authority became necessary after the apostolic era ended. Church leaders realized that a structure of offices and authority would be necessary to maintain consistent and authoritative teaching throughout the universal church. Beginning with the basic structure described in the Pastoral Epistles, namely the positions of bishop and presbyter, the church has developed into a highly organized, some might claim extremely complex, institution that allows for governance on the local, national, and universal levels.

Basic Roman Catholic Church Organization

The Roman Catholic Church as an organization is the most widespread in the world. As understood by church members, Jesus formed the church, centered about the apostles and St. Peter as the first leader, as the primary vehicle to continue the work he inaugurated during his earthly life. During the Christian era, Catholicism evolved and developed from a small band of Jewish men and women in Israel to a worldwide organization that today claims more than 1 billion members. Through its 2,000-year history, Catholicism has weathered many significant storms, beginning with local and universal persecutions by the Romans, numerous heresies, the Crusades, the Reformation of the sixteenth century, and the destruction of the French Revolution. While Catholics firmly believe that the church is inspired by the Holy Spirit, and guided and assisted by God, it must also be acknowledged on the human level that the church's structure and organization has helped to maintain continuity and maneuver her through many difficult periods of history.

Universal Roman Organization

Catholicism's central organization is found in Rome through the office of the pope and the Roman Curia. Beginning with St. Peter and continuing today under the reign of Benedict XVI, there have been 266 who have held the Chair of Peter and reigned as pope. While there have been challenges to this office, especially during the period of the Great Western Schism (see Chapter 1), papal succession has been continuous from the beginning. The pope has a large cadre of church officials who assist him with his many and complex duties in leading the universal church. First among these assistants is the Cardinal Secretary of State who is responsible for all political and diplomatic functions within Vatican City.

The Roman Curia, a series of offices generally headed by cardinals, serves as the core of the church's universal organization. The Curia consists of nine Congregations, three Tribunals, eleven Pontifical Councils, plus numerous other commissions and offices. The Congregations, the highest level of order, are responsible to oversee specific aspects of church life, such as the Congregation for the Doctrine of the Faith, Congregation for the Causes of Saints, Sacred Congregation for the Clergy, and the Congregation for Divine Worship and the Discipline of the Sacraments. Tribunals, such as the Roman Rota, which oversees canon law, and Pontifical councils, such as the Council for the Laity, Council for Promoting Christian Unity, and the Council for Justice and Peace, are the second- and third-tier organizations. Pontifical Commissions such as the Biblical Commission and Theological

Commission serve as a fourth level of the Curia. In addition to the Roman Curia, the Synod of Bishops, (see Chapter 6) called into conference periodically by the pope, serves as an advisory body to the Holy Father.

QUESTION

What is a Roman Catholic cardinal?
A cardinal is a senior administrative official, appointed by the pope to oversee an ecclesiastical office. Generally speaking, over history most of these men have also been bishops, but this is not necessary. The College of Cardinals collectively has the solemn responsibility to elect the popes.

Local Organization

Beyond the central Roman Curia, Catholicism is structured on the local level as well. Nationally, most countries, and in certain cases geographic regions, have conferences or councils of bishops, often canonically (official church status) established, that make policy for the geographic region alone as well as carry out edicts of the pope for the local church. Below the national level, the church is organized by dioceses, local geographic regions that are headed by a bishop. Some dioceses, due to historical significance and/or large population centers, serve as archdioceses. Each archdiocese, called the metropolitan, has a certain number of regional or suffragan dioceses under its overall administrative control.

The day-to-day life for Roman Catholics is not concerned with the Roman Curia, USCCB, or even the regional diocese, but rather with the local parish. Headed by a pastor who is generally assisted by other clerics and, most especially today, a staff that includes laymen and laywomen, the parish serves to meet the spiritual needs of Roman Catholics. Services such as sacramental preparation; religious education for youth and adults; counseling and spiritual guidance; as well as social networking and outreach programs to various groups, including people with addictions or assistance to the poor and marginalized of society, are common to most parishes. It is through the parish that most Roman Catholics hold a connection to the universal church.

Models of the Church

The traditional four marks of the church (one, holy, Catholic, and apostolic) and how the Church is organized (universally, nationally, and locally) are understood and lived on a day-to-day basis by Roman Catholics in varied ways. History, theological perspective, as well as local culture and customs are only three of several factors that have generated various understandings of the purpose and responsibility of the church today. These perspectives, which came to the forefront as a result of Vatican II, were formally described in a seminal book, *Models of the Church*, by Father (later Cardinal) Avery Dulles, SJ. In this monograph and a supplementary effort, *A Church to Believe In*, Dulles outlined several models to demonstrate the church's purpose and to understand her function.

Church as Institution

The longest standing and most traditional perspective on the church is to see it as a hierarchical institution. Geometrically this understanding can be modeled by a pyramid. The top apex of the pyramid represents the pope and the Roman Curia. Below this level, as the triangle broadens, lies the national and diocesan levels of the church. As the pyramid reaches its base and broadest point we find the parish level, including the role of the laity. Church history clearly indicates that this model has been operative for the majority of the Christian era; the model continues to function today and is considered by many as the standard. The institutional model suggests that the church functions and serves its people best through strict authority.

The Church as Sacrament

The sacraments, as we recall from Chapter 11, are special signs instituted by Christ that bring grace. While acknowledging the seven traditional sacraments, many Roman Catholics view the church itself as a sacrament, a sign to the world. As such the church must be a witness that brings the message of Christ to a world badly in need of his teaching. This perspective holds the church to be the responsible agent of proper Christian life and belief. Such a perspective quite obviously holds great responsibility for the church. As possibly the primary sacrament, it must be a witness, through its daily decisions and policies, to the message of Christ as articulated in the Gospels.

The Church as Herald

Roman Catholicism is quite obviously a huge faith community with numbers and influence in every part of the globe. Its size, historical significance, and authority in the minds of many make it the perfect vehicle to speak on behalf of its members. As the gospel evangelists and St. Paul fearlessly and courageously preached and wrote about the message of Jesus and supported the fledgling church in its infancy, so the church today is asked to speak on behalf of those throughout the world who have little or no voice. Additionally, the concept of herald requires the church to continue to proclaim the good news of Jesus Christ. Rather than concentrating on authority or serving as a sign, this model believes the church's greatest responsibility is to speak, even in the face of opposition, standing forthrightly in support of Jesus' message and for the rights of its members.

FACT

Liberation theology, rejected by Popes John Paul II and Benedict XVI, but nonetheless popular in Latin America where it was most manifest, stresses the models of church as herald and servant. Emphasizing outreach to the poor, this theology, influenced by Marxist principles, professes that the church must be an advocate for the oppressed and downtrodden in society.

The Church as Servant

A fourth operative model views the church as a servant. Using Jesus' words as its creed, "The Son of Man came not to be served but to serve, and to give his life [as] a ransom for many" (Mark 10:45), this model understands the church's primary responsibility is to serve its people. In the post–Vatican II church, this perspective has been broadly touted by those who believe the church must be a strong advocate for the poor. Not only must the church speak on behalf of those who have no voice, it must actively serve the needs of its people, both spiritually and physically. As a strong and economically prosperous institution, the church as servant seeks to emulate the life of Jesus, who constantly in a proactive way fed the hungry; cured lepers as well as the blind, deaf, and mute; and gave spiritual solace to those in need.

The Church as a Community of Disciples

The most contemporary church model offered by Dulles is that of a community of disciples. Instead of the geometric pyramid of the hierarchical model, this perspective sees the church in the shape of a circle. The church is not viewed as a top-down structure but rather as a community in which all people, whether they be popes, bishops, priests, religious, or laypeople, are no more or less important. Positions, ministries, and roles in the church will be different, but the idea that one is more important than another is rejected. Many contemporary Catholics, products of the 1960s and its rejection of authoritarianism, are strongly attracted to this model. Vatican II's use of the term "people of God" as a metaphor for the church also speaks to this particular model. Additionally, this perspective stresses inclusivity rather than exclusivity, a concept that has many adherents today.

CHAPTER 17

Priesthood, Religious Life, and Lay Ministry

Ministry, the active apostolic efforts of Roman Catholics, is practiced in several ways within the church. Clergy and religious are those who have traditionally provided lifetime service in formal ways. Today, however, in the post–Vatican II era, dedicated laity, both men and women, while not under religious vows, serve nonetheless in many capacities, often in positions formerly held by priests and religious. This study of Catholicism must look at the historical development of ministry, clerical and lay, seeing both means as significant contributions to the contemporary church.

The Sacramental Priesthood

Priests, who have always been male and from approximately the twelfth century forward celibate, have and continue to play a central role in the everyday life of Roman Catholics. They serve primarily as sacramental ministers but also in numerous auxiliary roles as counselors, chaplains, teachers and professors, social workers, and administrators. The understanding and function of the priest, finding roots in the Scriptures, has, like the church in total, evolved and developed through the Christian centuries.

Jewish Presbyters

Frequent references to presbyters or *zeqenim* are found in the Hebrew Scriptures. Sometimes referred to as elders, they generally hold the role of a representative of the people in political and religious matters. This concept is first seen and aptly illustrated by the college of seventy elders appointed by Moses (Numbers 11:16–17). Severely burdened by his task of leading some 600,000 Israelites from Egypt through the desert to the Promised Land, Moses asked God for assistance. God responded by telling his chosen deliverer to appoint seventy elders of Israel upon whom God would bestow some of Moses' spirit. These were to serve the people, making decisions in less important matters. This event was important in inaugurating the concept of presbyter for both Jews and Christians.

QUOTE

Numbers 27:18–20 illustrates the ancient rite of laying on of hands: "The Lord said to Moses, 'Take Joshua son of Nun, . . . and let your hand upon him; having to stand before Eleazar the priest and all the congregation, and commission him in their sight. You shall give him some of your authority so that all the congregation of the Israelites may obey.'"

By the time of the Roman occupation of Palestine, every Jewish community had its Sanhedrin of *zeqenim* who were elected by the people, all of whom had some voice in this process. During the Roman Empire, Jewish presbyters were ordained by the laying on of hands, an ancient custom dating back to the time of Moses. As with the elders in the desert, these officials were responsible chiefly for civil and judicial matters. The New Testament speaks of the Sanhedrin as consisting of chief priests and scribes (Luke 22:66), rulers, elders, and scribes (Acts 4:5–6), and high priests and elders (Acts 4:33, 5:21).

Christian Presbyters in the New Testament

The work of Jewish presbyters in the nascent Christian community is particularly well illustrated by the ministry of St. Paul. Commissioned by Christ himself (Acts, Chapter 9), Paul saw himself as an apostle, but his many tasks were similar to members of the Jewish Sanhedrin. For example, he served as judge (I Corinthians 5:1–13), reconciler (II Corinthians 1:23–2:11), punisher and admonisher (I Corinthians 6:1–8), official who settled marriage problems (I Corinthians 7), and raiser of funds (I Corinthians 16:1–4; II Corinthians 8–9). However, his primary apostolic duty was to proclaim the Gospel. In his letters Paul mentions several ministries, including apostles, prophets, teachers, healers, wonder workers, and administrators. He did not specifically mention presbyters, which seem to be subsumed under the titles of guardians and deacons.

ESSENTIAL

I Timothy 3:1–7 speaks of the office of bishop, *episkopos*. While this office seems to be distinguished from the court of elders and, therefore, presbyters, the position had not reached the concept of a more monarchical episcopacy of the second century. At this stage the office of bishop was the same as the priest today.

The function of Christian presbyters becomes more distinct in the Pastoral Epistles (I and II Timothy and Titus). Moving from Paul's understanding of presbyter as guardian of the tradition and one who gave good example to younger members of the community, the author of the Pastoral Epistles says that the essential function of presbyter is to preside. In I Timothy 3:1ff, some of the important qualities and specific works of elders (presbyters) are described, especially teaching and preaching. I Peter 5:2–5 says presbyters are to be humble and to be models of Jesus Christ. Each presbyter takes the place of Christ as pastor and guardian of souls.

Presbyters in the Early Patristic Church

As the church moved beyond the apostolic era, the role of the presbyter began to expand in new directions and become much more specific in action. Clement of Rome (circa 90–97) describes presbyters in ways very similar to the Pastoral Epistles but adds that they give council to mission churches. The Shepherd of Hermas, the prophet and presbyter of the Church of Rome (circa A.D. 140), says presbyters were responsible for reading the sacred books at the weekly liturgical prayer, the celebration of the Eucharist. Justin Martyr (d. 165) in his *First Apology* provides significant insight into the typical Sunday liturgy of his day. The presbyter presided over a service of readings. Additionally, he gave a homily and offered bread and wine to the congregation, which assented with "Amen." Justin also speaks of the presider's responsibility for the care of orphans, widows, the sick, and prisoners. The *Didache* (late first and early second centuries) presents a twofold ministry for the presbyter: the role of an itinerant charismatic apostle, prophet, and teacher, and the more recently developed liturgical ministers: prophet and later resident and elector of guardians, bishops, and deacons. St. Ireneaus of Lyon (d. 202) used the term "presbyter" to refer to church leaders who were disciples of the apostles and guardians of the tradition.

FACT

Early Christian communities practiced a ritual meal known as the *agape* feast held on Sundays, which became known as the Day of the Lord. This recalled not only the resurrection but other significant events, such as the Lord's appearance to Thomas and the Pentecost event, all of which happened on Sunday. This celebration evolved into the Roman Catholic Mass.

In the third century we first see the concept of priest presbyter as part of church order. In his famous *Apostolic Tradition*, Hippolytus (d. 235) reveals some of the functions of the priest presbyter in his era. The presbyter is responsible for giving the blessing at the *Agape* (today the Mass) if the bishop is not present. At this same celebration presbyters imposed hands on the offering with the bishop and administered the chalice. It does not seem, however, at this time that they presided at the celebration of the Eucharist in the absence of the bishop.

Additional church fathers of the third century addressed the role of presbyter. Tertullian in his *Apology* 39 said presbyters were chosen by the people. In union with the bishop, they exercised the *sacerdotalia munera*, the office to teach, preach, and to baptize. Cyprian, a student of Tertullian and later Bishop of Carthage (249–258), said presbyters were responsible to take care of widows, teach catechumens, and to receive penitents in private. Clement of Alexandria (d. 215) saw little distinction between the bishop and a presbyter. The bishop was only a presbyter who had been chosen to lead. Origen, Clement's student, on the other hand, makes a more clear delineation between bishops, presbyters, and deacons. Insofar as presbyters were in union with the bishop and received their ministerial mandate from him, they were priests.

By the time of the Council of Nicaea (325), there is a clear distinction between offices of bishop and presbyter. Bishops in the fourth century were responsible for local Christian communities, but they often delegated much of their priestly power to presbyters, except that of ordination. As the formal Christian ministry developed, its members moved further away from secular occupations; certain occupations, such as participation in the military, were even proscribed for those who wished to enter the presbyterate. The expansion of Christianity throughout the empire gave greater privileges to the clergy.

At this time as well a tradition arose for presbyters to practice abstinence in marriage or even celibacy. At the outset Christian presbyters were married along with their Jewish counterparts, but as the fourth century dawned the discipline of marital continence and celibacy began to grow in the West. Historians agree that the council fathers at Nicaea were interested in passing a law of celibacy, but this was not done. By the end of the fourth century the role of priest presbyter had emerged in its own right.

Religious Life—Concept of the Consecrated Life

As described in Chapter 12, priesthood is conferred upon and through the sacrament of Holy Orders, one of the two sacraments of commitment. How priesthood developed has been explained earlier, but it is essential in any study of this subject to understand and review the history of religious life, a concept related to and at times overlapping with priesthood. Religious life in Roman Catholicism is a particular vocation whereby men and women willingly choose to live in community and under the common structure of the evangelical counsels, namely the vows of chastity, poverty, and obedience. Religious life is a basic call, which for many men is lived through the sacramental priesthood. However, male and female religious who are not ordained, commonly referred to as brothers and sisters, serve the church institution and God's people in selfless lives of service and ministry.

History of Religious Life

Over the course of Roman Catholic history, men and women have sought to live religious life in varied ways. Different styles of religious life, based on the needs of those seeking this vocation and those whom religious serve, have arisen over time. The advent of new forms of religious life has not obviated earlier ways to lead this life but rather has led to new horizons and greater numbers of those who seek this vocation. Thus, various religious orders have arisen to meet the needs of the day. In some cases, when the need was specific and time-dependent, religious communities have died. Today the numbers of religious, especially women, have dropped rather precipitously; new recruits to religious communities are also few in number. Nevertheless, the service of men and women religious over the centuries of Catholic history has been and continues to be highly significant.

The common ground for all religious are the vows of celibacy, poverty, and obedience, referred to as the evangelical counsels. Men and women religious, after at least three years of intense preparation, take these vows perpetually to God. The theology of the vows is extensive, but in essence these commit the religious to live simply, depending of the religious community for sustenance, to forego sex and marriage, and to relinquish self-autonomy, being obedient to all religious superiors.

Monasticism

The first form of religious life, monasticism, emerged in full in the sixth century, but it had some very significant precursors that set the basic tone for future religious congregations. During the mid to late third century, some Christians, in an effort to seek greater personal unity with God, left their livelihood and journeyed to the desert to live in solitude. One of the most famous of these early desert dwellers, collectively called *anchorites*, was St. Antony of the Desert (251–356). Antony, and like-minded men and women, found their calling in life to be in constant prayer, meditation, and reflection. The desert provided them the environment to rid themselves of outside distractions.

FACT

In his biography of St. Antony, St. Athanasius describes how the former found his vocation. One day when passing by a church he heard the Gospel message proclaimed: "Go, sell what you own and give the money to the poor, and you will have treasure in heaven; then come, follow me." (Mark 10:21). Antony followed the challenge literally, after making arrangements for the care of his sister, by living in solitude in the desert.

The second group that preceded the sixth-century monastics was another band of desert dwellers called Cenobites. Pachomius (290–347), like Antony, followed the call to solitude in the desert, but rather than living a solitary existence he chose to create a community that would live a form of common life. Such an existence would bring the possibility of greater growth through the community's strength through numbers.

QUOTE

The Rule of Benedict, Chapter 48, reads in part: "Idleness is the enemy of the soul. Therefore the . . . [brothers] should be occupied at certain times in manual labor, and again at fixed hours in sacred reading. To that end we think that the times for each may be prescribed as follows." The Rule provides a total road map for day-to-day life.

This concept of searching for God away from society, what became known as monasticism, moved from the eastern desert to the western part of the empire through the actions of such people as St. John Cassian (365–435). As a formal part of religious life in the West, monasticism was inaugurated by St. Benedict of Nursia (480?–543), who founded his famous monastery at Monte Cassino in 529. Gathering a group of men around him, Benedict wrote a Rule that became the general pattern of life used by Benedictines and many other communities who followed the basic monastic way of life. The Rule calls for a strong abbot, stable residence, and the centrality of common prayer for all in the monastery. In addition to the three basic vows, Benedict insisted his monks add a vow of stability, meaning that a monk would live his entire life in one monastery. The model created by Benedict was for a self-sustaining community where monks could work at various activities during the day, coming together regularly for common prayer, meals, and recreation.

The Mendicant Orders

The twelfth century saw the first great innovation in religious life from its original manifestation in monasticism. Seeking to move beyond the walls of the monastery in order to serve God's people in a more public way, groups of religious gathered together as community, but sought their daily sustenance and needs from the people they served. Collectively referred to as the Mendicant orders, meaning beggars, each religious stressed the virtue of poverty and the active ministry of preaching. Because these groups sought the generosity of others to sustain their daily needs, Mendicant orders were urban; they did not live away from society as did their monastic predecessors. The two most famous Mendicant communities were the Franciscans and Dominicans. Today these orders continue their traditional charisms. Franciscans emphasize the simplicity of life as expressed by their founder, St. Francis of Assisi; Dominicans are well known for their eloquence in preaching.

QUESTION

Why do Dominicans use the letters O.P. as a designation for their religious order?
Most religious orders use letters that speak of their actual name or possibly their founder. The Dominicans, founded by the Spaniard, St. Dominic Guzman, specifically to preach against the heresy of the Albigensians (commonly known as the Cathars), use the letters O.P. to designate their ministry—Order of Preachers.

Apostolic Congregations

The Reformation of the sixteenth century was the primary catalyst to the creation of a third major category of religious, the Apostolic orders. We recall that the Counter Reformation (see Chapter 2) featured the rise of the Society of Jesus, commonly known as the Jesuits. The Apostolic orders in general were a response to the social and religious upheaval of the Reformation. A new environment had been created, and people like St. Ignatius of Loyola responded by establishing groups of religious who were totally free from enclosures, more mobile, and with a spirituality strongly oriented toward outward service. The Jesuits were undoubtedly the most famous of these new orders, but they were only the vanguard of a plethora of religious communities that were established when needs arose. In contrast to monastic orders, who lived in an enclosure and centered themselves on prayer, silence, and daily work, and the Mendicant orders that, while ministering to others, were totally dependent on local community for their daily needs, the Apostolic orders were much more independent. These religious were able to function in ministries that compensated them sufficiently so that collectively their communities could operate as independent congregations.

Post–French Revolution Orders

The French Revolution, a seminal event in world history, was extremely destructive to the Roman Catholic Church in Europe. Not only did one pope, Pius VI, die in prison, but the Concordat (1801) between Pope Pius VII and Napoleon in many ways placed the church in a subservient position to the state. Religious orders also suffered greatly during this period. Wellington's victory at Waterloo in 1815 and the downfall of French rule provided a new environment for the development of religious communities. The growing gap between the church and large sections of people in industrial centers raised a new and acute social and educational dilemma. In response to this need, many religious communities, especially communities of women who broke out from their enclosures, became involved in teaching, both secular subjects and catechesis. Additionally, European colonial expansion in Africa and Asia saw the development of many specialized missionary congregations who went to these foreign lands to evangelize the native peoples.

ESSENTIAL

It is important to understand that while male religious communities became more apostolic beginning in the sixteenth century, such was not the case with congregations of women religious, who remained basically cloistered. Some orders of women religious assisted through nursing and teaching, but the general trend, even with these groups, was to have little contact with the outside world.

Status of Priesthood and Religious Life Today

Throughout the world and in the United States specifically, priests and religious continue to serve God's people in many significant ways. Parishes provide the faithful with the sacraments, including their preparation, religious education, and numerous social programs, both for the poor and others in need. Educational institutions on the primary, secondary, and university levels serve to prepare young people to lead good and productive lives that are imbued with the Roman Catholic Church's ethic of life. Hospitals, charities, and other significant institutions also continue the important work that has characterized their service for centuries.

Why was there such a precipitous loss of priests and religious and subsequent fewer vocations in the wake of Vatican II?
The answers are complex, but they center about two points. First, Vatican II itself was for many priests and religious a divisive event, causing confusion and uncertainty. Second, the upheaval of the 1960s, including the challenging of all norms, including authority, and the general prosperity, especially in the United States, was not an environment conducive to considering religious vocation.

It must be acknowledged, however, that the contemporary church suffers from insufficient numbers of priests and religious and, in the minds of many, the perceived lack of direction of many who serve in these various congregations. The post–Vatican II church has seen a significant loss in the numbers of priests and religious worldwide. Additionally, vocations to these specialized ministries have also dropped significantly. As the Catholic population continues to grow and the number of ordained clerics and religious continues to drop, the ability of the church to meet the needs of its members becomes a significant challenge. The situation has been the topic of wide conversation with many varied solutions suggested.

The Permanent Diaconate

One very positive response to the present shortage of priests and religious is the significant rise in the number of permanent deacons. Deacons are ordained (Sacrament of Holy Orders) men who possess certain faculties (authorization) to perform sacraments and to assist priests in their day-to-day work. The order of deacons has for centuries been a steppingstone to priesthood. Additionally, during the patristic era, deacons had functioned in multiple and varied ways. However, over time the permanent diaconate dissolved, being basically absorbed into priesthood. However, the Vatican II document *Lumen Gentium*, paragraph 29, provided the catalyst for the restoration of the permanent diaconate by Pope Paul VI through documents he issued in 1967 and 1972. Deacons can baptize, officiate at marriages, preach, and conduct wakes and burials. Additionally, they can assist in numerous daily tasks in parishes and are invaluable in their service to the contemporary church. While the number of priests and religious is in decline, the permanent diaconate in the United States is flourishing, growing from 898 in 1975 (after its restoration) to 16,380 in 2009.

FACT

The precipitous drop-off in priests and religious after Vatican II can be seen in the following statistics concerning the Roman Catholic Church in the United States: (1) Diocesan priests in 1965—58,632; in 2009—40,666 (2) Religious priests in 1965—22,707; in 2009—13,072 (3) Religious sisters in 1965—179,954; in 2009—59,601 (4) Religious brothers in 1965—12,271; in 2009—4,863.

"Decree on the Apostolate of Lay People"

Peter Steinfels, in his book *A People Adrift: The Crisis of the Roman Catholic Church in America*, suggests the American Catholic Church over the next generation must successfully balance two key transitions: the passage from a pre–Vatican II generation with a foundational understanding of Catholicism to a new generation without that traditional background, and the passage of power from the clergy to the laity. It is Steinfels' second transition that many Roman Catholics suggest is the key to the church of the future. As the number of clergy and religious decrease, it will be necessary for the laity to take a more active role in meeting the ministerial needs of God's people. This transition, ongoing today, was in large measure inaugurated by Vatican II's "Decree on the Apostolate of Lay People."

This document, issued during the fourth session of the council in the fall of 1965, presented many new and at the time highly progressive ideas with respect to lay activity in the church. From the outset the decree speaks of the need for the lay apostolate to be broadened and intensified. All people are called, through the sacrament of baptism, to be a leaven to the world. This new activity must be manifested in spiritual and temporal realms, but emphasis is clearly placed on the latter. Catholics are called to serve by witnessing their faith to others and by spreading that faith through evangelization. In other words, the decree calls Roman Catholics to an active living of their faith. The laity are challenged to point people toward God and move them away from the temptations of the temporal world.

QUOTE

The "Decree on the Apostolate of Lay People" (paragraph 1) reads in part: "In many regions where priests are very scarce or (as is sometimes the case) deprived of the freedom they need for their ministry, it is hard to see how the Church could make her presence and action felt without the help of the laity."

The methods to be used by the laity to effect their role in the active apostolate are multiple and varied. Laymen and -women can act individually, but they also have a powerful witness when joined in a communal effort. The decree specifically promotes the work of Catholic Action. It is essential that the work of the laity be incorporated into the ministry of the church universal.

In order for the laity to participate along lines suggested by the decree, it is necessary to generate a training or formation program. Such formation must be spiritual as well as doctrinal in theology, ethics, and philosophy. Such training must begin from childhood; adolescents and young adults must be especially imbued with the spirit of the active apostolate.

Lay Ministries in the Church

The Roman Catholic Church today is buoyed and in certain ways sustained by the activity of laypeople in almost every ministry save administration of the sacraments. In a typical parish it is common to find laypeople serving in liturgical ministries such as lectors, lay Eucharistic ministers, music ministers, and ushers. Additionally, many laywomen and -men assist with sacramental preparation, such as baptism, confirmation, and marriage, as well as leading efforts in direct service to the poor through such organizations as the St. Vincent de Paul Society. It is not uncommon at all for laypeople to serve as pastoral associates, assisting the pastor with many administrative tasks as well as training other laymen and -women for their ministries in the parish. Possibly most importantly, religious education today is almost totally in the hands of laypeople. Generally it can be said that many functions previously conducted by priest curates (associate pastors) are now exercised by the laity.

FACT

Catholic Action, originating from *Ubi Arcano*, an encyclical letter of Pope Pius XI (December 1922), is defined as the work of the laity in conjunction with the hierarchy. In practice, Catholic Action reached its heyday in the 1930s through the work of such popular groups as the Catholic Worker, Friendship House, Young Catholic Workers, Christian Family Movement, and Grail.

Laymen and -women are also active on diocesan and national levels of church organization. Many administrative positions that require financial, organizational, or legal expertise are held by qualified laity. Additionally, bishops often invite laymen and -women with specialized training and gifts to serve on boards and to be consultants to the church on a whole variety of issues that seem to become more complex with the passing of time.

The Question of Women in the Church

The post–Vatican II era, with its emphasis on greater participation by the laity, has needed to address the role of women, especially in the light of changing attitudes in contemporary society. The issue of equality, raised so prominently through the women's movement of the 1960s, lies at the heart of the concern of many Roman Catholics, both men and women. In order to appreciate the laity and the gifts given by God to all, it is suggested by some that women must be given more equal roles in the church. Again, in line with contemporary society, some suggest the equality of women is an issue of justice. The questions involved with women in the church are quite complex and require treatment beyond the scope of this book, but it is important to outline the basic issues and how they have been addressed by the church to date. Chapter 22 will address the contemporary question of women's ordination.

The Question of Language

One contemporary issue raised by women (and some men) is that of inclusive language. This issue is on two levels: horizontal and vertical. Horizontal inclusive language suggests that words such as *mankind, man*, and *sons of God* can be made more inclusive, and in the minds of many more equitable and just, by substituting *humankind, men and women*, and *children of God* for the aforementioned terms. It is suggested that these latter expressions are not only not offensive to many, but equally important, are more accurate. The other form of inclusive language, vertical, is language associated with God. Traditionally God has always been referred to using the male pronoun "He." This is understandable from the perspective both of a patriarchal society and the limits of the English language. However, some suggest that since God is neither male nor female (rather beyond sex), such words as *God* or *Lord* should always be used in place of "He." Many experts, including Steinfels, suggest that horizontal inclusive language should be applied, but within the limits of language there is no simple way to correct language toward God.

The Four Categories of Roman Catholics

What is a religious and how is this individual differentiated from other Roman Catholics? The diagram and explanation below show how all Roman Catholics are divided into four basic groups with respect to religious vocation.

Number 1: Lay and secular. This is an individual who is not a religious (a person under vows) and is not a cleric (ordained priest). This represents the vast majority of Catholics.

Number 2: Religious and priest: This is a priest who is a member of a religious congregation, such as the Jesuits or Franciscans.

Number 3: Religious and lay: This is a person under vows (religious) but is NOT a cleric (priest) and is thus a layperson. This would be a sister or brother in a religious community.

Number 4: Cleric and secular: This is a priest who is NOT a member of a religious order, that is a diocesan priest. By far most priests in the world are diocesan.

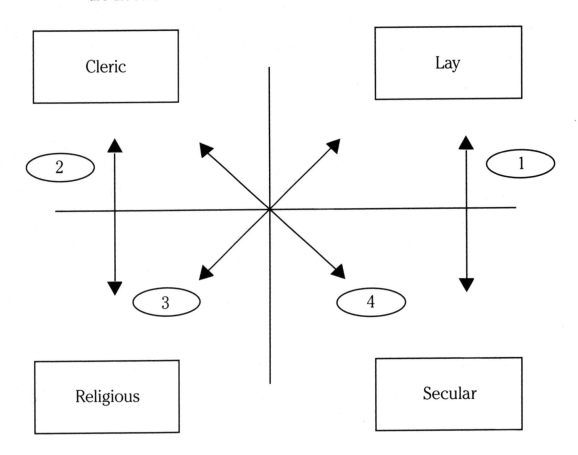

CHAPTER 18

Life of Prayer

Prayer is central to all peoples of faith. Roman Catholics view prayer as the primary vehicle to remain in communication with God. Forms of prayer vary greatly; some are very public and others private. For Catholics the formal and programmed prayer of the Mass and other sacramental rites are complemented by the spontaneous outpouring of individuals or groups who raise their needs as well as thanks and praise to God. The prayer life of Catholics, both personal and communal, bridges the institutional church with its members, the people of God.

What Is Prayer?

An ancient dictum of the Roman Catholic Church says *lex orandi, lex credendi,* the law of prayer is the law of belief. This expression says something very fundamental about how Catholics have traditionally viewed prayer. Prayer has always been the central hub that holds together the spokes of many beliefs, allowing the wheel of the church to turn successfully and move the faithful forward in their quest to find eternal life with God. This maxim clearly presents how belief finds its root in the ways people pray. In other words, the approaches Catholics take in their daily conversations with the Lord manifest themselves in various teachings that have been defined from the one deposit of Revelation.

ESSENTIAL

The Catholic Tradition says that when Jesus was in the Garden of Gethsemane, his prayer was so fervent and human fear so great that he sweated drops of blood. Today Catholics are encouraged to remember this event by praying at the altar of repose set up at the conclusion of the Mass of the Last Supper, celebrated on Holy Thursday.

Prayer, basically defined as one's efforts to communicate with God, is described in the Scriptures as absolutely necessary for Christians. Jesus prayed often and exhorted his apostles and disciples on numerous occasions to pray for various needs. The Gospel evangelists often describe Jesus moving away from crowds and even his close friends to pray to his Father in private. Mark 1:35 reads, "In the morning, while it was still very dark, he got up and went out to a deserted place, and there he prayed." Similarly Matthew 14:23 states, "And after he had dismissed the crowds, he went up the mountain by himself to pray." Certainly the most famous manifestation of Jesus' prayer was in the Garden of Gethsemane just prior to his arrest. St. Matthew (26:36–46) reports that Jesus prayed for deliverance from his fate, but in the end accepted God's will: "My Father, if it is possible, let this cup pass from me; yet not what I want but what you want."

Jesus' Instructions for Prayer

On two occasions Jesus gave very significant instructions to his apostles and disciples on prayer. The Sermon on the Mount (Matthew 6:5–15) provides specific instructions. Jesus told his apostles that there was no need to make a show of one's prayer on street corners or in synagogues, but rather one should go to one's room and speak to God privately. Additionally, he suggested that the multiplication of words was not what pleased God in prayer; rather Jesus succinctly taught his followers what to say. In the Gospel of Luke the disciples specifically ask Jesus, "Lord, teach us to pray, as John taught his disciples." Jesus responds with the Lord's Prayer.

QUESTION

Both Matthew and Luke present versions of the Our Father. Which is the most original?
Most scholars suggest that Luke 11:2–4 is the most authentic. Exegetes state that it would be inconceivable for anyone to add words to Jesus' lips. The reason Matthew's version is the one memorized by Christians is because of its inclusion in the Roman Mass.

While the Lord's Prayer summarizes in a beautiful way the basic reasons for prayer, Jesus also specifically addresses what and for whom his disciples should pray. Jesus exhorts his followers to ask for their needs. Again, in the Sermon on the Mount, he stated, "Ask, and it will be given you. . . . For everyone who asks receives." (Matthew 7:7a, 8a). Later Jesus said, "Again, truly I tell you, if two of you agree on earth about anything you ask, it will be done for you by my Father in heaven." (Matthew 18:19) All three Synoptic evangelists (Matthew 26:41; Mark 14:38; Luke 22:40) report Jesus' exhortation to pray that one will be delivered from serious trial. St. Mark recounts Jesus' words: "Keep awake and pray that you may not come into the time of trial; the Spirit indeed is willing, but the flesh is weak." Jesus goes so far as to tell his followers that they must pray for their enemies: "Bless those who curse you, pray for those who abuse you." (Luke 6:28) Additionally, Jesus strongly advocates persistence in prayer. In Luke 18:1–8, Jesus tells the story of the persistent widow who sought justice from a local judge. Importantly,

Luke (18:1) prefaces the story by saying, "Then Jesus told a parable about their [the Apostles'] need to pray always and not to lose heart."

The commands and exhortations of Jesus for prayer were brought by St. Paul to the Gentile world. Paul admitted that we often do not know for what we should pray (Romans 8:26), but he consistently encouraged and instructed the Christian communities to whom he wrote to pray without ceasing. In his letter to the Colossians (4:2), Paul wrote, "Devote yourselves to prayer, keeping alert in it with thanksgiving."

Prayer for Catholics Today

The challenge offered by Jesus and Paul (and others) in the Scriptures concerning prayer is manifest for Catholics today in prayers of praise, thanksgiving, and petition. Both publicly and privately, Catholics raise their minds and voices in praise of God. The celebration of Mass (described following) is the most obvious public means for Catholics to praise and give thanks to God. Mass, specifically the celebration of the Eucharist, is the common thanksgiving in which all Catholics are asked to participate each Sunday and special holy days sprinkled throughout the liturgical calendar. Privately as well, prayers of praise and thanksgiving as well as those of petition are raised to God. People pray for their needs as well as those of family and friends; people pray for the world in which we live.

It is important to understand that since prayer is a person's conversation with God, it is necessary to listen as well as speak. Traditionally Christians practice prayer of listening through the ancient practices of *lectio divino* and *lectio continuo*. Similar in their method, these practices, drawn from the monastic tradition of religious life, ask individuals to read Scripture, either until one finds a passage that brings meaning or for a specific amount of time. When the passage or time limit is reached, one prayerfully and in silence does his best to listen to the response of God.

Popular Devotions

Devotions are prayer forms that, while not part of the official public liturgy of the church, are nonetheless popular ways that Catholics over the centuries have expressed the basic exhortation of St. Paul to pray always. Many of these devotions, while fostered by the church for their ability to enhance the spirituality of Catholics, are not considered necessary for salvation. Many of these devotions have association with sacred images, reports of miraculous apparitions, or specialized prayers that have evolved over time into a ritualized pattern. Some devotions have a direct link historically with a religious order. Several popular devotions are associated with the veneration of specific saints. The post–Vatican II church has clearly seen a diminution in emphasis toward popular devotions, but these remain a vital part of Catholic Tradition and are utilized by many members of the faithful on a daily basis. Indeed, Pope John Paul II in an apostolic exhortation *The Church in America* (January 1999) stated concerning popular devotion: "These and other forms of popular piety are an opportunity for the faithful to encounter the living Christ."

Specific Popular Devotions

Many examples of Catholic devotions exist. These center about four orientations: devotions to Mary, Jesus, the Blessed Sacrament, and saints.

Devotions to Mary

Devotions to the Blessed Virgin Mary have always been prominent within Roman Catholicism. In Chapter 15, several of these specific practices, especially the rosary and Divine Chaplet, are discussed in some detail. Additional devotions to the Blessed Mother have developed with time. Use of the scapular, originally a Christocentric devotion, became standard in devotion to Mary beginning in the eighteenth century. The scapular is a pair of religious patches, one worn on the breast and one on the back, that are connected by cords in a configuration similar to a necklace. The Blue Scapular of the Immaculate Conception and the Scapular of Our Lady of Mount Carmel, the so-called Brown Scapular, were very popular by the early twentieth century. The Scapular gained further momentum after the apparitions of Mary at Fatima (1917) when the Virgin appeared to the three children holding a Brown Scapular in one hand and a rosary in the other.

A second significant Marian devotion, based on the apparitions at Fatima, is celebration of the Five First Saturdays of the Month. On February 15, 1926, Sister Lucia Santos, one of the three child seers at Fatima, received a vision of Mary holding the child Jesus. Mary was holding a heart in her hand surrounded by thorns. She told Lucia that she would help at the hour of death with the graces needed for salvation anyone who on the first Saturday of five consecutive months would: go to confession and receive Communion; recite five decades of the rosary; keep her company for fifteen minutes while meditating on the mysteries of the rosary for the purpose of reparation to her.

QUESTION

Why was devotion on five consecutive first Saturdays Mary's request?
It was to atone for attacks upon Mary's Immaculate Conception; attacks against her Perpetual Virginity; attacks upon her Divine Maternity and the refusal to accept her as the Mother of all humanity; for those who try to publicly implant in children's hearts indifference, contempt, and even hatred of this Immaculate Mother; for those who insult her directly in her sacred images.

Devotions to Jesus

The multiple devotions to Mary are complemented by those to Jesus. Devotion to his Sacred Heart, traced most significantly to St. Margaret Mary Alacoque (1647–1690), a French Visitation nun, is one of the most popular devotions to Jesus. During a series of apparitions from Jesus (approximately 1673–1674), the Lord promised her that any individual who completed devotion to his Sacred Heart would be granted final repentance and would not die without receiving the sacraments. Those completing the devotion must receive Holy Communion on the first Friday of nine consecutive months, with the proper disposition and with the intention of making reparation to the Sacred Heart of Jesus. In all, St. Margaret Mary reported twelve specific promises that would be granted to those who completed this devotion.

The Stations of the Cross, a devotion with roots tied to pilgrimages to Jerusalem, is a second significant devotion to Jesus. In an effort to reproduce the holy places traversed by Jesus during his passion, many locales constructed shrines and other small religious edifices. Devotion to the *Via Dolorosa*, the way of the cross, was developed by Franciscan friars in 1342 after they were granted administration of the Christian holy sites in Jerusalem. Two centuries later, Franciscans began to build outdoor shrines in various locales seeking to duplicate what was in the Holy Land. The stations consist of fourteen specific events that commemorate his salvific death for humanity, beginning with Jesus' condemnation to death and ending with his deposition in the tomb. In contemporary Catholicism, the Stations of the Cross are often celebrated during Fridays of Lent, especially Good Friday.

Devotions to the Blessed Sacrament

Eucharistic devotion was popularized through Exposition of the Blessed Sacrament and Benediction. Faithful Catholics often spent hours praying in the presence of the Eucharist. One specific manifestation of Eucharistic devotion was The Forty Hours Devotion, introduced at Rome by St. Philip Neri in 1548. This was a collective adoration of the exposed Eucharist for forty hours, in honor of the time Jesus spent in the tomb. Although rarely seen today, this practice was very popular prior to Vatican II, generally with each parish scheduling this devotion twice annually. Parishioners were asked to spend what time they could in prayer before the Eucharist.

Saints

Honors and prayers to saints are also a long-standing part of Catholic culture and devotional life. This devotion is recognized in the church in both formal and informal ways. Throughout the liturgical year, canonized saints (those officially recognized by the church for this honor) are commemorated. On November 1 the church celebrates the Feast of All Saints, a remembrance of all men and women whose lives have been crowned with the privilege of eternal life with God. In popular devotions, saints play an important role in the day-to-day life of Roman Catholics. Saints are often invoked for all sorts of different reasons and intentions. It is important, therefore, to understand Catholicism's strong emphasis on these devotions.

The Communion of Saints

In the Nicene-Constantinopolitan Creed, Catholics profess that they believe in "the communion of saints." This concept refers to the spiritual solidarity, which binds together practicing Catholics today with those men and women of the past who have already or will at some future time (namely those in purgatory) enjoy the Beatific Vision through the attainment of salvation. While the church formally recognizes the sanctity of men and women who in some way have distinguished themselves in the service of God and God's people, the communion of saints includes all who partake in the fruits of redemption.

QUOTE

The *Catechism of the Catholic Church*, number 947, reads in part: "Since all the faithful form one body, the good of each is communicated to the others. We must therefore believe that there exists a communion of goods in the Church. But the most important member is Christ, since he is the head." This statement describes the unity of the communion of saints with Christ as the leader.

The concept of the communion of saints has evolved over time but continues today as an integral part of Catholic belief. Evidence exists that belief in the communion of saints began in the early patristic church, with a more formal presentation of the dogma in the writings of the late fathers of the church in the third century. St. Thomas Aquinas in the thirteenth century presented the most thorough theological study of this dogma. The recent *Catechism of the Catholic Church* (1994) addresses this belief in several articles. The catechism refers to the church as the communion of saints, forming one body where the good of each is communicated to the whole.

Patron Saints

The theological significance of the communion of saints is complemented by the common devotion that Catholics hold for various saints. Patron saints are prominent in three different categories: patron saints of ailments and illnesses, of occupations and activities, and of places. Based largely on what is historically known about saints, individuals have been "assigned" as patrons. For example, the recently canonized (October 2009) Saint Damien of Molokai is the patron saint of leprosy as a result of his life of working with lepers. Similarly, St. Cecilia is the patron saint of musicians because the tradition says that at her wedding musicians played and Cecilia sang to the Lord in her heart. St. Rose of Lima, who lived her entire life in Peru, is the patron saint of that nation. While in the wake of the Second Vatican Council emphasis on patron saints may have waned somewhat, the practice is still popular. One can pick up any major daily newspaper and find in the want ads section many messages of thanks to St. Jude, the patron saint of hopeless causes.

FACT

Saints are proclaimed by the church through a process governed by the Congregation for the Causes of Saints, part of the Roman Curia. A thorough investigation of the heroic virtue of one's life is made. Once this is verified, one can be called "Venerable." When a miracle attributable to the individual is verified, the person is granted the title "Blessed." A second miracle completes the process of canonization, with the individual receiving the title "Saint."

The intercession of saints is highly encouraged by the contemporary church. The catechism (number 956) teaches that the saints, due to their proximity to Christ, assist the whole church to become more holy. These saints, "do not cease to intercede with the Father for us, as they proffer the merits which they acquired on earth through the one mediator between God and men, Christ Jesus."

Sacramentals

The sacraments (see Chapter 11), special signs instituted by Christ that bring grace, are accompanied by various sacramentals. These can be actions or objects that remind one of the power and presence of God in one's life. Certain acts, such as a profession of faith or confession of sin, can serve as sacramentals, but by far the most common manifestation is through objects. In the celebration of baptism, several sacramentals are used. The oil of chrism is used to anoint the child; water is used in the ritual baptism bath. A candle, lit from the Easter paschal candle, and a white garment placed on the child are additional sacramentals. Each of these objects has significant value for its ability to communicate the presence of God in the sacrament of baptism. Similar sacramentals, such as rings in weddings, oil in confirmation and anointing of the sick, and the laying on of hands in ordination, are found in all sacraments.

FACT

The first commandment's injunction to worship no strange gods was translated by Jews and early Christians to reject any sacred images. In the eighth century of Christian history this controversy, known as iconoclasm, required resolution. In 787, the Second Council of Nicaea met and declared that icons and sacred images did not violate the precepts of the Ten Commandments. Thus churches and Catholic homes today often feature images and statues of Christ, the Virgin Mary, and various saints.

In addition to their value in the seven sacraments, sacramentals are found and utilized in everyday Roman Catholic practice. Typically all Roman Catholic churches have a crucifix, a few statues of saints, votive candles, and holy water fonts, in addition to Bibles and other sacred books. In a similar way members of the faithful often have many of these same sacramentals in their homes. They may also carry on their person a rosary, holy card, or other personal reminders of their faith. In more recent times, icons, which are essential to Orthodox faiths, have become more popular in Roman Catholicism.

The efficacy of sacramentals has been manifested in many forms. Such objects were often used to drive away evil spirits and to combat mysterious and problematic situations. Another effect of sacramentals was to deliver one from sin and the penalties to be incurred from such sin. Lastly, sacramentals were often employed to obtain temporal favor, since these objects are often blessed by a priest or deacon.

The Mass

When speaking of prayer there is no more central and vital manifestation than Mass, the celebration of the Eucharist. Indeed, Catholics gather each Sunday to be one with each other and Christ as Jesus suggested, "that they may all be one." (John 17:21a) Mass is a communal thanksgiving to God for all humanity has received.

The Liturgy of the Word

Mass, which is divided into two major sections, begins with the Liturgy of the Word. After an introductory greeting, penitential rite, and recitation of the Gloria and opening prayer, the Word of God is proclaimed. On Sundays, the Biblical readings at Mass are preprogrammed on a rotating three-year cycle, designated as years A (using the Gospel of Matthew), B (using the Gospel of Mark), and C (using the Gospel of Luke). The first reading, which is always drawn from the Old Testament (save during the Easter season), is specifically chosen to be thematically similar to the Gospel, proclaimed at the same celebration. A psalm, which thematically responds to the first reading, is next proclaimed. The second reading, drawn from the New Testament and often from the letters of St. Paul, is a semicontinuous reading of one text; it is not specifically chosen to agree thematically with the other chosen readings. The Gospel, read in a semicontinuous manner, is the final Scripture reading proclaimed. The Liturgy of the Word concludes with the recitation of the Nicene-Constantinopolitan Creed and the Prayers of the Faithful, a series of congregational prayers for the needs of the world.

During weekdays, depending on the sanctoral cycle and liturgical season (see Chapter 19), the Liturgy of the Word usually comprises two readings, one from the Old or New Testament (proclaimed in a semicontinuous manner) and the Gospel reading. For weekdays, a two-year cycle, referred to as Year I (odd years such as 2009) or Year II (even years such as 2010), of readings is maintained.

ESSENTIAL

Catholics and non-Catholics alike can sometimes be confused when attending Mass when it appears that the priest celebrant has changed the order or content of the celebration in some way. "The Constitution on the Sacred Liturgy" of Vatican II directly addresses this concern. Paragraph 22(3) reads: "Therefore no other person, not even a priest, may add, remove, or change anything in the liturgy on his own authority."

Liturgy of the Eucharist

The second half of the Mass, the Liturgy of the Eucharist, centers on the celebration and reception of the Body of Christ. While the priest celebrant has various options with respect to the principal prayer of this section, known as the Canon or Eucharistic Prayer, the order, prayers, and general rubrics of the Mass are standard, although some variations exist for weddings and funerals. During the Eucharistic Prayer, through the process of transubstantiation (see Chapter 11), Catholics believe the bread and wine are transformed into the real sacramental presence of Jesus Christ.

The Spiritual Works of Mercy

Closely allied with the Corporal Works of Mercy (see Chapter 20), the Spiritual Works of Mercy are seven specific practices of charity that Roman Catholics demonstrate toward others. In this sense mercy is said to be a virtue that assists one in finding compassion for, and if possible, in minimizing or alleviating the suffering of another. Thomas Aquinas suggested that such mercy was a spontaneous product of charity. Still, it was a specialized virtue that was to be distinguished from charity. Traditionally these works are to convert the sinner, instruct the ignorant, counsel the doubtful, comfort the sorrowful, bear wrongs patiently, forgive injuries, and pray for the living and the dead.

CHAPTER 19

The Liturgical Year

Roman Catholicism celebrates its theology and Sacred Tradition by following a prescribed pattern of seasons and individual feasts throughout a yearlong cycle. Known as the liturgical year, these seasons celebrate the birth; life and ministry; and passion, death, and resurrection of Jesus. Individual feasts, fixed by the normal calendar year, celebrate the lives of saints and remember special Biblical and historical events. Governed by a hierarchy of priorities, the liturgical year organizes Roman Catholic celebrations that seek to unite the church, the people of God, as a community of faith.

Basic Premises of the Liturgical Year

The birth; ministry and message; and the passion, death, and resurrection of Jesus Christ are central events in the celebratory life of Roman Catholics. Through a series of liturgical seasons, these great events, commemorated in a fixed chronological pattern, form the basic format for the church year. Beginning with the season of Advent, and reaching its apex with the celebration of the Easter Triduum, the liturgical year recalls, through the use of Scripture and appropriate prayers, the life and death of Christ.

QUESTION

When does the liturgical year begin?
The liturgical year begins with the first Sunday of Advent, four weeks prior to Christmas, and the celebration of the Incarnation. On the calendar year this generally equates to the last Sunday in November or the first Sunday in December.

While the events of Jesus' life and death are central, the liturgical year also celebrates many special events, including significant feasts associated with the Blessed Virgin Mary, the lives of saints, and important events from the Sacred Tradition (see Chapter 5) of Roman Catholicism. These more specialized celebrations, based on historical facts and traditional practices, are interspersed throughout the various seasons of the liturgical year. Taken together, the liturgical seasons and individual feasts of the Lord, Mary, the Tradition, and saints form a unified and fixed calendar used by Roman Catholics for the celebration of the Eucharist.

Liturgical Seasons

The church year has as its base five liturgical seasons that recall the great events of Christ's life. Proceeding in historical order, Advent, the first liturgical season, prepares Roman Catholics for the celebration of the Incarnation, God becoming human, celebrated on Christmas Day. The Christmas season recalls Jesus' birth and the significant events of his early life, culminating in his baptism. After a brief period of Ordinary (ordinal) Time, a second great period of preparation, Lent, grooms the faithful for the celebration of the paschal mystery, the passion, death, and resurrection of Christ. The Easter season that follows recalls the resurrection of Jesus and his post-resurrection appearances leading eventually to his ascension to heaven and the celebration of Pentecost, the coming of the Holy Spirit. Lastly, Ordinary (ordinal) Time rounds out the liturgical year concluding with the celebration of the Feast of Christ the King.

Advent

Advent, a four-week season of preparation, actually challenges Catholics to prepare for two great events. During the first week of Advent, Scripture readings used in the celebration of Mass concentrate on the coming of Christ at the end of time, that is, the parousia or Second Coming. Christians in general spend little time thinking about the return of Christ, but the New Testament presents many stories, some told by Jesus himself, that tell us of this great event. Thus, the church in its wisdom prompts its members to consider their readiness for this great event. Jesus puts it this way: "You must be ready, for the Son of Man is coming at an unexpected hour." (Luke 12:40)

The central and most popular theme of Advent is preparation for the Incarnation. Scripture readings recall the prophecy from Isaiah that speaks of a Messiah who will come to the people of Israel. We are also told the important story of John the Baptist and his ministry as the one sent by God to prepare the people for Christ. On the fourth Sunday of Advent the story of the Annunciation is read, when Mary was invited to be the mother of God and the Lord came to Joseph, informing him to receive his betrothed into his home.

Christmas

Beginning with Christmas Day and concluding with the baptism of the Lord, the Christmas season recalls all of the great events of Jesus' birth and childhood until the onset of his public ministry. This liturgical season celebrates and commemorates several important events. The Sunday after Christmas is celebrated as the Feast of the Holy Family, recalling the joys and at times sorrows that were the life of Jesus, Mary, and Joseph. On

December 28, the church recalls the sacrifice of those children, called the "Holy Innocents," who died at the order of King Herod, who sought to destroy Jesus (Matthew 2:16–18). On January 1, the Feast of Mary, the Mother of God, one of the four Marian dogmas, is celebrated. The great feasts of the Epiphany (Matthew 2:1–12), when the three Magi from the East arrived in Bethlehem to worship Jesus, and the baptism of the Lord (Matthew 3:13–17; Mark 1:9–11; Luke 3:21–22) at the hand of John the Baptist, conclude the Christmas season.

FACT

The gifts presented by the Magi recognize three important aspects of his life. Gold represents recognition that Jesus is a king. Frankincense symbolizes that Jesus is God as well. Myrrh, an ointment used in burials, says that Jesus, Lord and King, will one day die for his people. Thus, Matthew's story demonstrates that Jesus, from the outset, was recognized for who he was and what he would accomplish.

Lent

Like Advent, Lent is a season of preparation that recalls Jesus' forty days and nights of fasting in the desert where he readied himself for his public ministry. All three Synoptic evangelists (Matthew 4:1–11, Mark 1:12–13, Luke 4:1–13) report that after Jesus' baptism in the Jordan River, he was led by the Spirit into the wilderness to be tempted by Satan. Matthew and Luke, using the "Q source,"(Matthew and Luke have several common parts; Biblical scholars conclude this common ground can be explained by one common source, referred to as the "Q," from the German word *quelle*, meaning source) report that after Jesus fasted for forty days and forty nights, he was tempted by Satan. Repudiating Satan's entreaties to turn stones into bread (power), to possess the kingdoms of the world (wealth), and to be saved from harm by his angels (prestige), Jesus was ready to begin his public ministry.

Lent begins on Ash Wednesday and continues for six weeks until the beginning of the Easter Triduum on Holy Thursday evening with the celebration of the Mass of the Last Supper. As proclaimed strongly in the Scripture readings used on Ash Wednesday, the three traditional disciplines upon which the church asks the faithful to focus during Lent are prayer, fasting, and almsgiving. Catholics traditionally make an extra effort to pray more; some attend daily Mass as a form of Lenten discipline. Fasting is sought in canonical and voluntary ways. For Catholics between the ages of eighteen and fifty-nine (save those with medical or special needs), Ash Wednesday and Good Friday are days of fast and abstinence; all Fridays during Lent the faithful are asked to abstain from meat.

ESSENTIAL

Modern rules for fasting and abstinence, promulgated by Pope Paul VI in 1966, have been adopted by the United States Catholic Conference of Bishops. Fasting requires that Catholics eat only one full meal a day; the other two meals should not equal one full meal. Abstinence is the discipline of refraining from consuming meat.

Holy Week and the Easter Triduum

Holy Week recalls the climax of Jesus' salvific life and death as reported by the Gospel evangelists. They narrate the events of Jesus' triumphal entry into Jerusalem and his eventual crucifixion five days later. On Palm Sunday, the church recalls when Jesus was welcomed into Jerusalem and hailed as a hero and champion. The apex of the Roman Catholic liturgical year is the celebration of the Easter Triduum, which commemorates the passion, death, and resurrection of Jesus.

The triduum begins with the celebration of the Mass of the Last Supper on Holy Thursday evening. Commemorating two important events, the institution of the Eucharist and the priesthood, the Mass recalls Jesus' final meal with his apostles, commonly called the Last Supper. Again, the Synoptic evangelists all report that after the Passover meal was completed, Jesus offered bread and wine to his apostles. Roman Catholics believe that Jesus' words, called the institution narrative, transformed these simple elements into the real presence of Christ. The Mass of the Last Supper also recalls Jesus' humble act of service when he washed his disciples' feet (John 13:1–20).

The Mass of the Last Supper concludes with a procession of the Eucharist to the altar of repose. This recalls that after the meal with his apostles, Jesus went to the Garden of Gethsemane, with Peter, John, and James, and prayed to his Father. He asked if possible that he be spared the cup of suffering he would soon endure, yet he was ready to embrace the will of the Father (Matthew 26:39). Those who attend the Mass are encouraged to pray at the altar of repose, being in solidarity with Jesus in his prayer.

FACT

> In order to emphasize the virtue of service, St. John's version of the Last Supper is proclaimed as the Gospel for Holy Thursday. The institution of the Eucharist is recalled during this Mass through the proclamation of the first chronological account of the event, given by St. Paul in I Corinthians 11:23–26. This was written approximately fifteen years before the work of St. Mark, the first gospel evangelist.

Good Friday, the most solemn day of the liturgical year, commemorates the painful and ignominious death of Jesus Christ by crucifixion. Although this is the only day of the church year when the celebration of Mass is not allowed, the faithful, nevertheless, gather to celebrate the passion and death of Jesus through a service of Scripture readings, prayers, and reception of the Eucharist that has been kept on reserve from the previous night's celebration. It is also very traditional for Roman Catholics to celebrate the Stations of the Cross on this day.

The Easter Season

The Easter season, comprising fifty days until the celebration of Pentecost, the arrival of the promised Holy Spirit into the world, begins with the Easter vigil, marking the apex of the Roman Catholic liturgical year. The vigil, beginning with the service of light, representative of the return of Christ, the light of the world, recalls through its readings and celebration the story of salvation history. Readings from the Hebrew Bible include the story of creation, the call of the patriarch Abraham, the escape of the Israelites across the Red Sea, and God's message of care as proclaimed by the prophets. The story of the resurrection, as written in the Synoptic Gospels, is also proclaimed. Since Vatican II and the restoration of the catechumenate, the vigil is also the celebration at which true catechumens, those who have not been baptized, receive the sacraments of initiation—baptism, Eucharist, and confirmation; converts to Catholicism are received into the church. The latter group also receives the Eucharist and is confirmed. Additionally, Roman Catholics who have not completed their sacraments of initiation and have journeyed with the catechumens during their period of preparation receive those sacraments necessary to be considered adults in the church.

QUESTION

Why is the passion narrative of St. John always proclaimed on Good Friday?
On Palm Sunday the Synoptic passion narratives are read, one each year, in a sequential and repetitive pattern. St. John's narrative is always used on Good Friday because, from this evangelist's perspective, Jesus' greatest triumph comes at the time of his crucifixion. For John, the cross becomes Jesus' throne as king.

The Easter season continues for a period of seven weeks. The initial eight days, known as the octave of Easter, are celebrated liturgically as Easter day. During this week Gospel readings recall the post-resurrection appearances of Jesus, culminating on the ensuing Sunday with the story of Jesus' encounter with the apostle Thomas (John 20:19–29). Forty days after Easter, the church celebrates Jesus' Ascension to heaven (Luke 24:50–53; Acts 1:6–11). Ten days later the Festival of Pentecost (Acts 2:1–13) closes the Easter season.

Ordinary (Ordinal) Time

The longest "season" of the liturgical year, which extends for a few weeks between the end of the Christmas season and the beginning of Lent, and for a much longer period from the celebration of Pentecost to the onset of Advent, is known as Ordinary Time. The name is a bit misleading as there is nothing ordinary about the church year. The name was derived originally from ordinal, as the Sundays during this season are numbered.

Since this period of the church year is not one of any special preparation, the name "Ordinary" has become the standard nomenclature. The Sunday celebrations, comprising a total of thirty-four weeks, actually commences after Pentecost with two special feasts, Trinity Sunday and the Feast of the Body and Blood of Jesus, traditionally known as *Corpus Christi*. Ordinary Time ends with the thirty-fourth Sunday, known as the Feast of Christ the King.

ESSENTIAL

Roman Catholicism accepts the baptism rite of other churches, so long as one is baptized in the name of the Trinity—the Father, Son, and Holy Spirit. Such converts must merely profess their faith in Roman Catholicism. For those who have never been baptized or for those not baptized in the name of the Trinity, baptism at the vigil is celebrated.

The Sanctoral Cycle

The liturgical year, celebrated through the various seasons previously described, is centered in Sunday worship. Christ's resurrection from death on the first day of the week set the standard for Christian worship on Sunday. Still, throughout the liturgical year, including the various seasons of preparation and Ordinary Time, the church celebrates various significant dates, events, and most prominently lives of saints. These days, while not of the highest order as the Sunday celebration, are nonetheless significant and play an important role for Roman Catholics. Geographic regions, many religious congregations, various nations, and certainly individuals have (for various reasons) special affinity to various saints.

Solemnities

The sanctoral cycle comprises five different celebrations that stand in a hierarchy of liturgical precedence. The most significant category of specialized celebrations is the solemnity. These celebrations include most of the significant Marian feast days, such as those that celebrate the four Marian dogmas (see Chapter 15), commemorations of the apostles Peter and Paul, and all special feasts of the Lord, such as the Feast of the Presentation (February 2), and Ascension Thursday (mentioned above).

Feasts

The second level of specialized celebrations in the sanctoral cycle is the feast. Like solemnities, feasts are marked with specialized prayers during the celebration of Mass. Feasts commemorate the lives of certain saints, including the apostles, the transfiguration of Jesus (August 6), the exaltation of the cross (September 14), and the commemoration of the archangels (September 29). With the exception of specialized Masses, such as a wedding or funeral, solemnities and feasts are required celebrations within the liturgical year.

QUOTE

"The Constitution on the Sacred Liturgy" of Vatican II (Section 106) describes Sunday as "the original feast day . . . ; other celebrations, unless they be truly of the greatest importance shall not have precedence over Sunday, which is the foundation and kernel of the whole liturgical year."

Memorials and Ferials

A third category of specialized celebrations during the liturgical year is the memorial. Memorials are further broken down into obligatory and optional. The former, like solemnities and feasts, are required celebrations during the liturgical year. Memorials principally celebrate the lives of saints and certain feasts of the Blessed Virgin Mary, such as Our Lady of Lourdes (February 11) and Our Lady of the Rosary (October 7). Optional memorials also principally celebrate the lives of various saints. This latter category of liturgical celebrations, while important, does not require a specialized celebration at Mass. The priest celebrant of the Eucharist has the option to use the prayers and optional readings if he desires, but it is not required.

Ferial days, the last category of liturgical precedence, are those days of the liturgical year that are not marked by one of the just-mentioned four specialized celebrations. As described in Chapter 18, the readings follow the pattern for Year I or II (odd or even).

ESSENTIAL

The Easter Triduum stands as the highest precedence in the liturgical year. Behind this are celebrations of Christmas, Epiphany, Ascension, and Pentecost. When important feasts, such as the Solemnities of St. Joseph (March 19) or the Annunciation (March 25) are usurped by Holy Week or the Easter Octave, these celebrations can be moved to an appropriate date after the period of higher precedence has passed.

Holy Days

Roman Catholicism holds Sunday, the Lord's Day, to be the primary day of worship. While the Eucharist is celebrated daily to commemorate events in salvation history, historical events, specialized devotion, and the lives of saints, attendance at Sunday Mass is considered normative and required. However, certain celebrations throughout the liturgical year are of a significance that the church also mandates the faithful to attend Mass. Traditionally known as holy days of obligation, these celebrations are Mary the Mother of God (January 1), the Ascension of Jesus into Heaven (variable, forty days after Easter), the Assumption of the Blessed Virgin Mary (August 15), the Feast of All Saints (November 1), the Immaculate Conception (December 8), and Christmas Day (December 25). In many countries today the celebration of these particular feasts has been moved to the nearest Sunday.

Liturgical Precedence and Order

Eucharistic celebrations, both those of the liturgical seasons and the sanctoral cycle, are governed by a precedence, established through the General Norms for the Liturgical Year and the Calendar. Often during any particular liturgical year, conflicts arise when a particular solemnity or feast falls either on a Sunday or during a period of specialized celebration, such as

Holy Week or the octave of Easter. In such cases the General Norms provide guidance as to precedence (which celebration is to be followed) for feasts.

Besides precedence, the church year is also governed by certain norms, namely the use of specialized Biblical readings and liturgical colors for the celebration of the Eucharist. As described in Chapter 18, the readings for Mass, both on Sundays and daily, are programmed on a fixed cycle of three years and two years (odd and even), respectively. This pattern is generally continued through the various liturgical seasons, but there are some significant deviations from the general pattern of Ordinary Time during specialized seasons. During the Advent, Christmas, Lent, and Easter seasons, daily Mass readings, both the first reading and gospel, are the same each year. The readings are chosen to be consistent thematically and to highlight ideas relevant to the season. The general pattern for Sunday Mass of a first reading from the Hebrew Bible and a second from the New Testament is modified during the Easter season when the first reading is proclaimed from the Acts of the Apostles.

PART VII

Contemporary Issues

CHAPTER 20

Social Catholicism

This book demonstrates that Roman Catholicism is a highly structured faith as manifested through sacraments, canon law, the hierarchy and papacy, and its doctrinal and dogmatic teachings. Catholicism, however, is much more than an inanimate structure; it is a very vibrant and lively faith that is expressed through an active engagement with society. Beginning overtly in the late nineteenth century, Social Catholicism puts into practice, in the everyday lives of people, the teachings of Jesus Christ, who came not to be served but to serve.

The Social Question in Christianity

Beginning in the seventeenth century, Western civilization began a revolutionary transformation that had significant influence on Roman Catholicism. The scientific revolution, with leading lights such as Copernicus and his heliocentric theory of the universe, Galileo, Johannes Kepler's laws of planetary motion, and Isaac Newton's groundbreaking approach to physics, forced the church to rethink some of its ideas. One century later, the free-thinkers of the Enlightenment, such as Rousseau, Voltaire, and John Locke, challenged many prevailing Christian concepts, suggesting that many of these teachings could not be verified by reason. Beginning in the late eighteenth and moving into the nineteenth centuries, the Industrial Revolution also demanded a response from the church.

ESSENTIAL

It is important to understand that Catholicism's response to the social question sought to counter the solutions proffered by various movements and entities of the day. These included socialism, communism, nationalism, and religious indifferentism. The church wanted to be a significant voice in stabilizing a society in flux.

The transformation of the Western world from a rural and agrarian society into one that was more urban and industrial generated many significant problems that required action for their resolution. Crowded cities and sweat-shop factories led to many personal and communal problems, including unemployment, disease, overwork, absence of workers' rights, poverty, and overcrowding, just to name a few. Viewing the situation as highly problematic, the church sought solutions to these problems. In order to find answers, however, it was necessary to evaluate modern society, not merely philosophically, but more importantly practically, so that the daily miseries experienced by many workers could be resolved. Thus, the "social question," that is, how to resolve contemporary problems of society, became a central issue for Roman Catholicism.

The Social Catholicism Movement

The Social Catholicism movement, as it came to be known, was initially led through the efforts of Father (later Bishop of Mainz) Wilhelm von Kettler. He saw the world as a place of great poverty caused in large measure by a gross inequality in power and wealth. In 1848 he addressed this issue in a series of sermons, delivered during the Advent season. In these sermons he provided some specific suggestions to address social problems of the day. First, he advocated the prohibition of child labor. Next, he suggested working hours should be limited for all, including Sunday rest. He also promoted the limited right for people to own private property. Lastly, he proclaimed that the state had an obligation to care for disabled workers.

Von Kettler's ideas became the catalyst leading to the foundation of the Fribourg Union, beginning in 1884. This "think tank" of theologians, political leaders, and the aristocracy (numbering between twenty and thirty-two) met annually each October from 1885 to 1891. The union's goal was to address social needs from a perspective of faith, using the philosophy of Thomas Aquinas as a base. The basic response of the union, in its efforts to answer the social question, was to steer a middle course between socialism and capitalism. Some of the important themes that the union proclaimed were the idea that charity (the philanthropic enterprise) is insufficient, the promotion of the concept of a just wage—just wages were to be determined by the minimum necessary to maintain a family in ordinary circumstances, —the idea that state intervention is necessary to correct social abuses and to assure people have subsistence, and the right to limited private property.

QUESTION

What is the principle of subsidiarity?
This concept refers to the basic procedure of seeking solutions to problems by starting at the lowest, most basic level and moving up the chain of command as necessary until the situation in question is resolved. Local authority can generally understand and find better solutions to specific problems.

The influence of the Fribourg Union was significant. First, it brought together the laity and clerics to find answers to social problems. The union brought forward into common discussion certain critical questions, including the social purpose of property, the positive but limited role of the state, the centrality of justice, the principal of subsidiarity, and the concept of the common good as a unifying force of the political community.

Rerum Novarum

On May 15, 1891, Pope Leo XIII issued *Rerum Novarum* ("On the Condition of the Working Classes"), a document that history knows as the first modern social encyclical. The document, which presents teachings that were revolutionary for their time, became the foundation upon which modern Social Catholicism is based. Utilizing many of the ideas that arose in the Fribourg Union, *Rerum Novarum* highlighted the plight of workers, the right of people to own property (an argument against socialism), and the role of the state to intervene to prevent class suffering by taking a middle ground between capitalism and socialism. In addition, the encyclical advocated a living wage, defined as sufficient money to live without hardship, and the right of workers to organize, and it promoted the rights of the church to speak on social issues.

FACT

Almost from the outset of his papacy in 1878, Pope Leo XIII published various pronouncements on labor and the evils of the present generation, all of which preceded *Rerum Novarum*. These documents highlighted the dignity and value of work, from both a metaphysical and material sense. He advocated that the burdens upon workers must be lightened.

What was Pope Leo's motivation for writing this first great social encyclical? His first reason was theological and moral. He believed that the church as an institution of moral guidance must be a major part of the solution to the social question. Secondly, from a pastoral perspective, Pope Leo feared that the church would lose workers to socialist movements if it did not speak. Lastly, from an ecclesial dimension, the pope did not want the position of the church in society to be weakened any further than it already had been from the events and movements prominent in nineteenth-century Europe.

Papal Encyclicals on Social Catholicism

Rerum Novarum, often referred to as the Magna Carta of Social Catholicism, was only the first of many encyclicals to be published throughout the twentieth century that continued to articulate specifics of Roman Catholic social teaching. On May 15, 1931, forty years to the date after the publication of *Rerum Novarum*, Pope Pius XI issued *Quadragesimo Anno* ("On the Reconstruction of the Social Order"). In the document the pope reinforced the teachings of Leo XIII but then moved forward giving additional specifics on the role of the state in its relations with workers and employers. This is the first papal document to use the term "social justice" to describe the need for the common good, that is, the good of each person.

QUOTE

As an example of the teaching of these social encyclicals, *Quadragesimo Anno* suggests wage levels should be set with public economic welfare in mind. Paragraph 74 reads in part, "To lower or raise wages unduly, with a view to private profit, and with no consideration for the common good, is contrary to social justice."

The combination of the Second Vatican Council, the ongoing Cold War, and the general greater awareness of people across the globe to social problems led in the 1960s to the generation of a series of papal documents that have become mainstays in the Social Catholicism literature. In 1961, Pope John XXIII published *Mater et Magistra* ("Christianity and Social Progress"), an encyclical letter issued in response to perceived imbalances between rich and poor in the world. The document placed heavy emphasis on human solidarity, especially between economically advanced and economically depressed nations. The church accepted its responsibility to do its share to aid needy people and nations. One year later Pope John issued the encyclical *Pacem en Terris*, which contends that peace can only be attained by observing the social order set down by God. Peace can be found when justice, truth, and charity are put into practice. Written in the wake of the 1962 Cuban missile crisis, the document made a major impact beyond the Catholic world. In 1967, Pope Paul VI wrote *Populorum Progressio* ("The Development of Peoples"), which speaks to the challenges of human development and explores the nature of poverty in the conflicts it produces. The pope spoke of the church's role in development, sketching a Christian vision of a more equitable world. He directly associates proper development with overtures toward peace.

The pontificate of Pope John Paul II included a series of encyclicals and other documents that addressed numerous issues pertinent to Social Catholicism. In 1981 he issued *Laborem Exercens* on the ninetieth anniversary of *Rerum Novarum*. The document emphasizes the dignity of human labor in four points: (1) It suggests that work must be subordinated to humanity. (2) It professes that the worker is more important than any instruments or environment that constitute the world of labor. (3) It recognizes the right of humans to determine socioeconomic, technological, and productive processes. (4) The document articulates certain elements that will assist people to identify with Christ through their labor.

In 1987, on the twentieth anniversary of *Populorum Progressio*, the pope issued *Sollicitudo Rei Socialis*. John Paul sought to advance the concept of development by application of the relationship between nations and major regions of the world. The document suggests that if the accumulation of wealth is gained at the expense of the development of the masses and without due consideration for the social, cultural, and spiritual dimensions of humanity, then such gain is sordid. In 1991 he issued *Centissimus Annus* ("One Hundredth Anniversary") that reinforced the ideas initially proclaimed in *Rerum Novarum*, on its centenary, and plowed new ground concerning significant social issues of the late twentieth century. Foremost among these new teachings was the promotion of families and social policies that have the family as their principal object.

Catholic Action

In December 1922, Pope Pius XI issued *Ubi Arcano Dei Consilio*, an encyclical letter that introduced the terms "Catholic Action" and "lay apostolate" into the literature. Technically, Catholic Action is the work of the laity in support of the hierarchy. However, over the next half century this more restrictive definition would be broadened through the efforts of numerous individuals and groups who in varied ways sought to manifest the social teachings of the church through direct service to the poor and those who lived on the margins of society.

The Grail Movement, the Young Christian Workers, and the Christian Family Movement

Catholic Action groups, especially in the United States, were quite prominent beginning in the interwar years and continuing to the onset of Vatican II. The Grail Movement, originally founded in Holland in 1921 by Jacques van Ginnecken, migrated to the United States in 1940 and was headquartered at Loveland, Ohio. This worldwide spiritual renewal assisted women exclusively in three specific areas. First, participants were encouraged to actively engage ecumenical dialogue. Secondly, women were educated to help them realize their full potential. Lastly, the Grail Movement promoted international and intercultural cooperation.

FACT

The YCW and CFM used a threefold system to effect social change: observe, judge, act. First, it was necessary to observe the situation. Secondly, members had to judge what plan of action could be brought to correct the observed problem. Thirdly, participants had to act in order to effect the necessary change.

The Young Christian Workers (YCW), originating in Belgium through the efforts of Father (later Cardinal) Joseph Cardijn was active as early as 1912. Known in Europe as the Jocists (JOC), the group came to the United States in the late 1930s with cells formed initially in Brooklyn, Toledo, and San Francisco. The group had a threefold purpose: formation of youth, service, and representation.

A third mainstream Catholic Action group was the Christian Family Movement (CFM). Started in 1943, this group used the same method of YCW to bring about social change. Instead of young workers, however, CFM involved couples where cells were established in geographic neighborhoods. A priest chaplain might be present at meetings, but lay couples ran the program. Their efforts concentrated on adult education and service.

Friendship House and the Catholic Worker

Historically the most famous Catholic Action groups were, coincidentally, more truly defined as alternative Catholic Action, for their genesis was found not with the hierarchy but with the laity. Baroness Catherine de Hueck, a Russian émigré to the United States, started the first Friendship House in the United States in New York City's Harlem district on February 14, 1938. Similar houses were established in Chicago, Washington, D.C., and Portland, Oregon. Friendship House assisted the African-American community specifically through the promotion of social action, publication of a monthly organ (*Community*), educational home visits, and weekend retreats and conferences.

QUESTION

Why was the Catholic Worker Movement so successful?
Dorothy Day's ability to promote her ideas and those of Peter Maurin, through their monthly newspaper, *The Catholic Worker*, was enhanced by the plight of millions during the Great Depression. The combination of published ideas and hands-on efforts to assist the poor brought great prominence to the movement.

Undoubtedly the most famous Catholic Action group in the United States was the Catholic Worker, founded through the joint efforts of Peter Maurin, a French émigré to the United States who possessed many ideas for social reform, and Dorothy Day, an American social activist who was a gifted journalist. Beginning on May 1, 1933, with the publication of the first issue of *The Catholic Worker*, Maurin and Day's work blossomed through its most notable work, the establishment of houses of hospitality, which provided food and shelter to the hungry and homeless in many major cities. Although less successful, the promotion of roundtable discussions, at which intellectuals sought solutions to social problems, and the formation of farm communes, were two additional features of the Catholic Worker Movement.

Catholics and Organized Labor

One of the most significant achievements of Social Catholicism in the twentieth century is the promotion of organized labor, but this support was a departure from a much more wary position toward unions taken by the church in the nineteenth century. At that time, due in large measure to European groups that sought to undermine the church, the Vatican held a general prohibition against all secret societies, including labor unions. In the United States both the Second (1866) and Third (1884) Plenary Councils of Baltimore reiterated the papal condemnation of secret societies, especially the Masons, but a special cautionary provision was made for labor unions.

The church's movement toward support of organized labor was prompted by the formation of the Knights of Labor in 1869. Ten years later, Terence Powderly, a Catholic, was made "Grand Master Workman," a position that brought both conflict and the possibility of amelioration with the church. Many American Catholic workers joined the Knights, which placed them in direct conflict with the Vatican. However, Archbishop (later Cardinal) James Gibbons of Baltimore wrote in defense of the Knights, stating that condemnation of the union would force many to abandon Catholicism, for workers considered their membership in the union to be a right. Two years later, in August 1888, the Vatican agreed with Gibbons' position so long as the constitution of the Knights was modified to eliminate secretive elements and references to socialism. Three years later Pope Leo XIII issued *Rerum Novarum*, which directly supported the right of workers to organize.

Using *Rerum Novarum* and *Quadragesimo Anno* as inspiration and starting points, a series of Catholic labor priests evolved throughout the twentieth century. Three of the most nationally prominent "labor priests" of the first half of the twentieth century were Fathers John Ryan, Peter Dietz, and Francis Haas. Ryan distinguished himself as the author of the "Bishop's Program for Social Reconstruction," (February 1919) a document that addressed specific social issues that had arisen in the wake of World War I, and as director of the Social Action Department of the National Catholic Welfare Conference, today the United States Catholic Conference of Bishops (USCCB). While Ryan was more a theorist, Peter Dietz was an organizer and frontline foot soldier for workers. His most significant contribution was his organization in 1909 of the Militia of Christ for Social Service, a Catholic umbrella union affiliated with the AFL. Francis Haas was noted during the

Franklin Roosevelt administration for his settlement of major strikes in Milwaukee and his participation on the National Labor Relations Board.

QUOTE

Among its many important ideas, the "Bishops Program for Social Reconstruction" (paragraph 24) states the following: "There is no longer any serious objection urged by impartial persons against the legal minimum wage." Many of the ideas of Ryan's program were later enacted as part of Roosevelt's New Deal. The similarity in approach is most likely not coincidental.

The second half of the twentieth century also produced numerous labor priests, but the career of Father George Higgins is probably most noteworthy. Higgins was active for close to three generations, using theory as a professor at the Catholic University of America and his weekly syndicated column "The Yardstick" to articulate his views on all sorts of issues pertinent to workers' rights, organized labor, and associated topics. However, Higgins was also a priest who stood side by side with those who directly fought for organized labor, such as Cesar Chavez and his United Farm Workers campaign in the 1970s.

Nine Basic Themes of Catholic Social Teaching

In his book *Living Justice: Catholic Social Teaching in Action*, Jesuit priest and scholar Thomas Massaro provides nine basic concepts that have characterized Social Catholicism since the time of *Rerum Novarum*.

1. **The dignity of every human person and human rights:** Made in the image and likeness of God, humans deserve respect and dignity from conception to natural death. This idea means Catholics reject abortion, euthanasia, and capital punishment. This teaching calls for equality on all fronts. Human rights are a way of expressing what belongs to humans by virtue of their dignity.
2. **Solidarity, common good, and participation:** This idea balances the first, rejecting rampant individualism. Solidarity means we are dependent

upon each other; we must be committed to the well-being of others. The common good, which seeks the benefit of all, and participation, meaning both the right and obligation, are part of our social life. Catholic social teaching says government is the privileged agent of the common good.

3. **Family life:** Family life is where people learn; it is the domestic church. Families are where God's unconditional love is reflected in everyday life and activity.

4. **Subsidiarity and the proper role of government:** Coined by Pope Pius XI in *Quadragesimo Anno*, subsidiarity speaks of the proper division of labor among human institutions, believing that those institutions closest to the people, that is the lowest level, should be engaged first. Government definitely has a significant role to play to coordinate and make things possible, but the state is only one facet of a larger society.

5. **Property ownership and modern society-rights and responsibility:** The church follows the middle road of Thomas Aquinas, who believed in the right of private property with consideration for the common good. From *Rerum Novarum* forward, the church has supported the right of private ownership of property. Still, the common good at times requires expropriation of lands from their owners.

6. **The dignity of work, the rights of workers, and support for labor unions:** Catholic social teaching suggests that despite some problems, a world without organized labor would be a less favorable environment for achieving justice and an equitable sharing of the earth's resources. Labor is believed to be something intrinsically good for humans; it allows us to use our talents to contribute to the wider society. Thus, human work is more than a commodity or a job; it is our vocation.

7. **Colonialism and the economic environment:** Disturbing inequities between rich and poor in the world prompt the church to offer two important teachings. First, the church says we have a moral obligation to care deeply about world poverty and to act to address this issue. Additionally, people are invited to ponder this issue and offer suggestions.

8. **Peace and disarmament:** Social justice has long been allied with peace. Two prominent teachings on peace are pacifism and the just-war theory. Advocates for pacifism have been rare, although more recently there has been a greater movement toward pacifism because many question the validity of the just-war theory and its application to contemporary

warfare. Nonetheless, the just-war theory has been used to justify Christian conflict for many centuries.

9. **Option for the poor and vulnerable:** This idea is relatively new, appearing in a church document only in 1979 and in a papal document in 1987. On the other hand, the sense of this teaching has been part of the church from the very outset. Living the Gospel message means simultaneously meeting people's spiritual and material needs.

The Corporal Works of Mercy

The corporal works of mercy find their Biblical origins in Isaiah 58:6–10, and Matthew 25:34–40. Conducted for the common good and basic human welfare, these special works are closely associated today with Catholic social justice. Indeed, Pope John Paul II in his encyclical letter, *Dives in Misericordia* ("Rich in Mercy"), paragraph 14, declared that: "Jesus Christ taught that man not only receives and experiences the Mercy of God, but that he is also called to practice mercy toward others." As Jesus says in the Beatitudes, "Blessed are the merciful, for they will receive mercy." (Matthew 5:7) Inspired by the Holy Spirit to commit to these works, Christians are called to respond to the needs of their poorest sisters and brothers worldwide. The traditional corporal works of mercy are feed the hungry, give drink to the thirsty, clothe the naked, shelter the homeless, visit the sick, ransom captives, and bury the dead.

CHAPTER 21

Contemporary Moral Issues

Many people today, Catholics and non-Catholics alike, see the face of Roman Catholicism in the many moral issues that grab headlines and are the subject of conversations at home and at work. Such conversations and the media frenzy around many hot-button issues are often slanted against church teaching due to ignorance of facts and poor understanding of the foundational principles upon which Catholic moral teachings are based. Thus, an exploration of contemporary moral issues that provides an accurate explanation of the church's teaching and rationale on these subjects is essential.

Birth Control

Sexuality, a basic and instinctual drive of all humans, and marriage are the roots from which many contemporary moral issues find their origins. Marriage, the central relationship of human sexuality, which has been sacramentalized in the Roman Catholic Church (see Chapter 12) and finds its crowning glory in the procreation and education of children, is a sacred bond of privilege and responsibility. During the early centuries of Christianity, however, marriage was not afforded the sacredness with which it is held today. St. Augustine, as an illustrative model, saw sex within marriage as a form of concupiscence, almost a necessary evil to continue the human race. This rather negative attitude toward human sexuality predominated in Roman Catholicism until the time of Vatican II.

QUOTE

Casti Connubii (Section 54) reads: "But no reason, however grave, may be put forward by which anything intrinsically against nature may become conformable to nature and morally good. Since, therefore, the conjugal act is destined primarily by nature for the begetting of children, those who in exercising it deliberately frustrate its natural power and purpose sin against nature and commit a deed which is shameful and intrinsically vicious."

Closely associated with the general topic of marriage is the concept of birth control. Since conjugal rights, freely given by man and woman to each other, bring the possibility of procreation, the question of artificially regulating pregnancy, commonly referred to as birth control, has been an issue for centuries. Genesis 38:7–11 speaks of the Lord's displeasure at Onan, for "he spilled his semen on the ground whenever he went in to his brother's wife." By the mid-twentieth century, more sophisticated means of artificial contraception, through the creation of prophylactic devices (and most especially the birth control pill), became commonplace. Such new methods of birth regulation prompted the church to respond. In December 1930, Pope Pius XI issued *Casti Connubii* ("On Christian Marriage"), which condemned all forms of artificial contraception.

Thirty years later, the church again addressed this same issue in a formal way. Believing that the issue of artificial contraception might bog down discussion on the council floor, Pope John XXIII decided to keep this issue off the agenda of Vatican II. However, in 1963, before his death that summer, Pope John formed the Papal Birth Control Commission, which was given the specific charter to review church policy on this issue and to make a report to the pope. This commission, which over time expanded in numbers and membership, including by the end of its investigation some lay couples, presented to Pope Paul VI in 1966 its majority report, "Responsible Parenthood." This document recommended that in some cases artificial contraception might be appropriate, even necessary, in order for couples to be responsible parents. Two years later, however, Pope Paul issued *Humanae Vitae*, which continued the long-standing Roman Catholic rejection of all forms of artificial contraception, labeling such action as "intrinsically evil."

QUESTION

What if a woman must use medication for a medical condition that renders her nonfecund?
The church has no restrictions in such conditions. The rationale for taking the medication is not to frustrate the procreative element of sex but rather to correct or alleviate some other medical condition. The woman's inability to conceive is only a side effect, not the intended purpose of the medication.

Church Teachings

Roman Catholicism teaches that artificial contraception is wrong because such procedures compromise the integrity of the conjugal act. The church teaches that each instance of sexual intercourse, as the highest expression of human love, has two important functions: unitive and procreative. Artificial contraception certainly does not compromise the unitive or love aspect of sex, but it does render such acts nonfecund, that is, not open to the possibility of conception. Roman Catholicism teaches that to frustrate this essential element of conjugal relations is an intrinsically evil act. Thus, the use of all forms of artificial contraception, including voluntary sterility, is rejected. However, natural family planning, because it does not frustrate either of the two basic reasons for sex, is approved.

Interception and Contragestation

Associated with, but oriented in a different way than those artificial contraceptive methods that frustrate fertilization, the medical techniques of interception and contragestation serve to control pregnancy after fertilization. Interception techniques, best illustrated by the intrauterine device (IUD) or the morning-after pill, do not allow a fertilized embryo to be implanted in the mother's uterus. Contragestative techniques cause the elimination of an embryo once implanted. Such methods are utilized when a delay in a woman's menstrual cycle is noticed. The stated goal of such technique is to re-establish menstruation, but the result is the abortion of an embryo recently implanted. Thus, both techniques of interception and contragestation are forms of abortion and, therefore, gravely immoral.

Alternative Reproductive Methods

Recent decades have witnessed significant advances in medical technology associated with human life in its initial stages. Some of these developments, such as prenatal care and new equipment and techniques that have saved from death premature infants and those born with treatable physical defects, such as heart malfunction, have certainly been positive and worthy of support, especially when they support the normal functions of human procreation. However, some advanced technologies that involve the destruction of human life or employ means that violate human dignity have also become common in human society. It is important, therefore, to recall the fundamental criterion expressed in the Instruction *Donum Vitae* (1988), which demanded that total and unqualified respect be given a human being from the moment of conception. Therefore, the human embryo possesses the dignity of a person from the very outset. This forms the premise upon which the church's teaching on various alternative reproductive methods is based.

In Vitro Fertilization

The treatment of infertility is one of the more common and highly developed of new medical techniques associated with the transmission of life. In September 2008, the Congregation for the Doctrine of the Faith, headed by American Cardinal William Levada, issued, "Instruction *Dignitatis Humanae*: On Certain Bioethical Questions," which addresses various contemporary moral issues associated with human infertility, gene therapy, and therapeutic use of stem cells. The document articulates three fundamental goods that must be held when considering if new medical techniques are morally sound. First, the right to life and to physical integrity of all humans, from conception to natural death, is paramount. Second, the unity of marriage maintains the right to become a father or mother is possible only with the other spouse. Third, the specific value of sexuality requires that procreation be the fruit of the conjugal act specific to the love between spouses.

ESSENTIAL

From the perspective of Roman Catholicism, the replacement of the conjugal act by a technical procedure, which reduces procreation to mere reproduction, leads to a weakening of the respect owed to every human being. Recognition of this respect, on the other hand, is promoted by the physical intimacy of married love.

In vitro fertilization is rejected by Roman Catholicism for two important reasons. First, frequently this procedure generally involves the destruction of human embryos. As such, these techniques proceed as if the embryo was a mass of cells to be used, selected, or discarded. Embryos produced *in vitro* with defects are almost immediately discarded. Ordinarily, professional ethics would obviate any procedure that involves a high number of failures and fatalities. Such is the case with *in vitro* fertilization. Moreover, this technique is morally unacceptable for it disassociates procreation from the personal conjugal act. Indeed, procedures that allow foreign embryos to be implanted based on genetic selection misconstrue and even invalidate true procreation.

Other Alternative Reproductive Techniques

Intracytoplasmic sperm injection (ICSI), a technique used with increasing frequency, is used to overcome various forms of male infertility. Just as with *in vitro* fertilization, the church considers this technique intrinsically illicit, as it manifests a complete separation between procreation and sexual intercourse. This procedure occurs outside the bodies of a couple where fertilization is entrusted to the power of medical personnel who hold total control on the origin and destiny of the embryo so created. Such fertilization is neither achieved by nor an expression of the conjugal union.

Cryopreservation, the process of freezing human embryos, a varied form of *in vitro* fertilization, is also morally unacceptable, due to its failure to manifest respect for the human person. The question of what to do with frozen embryos not used is highly problematic. Proposals to use these embryos for the treatment of human disease are unacceptable for they treat the embryo as mere biological material. These "abandoned embryos" present a problem that is not morally solvable. In order to avoid ethical problems associated with the freezing of embryos, some have suggested freezing only oocytes (female eggs). Again, however, such artificial procreation is not morally permissible because it violates the three basic premises mentioned above.

Preimplantation diagnosis is a process whereby embryos formed *in vitro* are genetically tested before being implanted into a woman's womb. This procedure is conducted to ensure that the embryo used is free from defects or has the sex or specific qualities desired. This procedure amounts to a form of eugenics that leads to selective abortion for all embryos discarded as unacceptable for whatever reason. Thus, this procedure is also morally indefensible.

Life and Death Issues

Another major category of contemporary moral issues, beyond those of sexuality, are life and death issues. As illustrated well by Cardinal Joseph Bernardin's concept of the "Consistent Ethic of Life," Roman Catholicism teaches that all life is sacred, from conception to natural death. Therefore, all actions that in any way terminate life, save actions of war or justifiable self-defense, are judged morally illicit. In 1995, Pope John Paul II in his encyclical letter *Evangelium Vitae* ("The Gospel of Life"), outlined the

Church's consistent arguments against abortion, euthanasia, and the death penalty. Describing contemporary society as a "culture of death," John Paul forcefully described the rationale behind the church's teaching, both in general and with respect to specific issues.

FACT

It is important to understand that Roman Catholicism does not teach that extraordinary means must always be applied to save life. Use of respirators, heart-pumping machines, and similar devices that can be used to prolong life need not be utilized if the individual or her cognizant representative decides such treatment is to be removed or not utilized from the outset.

From the perspective of Roman Catholicism, life and death issues begin with two basic premises. First, the sanctity of life must be protected from the first moment of conception to natural death. Second, life begins at the moment of conception. The church does not entertain various theories concerning when human life begins, but rather teaches that from the first moment of fertilization the embryo is human. Speaking of a fertilized ovum, Pope John Paul II in *Evangelium Vitae* (Section 60) stated, "It [the ovum] would never be made human if it were not human already." Additionally, the church teaches that God, and God alone, is the purveyor of life. Again, as the pope wrote in the same letter (Section 53), "God alone is the Lord of life from its beginning until its end: no one can, in any circumstance, claim for himself the right to destroy directly an innocent human being."

Using these premises as a base, the church teaches that abortion, euthanasia, and the death penalty, while understanding the various circumstances and nuances of these different issues, are all morally illicit acts. "The Gospel of Life" (Section 57) reads, "The deliberate decision to deprive an innocent human being of his life is always morally evil and can never be licit either as an end in itself or as a means to a good end."

Abortion and Euthanasia

Since the 1973 United States Supreme Court decision *Roe v. Wade*, which legalized abortion in the first two trimesters of a women's pregnancy, abortion has been a contentious issue in the United States on all fronts. The need to respect and treat as a human person any human embryo makes abortion, regardless of the situation, an act of murder, for it is the deliberate and direct killing by whatever means of a human being. Vatican II (*Gaudium et Spes*, Section 51) links abortion with infanticide as an "unspeakable crime."

Euthanasia and (physician)-assisted suicide are similarly rejected by the church as morally illicit acts. Citing the premise that God is the Lord of life, the church teaches that it is symptomatic of a "culture of death" that allows individuals rather than God to dictate when an individual will die. Defined as an action or omission that of itself and by intention causes death, euthanasia must be rejected due to its overt intention to bring death.

The Death Penalty

Like abortion and euthanasia, the death penalty is considered by Roman Catholicism to be taking an innocent life. While the situation of punishing a criminal is vastly different than abortion and euthanasia, nonetheless, Pope John Paul II teaches in "The Gospel of Life" (Section 56) that the extreme punishment of death should never be used unless there is no possible way to defend society against the individual. Indeed, *The Catechism of the Church* (#2267) states, "If bloodless means are sufficient to defend human lives against an aggressor and to protect public order and safety of persons, public authority must limit itself to such means, because they better correspond to the concrete conditions of the common good and are more in conformity to the dignity of the human person."

Homosexuality

During the last generation, homosexuality has moved from a topic rarely if ever addressed, even in private conversation, let alone a public forum, to an issue that often dominates headlines as a normal subject of discourse. The subject itself, as well as homosexual men and women, have moved from the darkness of the closet to the light of day. This significant shift in both the profile and general acceptance in society of homosexuality has undoubtedly been in part the catalyst to several statements and documents from various institutional church offices that address this issue and certain significant subissues that have arisen from it.

Roman Catholicism has addressed the issue of homosexuality by making a clear distinction between an individual's sexual orientation and homosexual activity. In 1975 in its document "Declaration on Certain Questions Concerning Sexual Ethics," the Congregation for the Doctrine of the Faith made a clear distinction between the homosexual orientation or tendency and individual homosexual actions, the latter being declared as "intrinsically disordered." While the document clearly states that the inclination of the homosexual person is not sinful, it is a strong tendency toward an intrinsic moral evil. Thus, "the inclination itself must be seen as an objective disorder." (Section 3) It is important to note, however, that homosexual persons have the same basic rights as all people. Therefore, any discrimination against such people is rejected.

QUESTION

With respect to the homosexual orientation, what does "objective disorder" mean?
This poorly understood concept means that the homosexual is objectively different from the majority, as a person born with a mental or physical handicap would be similarly objectively different from the majority of human births. Thus, the homosexual is seen as objectively different from the norm, that is the heterosexual.

Homosexual activity, however, is morally wrong for the same basic reasons that premarital sex or use of artificial contraception are intrinsically illicit. By its very nature, homosexual activity can never be fecund, open to the possibility of procreation. Additionally, such actions are not ordered among married couples. Since the two basic reasons for conjugal acts cannot be satisfied by homosexual couples, Roman Catholicism teaches that such activity between gay and lesbian couples is morally and intrinsically illicit.

Gay Marriage

While various forms of civil unions between gay couples had been enacted in various states, in May 2004, through the case of *Goodridge v.*

Department of Public Health, Massachusetts became the first state to legalize gay marriage. From this start, the issue has become widespread, being debated in several states, and implemented in some and the District of Columbia.

"Non-Discrimination Against Homosexual Persons" (Section 12), issued by the Congregation for the Doctrine of the Faith on May 30, 1992 reads: "Homosexual persons, as human persons, have the same rights as all persons, including the right of not being treated in a manner which offends their personal dignity."

The church's response to this new development is completely consistent with its general teaching on the sanctity of marriage and the purposes of the conjugal act. Roman Catholicism teaches that marriage is a union between one man and one woman, joined in an intimate partnership of love for life. As stated above, one of the primary reasons for marriage, the procreation and education of children, is clearly not possible in any type of homosexual union. Thus, the unique manifestation of creation and potential of what marriage should be is not possible in such a union. Regarding this issue, in June 2003, the Congregation for the Doctrine of the Faith, in a document "Considerations Regarding Proposals to Give Legal Recognition to Unions Between Homosexual Persons" (Section 3), states, "There are absolutely no grounds for considering homosexual unions to be in any way similar or even remotely analogous to God's plan for marriage and family." The document goes on to say that laws that favor such unions are "contrary to right reason." (Section 6)

Manipulation of Human Genetics

A significant area of modern medical technology that has once again raised new moral questions is that of the manipulation of human genetics. Gene therapy, the name commonly given to various genetic engineering techniques, is today being applied to human beings for therapeutic purposes. Such technology seeks to mitigate or eliminate genetic effects in nonreproductive cells. Thus, this procedure aims to positively enhance a single person. These methods are undertaken on a fetus before his or her birth in the uterus or after birth of a child or adult. The church teaches that strictly therapeutic procedures are in principle morally licit, for they seek to restore the normal genetic configuration or to counter damage caused by genetic anomalies related to other medical problems.

Germ line cell therapy, which aims to correct genetic effects with the purpose of transmitting this result to offspring of the individual, is understood differently. Because risks associated with genetic manipulation are considerable and not fully controllable, the church, under the present state of research, does not consider it morally licit to use such therapy due to possible harm to resulting progeny.

Cloning

Cloning is another moral issue associated with human genetics. Medical science has proposed cloning for two basic purposes: reproduction, namely to obtain the birth of a child with specific traits, and medical therapy. Cloning has generated significant concern throughout the world, with many nations and organizations expressing negative judgments on such procedures. Roman Catholicism teaches that human cloning is intrinsically illicit because it takes techniques of artificial fertilization to their extreme, giving life to a new human with no connection to an act of reciprocal self-giving and without any link to human sexuality. Such techniques greatly abuse human dignity.

ESSENTIAL

The church suggests that stem cells obtained from adult organisms, the blood of the umbilical cord at time of birth, or fetuses that die of natural causes can be used in medical research. However, the common criteria of medical ethics must always be respected, including scientific rigor and prudence in reducing to a bare minimum the risk to any human.

Therapeutic cloning is even more problematic from an ethical perspective. Such procedures require the creation of embryos, many of which will be destroyed. Such ethical objections have led some researchers to propose new techniques that can generate embryonic stem cells without the destruction of human embryos. Still, these techniques stand on shaky moral ground if even the possibility of killing a human embryo is at stake.

Questions concerning the therapeutic use of stem cells arise directly from the issue of human cloning. Stem cells are undifferentiated cells that possess two qualities: the prolonged capability of multiplying themselves while maintaining their undifferentiated state and the capability of producing cells from which fully differentiated cells can descend. The principal moral question is how such cells can be obtained. Methods that do not cause serious harm to the individual from which stem cells were taken are considered by the church to be licit. Obtaining stem cells from a living human embryo, on the other hand, invariably causes the death of the embryo and is, therefore, considered morally illicit.

CHAPTER 22

Dissent in the Church

The post–Vatican II era has seen major shifts in many aspects of Roman Catholicism, some rather subtle, others more obvious. Liturgical changes in the celebration of the sacraments, significantly fewer priests and religious, and, as a consequence, fewer Catholic schools are overt and visible changes. However, a more subtle, yet possibly more significant shift is found in the general acceptance of dissent in the church. While certainly part of Catholic history, dissent today is not only widespread, but it is manifest in nearly every aspect of the faith.

Pay, Pray, and Obey

The Second Vatican Council and the era of the 1960s provided a point from which a clear separation in thought—socially, culturally, and theologically—can be drawn. Indeed, as researchers William D'Antonio and associates have pointed out in their book *American Catholics Today*, significant differences exist in how groups of people understand Roman Catholicism based on their categorization as pre–Vatican II, Vatican II, or post–Vatican II Catholics. Those Roman Catholics educated in the faith prior to Vatican II hold a more conventional view of the church, one that emphasizes the basic doctrinal and dogmatic teachings as well as a spirituality that has strong links to popular devotion. As the generations move to the more contemporary period, D'Antonio and his colleagues have found that traditional views and practices are subjugated to issues that find greater resonance with contemporary society. This movement from a more traditional to a more progressive understanding of Roman Catholicism demonstrates how Catholicism today is understood in many different ways, leading to the presence of dissent as a common everyday reality in Catholicism.

ESSENTIAL

As an example, D'Antonio and coauthors show that 52 percent of pre–Vatican II, 40 percent of Vatican II, and 42 percent of post–Vatican II Catholics believe the teaching authority claimed by the Vatican to be "very important to them." However, only 27 percent of millennials, the generation born after 1980, believe the Vatican's teaching authority to be important to them.

In order to understand and appreciate how Catholicism is practiced today, and the significant change that today's church represents from earlier generations, it is essential to gain an appreciation for the pre–Vatican II era. As described in Chapter 4, Catholics prior to Vatican II were strongly united. When one Catholic was cut, the whole community bled; when one member of the faith was exalted, the church collective rejoiced. The unanimity and close ties that characterized the Roman Catholic community of this era are well illustrated by the phrase "pay, pray, and obey." In general, Catholics were a very cohesive and contented group.

While anti-Catholicism never left, the post–World War II American Catholic Church experienced a renaissance of sorts. Catholics were better accepted, had greater opportunities for education (especially college and university education), and economically moved into the growing middle class. Riding on a wave of greater general acceptance within society, Catholics were equally satisfied with the day-to-day operations of their church. They supported the church financially, not only through monetary donations, but additionally through support for Catholic institutions, such as

schools and hospitals. In other words, the people were happy to pay to maintain the vibrancy of their church.

The faithful were also more than willing to pray; their participation in the formal sacramental and devotional aspects of the faith was consistently strong and vibrant. People willingly and seemingly with great joy participated; the local parish was the center for the typical family, providing education, social interaction, recreation, and most importantly worship.

Lastly, pre–Vatican II Catholics had no problems with the concept of obedience. As the title of the popular 1950s television show *Father Knows Best* indicated, Catholics as a group placed total trust and confidence in their local pastor (their spiritual "Father") and his associates. Happy people generally do not make waves; such was the reality for Catholics prior to Vatican II. The faithful had no problem with obeying, doing as they were asked or told. The concept that one might differ with an official opinion issued by an institutional church authority figure was not a serious consideration at the time.

Vatican II, *Humanae Vitae*, and Licit Dissent

Roots to today's multiple understandings of Roman Catholicism are found during the era of the 1960s, which included Vatican II (1962–1965). While many have attributed the contemporary status of Catholicism to the council, one cannot disassociate Vatican II from its historical context. The combination of the Cold War, a counterculture that challenged all authority, Vietnam, and the rise of women in society, among other factors, created an environment ripe for the splintering of unity on many fronts, including the church. As described in Chapter 4, while Vatican II was received in different ways by various individuals and groups, its efforts at *aggiornamento* and reform certainly created, from both inside and outside perspectives, a new look for Catholicism. The perceived changes in church teaching, its new orientation toward other peoples of faith, and acceptance of new models for Catholicism, ones that provided for greater participation by the laity, added fuel to an already burning fire that soon would become a conflagration in 1968.

FACT

"Responsible Parenthood's" conclusion that, in certain cases, artificial contraception was appropriate was rejected by *Humanae Vitae*, which maintained the long-standing church tradition that every act of sexual intercourse must be fecund, that is, open to the possibility of conception. To frustrate this primary reason for sex renders such action "intrinsically evil."

Perhaps no better illustration for the rise and rapid growth of dissent within Roman Catholicism is found than the publication of *Humanae Vitae*, Pope Paul VI's encyclical that continued the Church's long-standing prohibition of artificial contraception. As described in Chapter 21, the papal Birth Control Commission's position in "Responsible Parenthood" was contradicted in *Humanae Vitae*. This generated a firestorm of dissent that has ebbed and flowed for over forty years.

The Clergy's Dissent

The dissent that arose in the wake of the publication of *Humanae Vitae* was certainly unprecedented for the era and was, most probably, fueled at least in part by unfortunate timing. The most unique aspect of this dissent was that it was led by members of the clergy. In the United States, Father Charles Curran, a professor of moral theology at the Catholic University of America, was the chief spokesman for those who disagreed with the teaching of the encyclical. Using the rationale that *Humanae Vitae* was not a dogmatic proclamation, as defined at Vatican I in 1870, Curran and his allies suggested that Roman Catholics could in good conscience dissent from the pope's teaching and still be faithful members of the church. Deep divisions within the clergy and the laity ensued. Many priests publicly and privately encouraged their congregations to act according to their conscience with respect to using artificial contraception. Active and vocal dissent from the ranks of the clergy emboldened the rank-and-file Catholic faithful to express their dissent, beginning with artificial contraception but then moving rapidly and widely to many other teachings and practices that for generations had never been challenged.

Timing

It is probable that the timing of the publication of Pope Paul's views contributed to the negative reaction it received. *Humanae Vitae* was published in late July when the United States was already reeling from the April and June assassinations of Martin Luther King Jr. and Robert Kennedy, respectively. The general frustration of the nation and desire to strike back at those who had destroyed the hopes of millions through the murders of two great champions of civil rights and politics most assuredly brought at least a subtle boost to the general feeling of malaise that pervaded the nation. From the perception of some, the pope's rejection of the Birth Control Commission's majority report only exacerbated an already problematic situation.

Norms for Licit Dissent

The firestorm generated as a result of *Humanae Vitae* forced the institutional church to respond. In the same critical year of 1968, the National Conference of Catholic Bishops (NCCB) published norms for licit dissent.

Intended to corral growing dissent and to present a very clear method for those who believed that dissent was necessary, the norms are principles that provide an opportunity for theological discussion of noninfallible teaching. The bishops start with a presumption in favor of the magisterium. While noninfallible doctrine may admit to development, or even to a call for petition or revision, it remains binding and carries moral certitude when it is addressed to the universal church. However, theological dissent from the magisterium is in order if: the reasons are serious and well-founded, if the manner of dissent does not question or impugn the teaching authority of the church, and such dissent does not give scandal.

Role of the Theologian

The issue of dissent raises an important question: What is the role of the theologian in Roman Catholicism today? Is a scholar theologian one who pushes boundaries, and at times steps over them, in order to discover new vistas and religious understandings, or are these academics people who through their research find their *raison d'être* in support of magisterial teaching? Forces stand arrayed on both sides of this contentious issue. A significant percentage of theologians who write on this subject today stand on the more progressive side, believing that the only way to further theology is, in a professional and courteous manner, to challenge noninfallible teachings, seeking dialogue with those on the other side of the divide. Inevitably, such a position generates pluralism.

The position of those who believe the theologian's role is more to articulate and make clearer magisterial teaching is best represented by a document published by the Congregation for the Doctrine of the Faith in 1990. The "Instruction on the Ecclesial Vocation of the Theologian" (paragraph 6) states: "His [the theologian's] role is to pursue in a particular way an ever deeper understanding of the Word of God found in the inspired Scriptures and handed on by the living Tradition of the Church. He does this in communion with the Magisterium which has been charged with the responsibility of preserving the deposit of faith."

The question at the heart of this debate is: What freedom does the theologian have to dissent against noninfallible teaching? Both sides of this debate acknowledge that dissent against infallible dogmatic teachings is inconsistent with the role of the theologian, but the issue with respect to noninfallible teaching is more open to debate. The more conservative position holds that, while not infallible, all church teaching is authoritative and, therefore, only open to debate and dissent along lines issued by the NCCB in 1968. The more progressive camp, however, while offering deference to the magisterium, seeks greater independence of thought, research, and inquiry. This difference of opinion has led, unfortunately, to some celebrated breaks between the institutional church and specific theologians. Thus, efforts must be made to bridge this divide and bring greater unity to Catholicism, both on the local and universal levels.

Catholic Common Ground Initiative

Inaugurated on August 12, 1996, the Catholic Common Ground Initiative is an effort to lessen polarities and divisions, often seen in the form of dissent that jeopardized the unity of the faith and often placed people on opposite sides of many significant issues. The man most associated with this initiative was Cardinal Joseph Bernardin of Chicago. In 1992, Bernardin issued to his parishioners a short reflection, "The Parish in the Contemporary Church," which called parishes to foster a spirit of cooperation among their members concerning the varied understandings of the church.

QUOTE

"Called to Be Catholic" reads in part, "American Catholics must reconstitute the conditions for addressing our differences constructively—a common ground centered on faith in Jesus, marked by accountability to the living Catholic Tradition, and ruled by a spirit of civility, dialogue, generosity, and broad and serious consultation."

Through the efforts of the National Pastoral Life Center, to which Bernardin sent a copy of his statement, a series of meetings to discuss common ground in the church was initiated. No subject was off the table; the only rule was candor and confidentiality were expected. Eventually, participants suggested that a formal statement of their ideas be published. It was to be an appeal to reflect upon and discuss criteria for authentic and effective dialogue with individuals and groups within the church. Thus, the idea of the Catholic Common Ground Initiative was born. The initiative planned periodic conferences on pursuing common ground and encouraged constructive dialogue among peoples representing different perspectives and positions in the church. Additionally, occasional publications were considered a future possibility.

On October 12, 1996, the National Pastoral Life Center, after consultation with various individuals and groups and with great sensitivity to the diversity of Catholicism in the United States, issued "Called to Be Catholic: Church in a Time of Peril." Led by its principal spokesman, Cardinal Bernardin, this initial statement of the Catholic Common Ground Initiative suggested that in order for the church to be a leavening force in society, common ground had to be found. Otherwise, a defensive position, born out of dissension, would prevail. The church needed to confront its challenges with honesty and imagination in order to reverse the rising state of polarization that inhibits discussion and creates camps of diverse opinion.

The Question of Women's Ordination

While the breadth and tenor of dissent within the church is on many fronts, the question of women's ordination serves as an excellent illustration of the gap between the opposed sides and constitutes a lightning rod issue for many Roman Catholics today. From the apostolic era forward, Roman Catholicism has maintained the tradition of an all-male clergy. As described in Chapter 17, the policy of celibacy was evolutionary, but the priesthood has been exclusively male from the outset. Beginning at the approximate time of Vatican II, several forces converged to raise the question of women's ordination. The 1960s environment that questioned authority, the rise of the women's movement, the beginnings of open theological dissent, and a significant reduction in the numbers of clergy and religious were four factors that caused people to ask if the tradition of an all-male clergy was reformable.

The documents of Vatican II raised the question of the role of women in the church in several significant ways. The basic dignity of the human person was strongly emphasized. *Lumen Gentium* ("The Dogmatic Constitution on the Church") spoke of the "priesthood of the faithful," a different but nonetheless important role along with the ministerial priesthood. The overall role of the lay apostolate was also accentuated. These important points, combined with changing roles in society for women on many fronts, added more ammunition to those who questioned the need to continue the tradition of an all-male clergy.

QUESTION

Why did the church speak on this issue in 1976?
That year the Anglican Church first ordained women to the priesthood. In response to this decision, Pope Paul VI believed it was imperative for Roman Catholicism to clarify its position on the issue.

In response to the significant questions raised concerning women's ordination, the church has issued two documents that address in specific ways the issues raised by those advocating change. In 1976 Pope Paul VI issued *Inter Insigniores*, which articulates the church's position while simultaneously responding to questions and concerns raised by those advocating change. The document states that the church has never validly conferred ordination on women, and, thus, this stands as the tradition. Next, the pope says that it was the attitude of Christ not to choose women for the ministerial priesthood. While Jesus reached out in many ways to women, he did not call them to be apostles. Third, this practice was continued by the apostles. While considerable evolution with respect to the customs of Judaism occurred, the apostles did not break with Mosaic practice concerning women and the church. *Inter Insigniores* states that priests and bishops exercise their ministry, not in their own name, but *in persona Christi*. In other words, the priest is another Christ; therefore, only men can serve in such a role. Lastly, the document says the human rights argument that suggests ordination should be open to women is flawed. Rather, the ministerial priesthood is not a human right. Equality in the church does not require specialized identity; each person has his or her own role.

In May 1994, after debate on this issue again reached fever pitch, Pope John Paul II issued *Ordinatio Sacerdotalis*. This much shorter document succinctly reiterates the basic message of *Inter Insigniores* but forcefully suggests that the church has no authority to confer ordination on women.

Catholicism Divided

Theological dissent has created various camps within the Roman Catholic community, even to the point of schism. Arising in the wake of Vatican II, these groups, with the passage of time, have become more clearly defined and possibly more strident and unbending in their theological positions. Two distinct positions within Roman Catholicism, loosely distinguished by the terms conservative and liberal, are joined by a third perspective, traditional Catholics, who as a result of a staid view that rejects the present pope and the teachings of Vatican II, have been labeled a schismatic group since 1988, although in 2009 Pope Benedict XVI initiated dialogue seeking reconciliation.

QUOTE

Ordinatio Sacerdotalis (Section 4) reads: "Wherefore, in order that all doubt may be removed regarding a matter of great importance, a matter which pertains to the Church's divine constitution itself, in virtue of my ministry of confirming the brethren (cf. Luke 22:32) I declare that the Church has no authority whatsoever to confer priestly ordination on women and that this judgment is to be definitively held by all the Church's faithful."

Conservative Catholics

Conservative Catholics are those members of the faithful who seek to defend, advance, and live the teachings of the church through the proper implementation of the documents of Vatican II. While most members of this camp would not expressly describe themselves as "conservative," the name has been given as a result of a specific group whose philosophy of the Catholic faith generally adheres to this more conventional understanding of the church. Catholics United for the Faith (CUF), a formal organization started in August 1968 by H. Lyman Stebbins, is characterized by loyalty to the Vatican and a spirit of cooperation with Catholic religious authorities. The organization sees Catholicism as a religious bulwark against modernity and as a corrective to the dissent generated in the wake of *Humanae Vitae*. The communitarian aspect of CUF is important; it does not see itself as an organization of ideas alone. Membership in CUF is small, with nine chapters, attached to specific parishes, in the United States.

Conservative Catholics in general believe that many of the new ideas that have arisen in the church since Vatican II have led to widespread doctrinal illiteracy and religious indifferentism. Those associated with this perspective believe authority in the church has been compromised. In response, adherents suggest complete faithfulness to magisterial teaching is necessary; no one has the right to pre-empt church teaching or go beyond what the church has stated.

Progressive Catholics

By far today the vast majority of Roman Catholics in the United States are found on the opposite side of the religious ideological spectrum. Often referred to as progressive Catholics, these members of the Catholic faithful are content to live in the "spirit of Vatican II" and thus do not feel constrained to follow magisterial teaching absolutely. Proponents of this perspective view the church in a more inclusive way. This group feels free to dissent from church teaching, accepting certain teachings but rejecting others. Members of this camp believe Vatican II freed church members to prayerfully and in conscience make prudent decisions on how to live and practice their life of faith.

Traditionalists

Catholic traditionalists actually are two groups in one. The majority of this group accepts the authority of and claims union with the pope. They do, however, reject the liberal tendencies of certain members of the hierarchy and their teachings. A second group, whose first great champion in the hierarchy was Archbishop Marcel Lefebvre, seeks to arrest and reverse religious change among Catholics and to preserve the ideological, organizational, and cultic patterns of the church that were present before the Second Vatican Council. This second form of traditionalism is a protest against the blurring of Catholic identity and the loss of Roman Catholic hegemony in the world. The movement began somewhat underground, but by the mid-1970s had gained worldwide support by its return to the pre–Vatican II (Tridentine) Mass.

The Catholic Traditionalist Movement (CTM) in the United States was inaugurated in March 1965 by Father Gommar De Pauw, a professor at St. Mary's Seminary and College in Emmitsburg, Maryland. CTM's theology is a radical departure from Roman Catholicism, although it claims that the Roman Church has moved far astray from its tradition. The CTM rejects Vatican II, including the contemporary Mass, casting aspersions on its doctrinal integrity. Its ideology is animated by a conspiracy theory and apocalyptic imagery of the Great Apostasy.

ESSENTIAL

Pope Benedict XVI has made overtures toward reconciliation with the traditionalists. He has allowed wider celebration of the Tridentine Mass, removed the excommunication from the four bishops ordained by Marcel Lefebvre in 1988, and inaugurated dialogue that seeks re-union as a goal.

The CTM believes that the papacy is *sede vacante* (seat is empty), believing that all popes after John XXIII were imposters. Through the work of Archbishop Lefebvre in France, clerical societies, the Society of St. Pius X, the Society of St. Pius V, and the Society of St. Peter, became part of the traditionalist movement. In 1988, against the orders of Pope John Paul II, Lefebvre ordained four bishops in the Society of St. Pius X, leading to his excommunication and placing the traditionalist movement in schism.

CHAPTER 23

Catholics and
Other Religions

From the time of Christ, Roman Catholicism has held historical primacy among Christians. Catholicism understands itself to be the church founded by Christ, what is labeled in the Acts of the Apostles (11:26) as "Christians." Historically, through the breakoff of the Orthodox traditions in the eleventh century and the Protestant Reformation of the sixteenth century, Catholicism maintained its direction and posture of primacy. In the wake of Vatican II, however, the church has become more open to contact and dialogue with peoples of other faiths, Christians and non-Christian alike.

Catholics and Other Religions: An Historical Overview

The Biblical message presented by Jesus Christ was always one of inclusion. In his public ministry, Jesus regularly reached out to individuals and groups who had been placed on the margins of Hebrew society. Ignoring the ritual purity laws of his day, Jesus touched lepers (Matthew 8:1–4; Mark 1:40–45; Luke 17:11–19) and healed them, allowed a woman who suffered from a hemorrhage for twelve years to touch him (Mark 5:25–34, Luke 8:43–48), and told a parable, the Good Samaritan (Luke 10:25–37), that proclaimed one of the most despised in society to be a hero while simultaneously critiquing religious elites who chose ritual purity over compassion. Christ also took his ministry to people outside the purview of Jewish society. He proclaimed that a Roman centurion had greater faith than any he had seen in Israel (Matthew 8:5–13; Luke 7:2–10), held an in-depth conversation with a Samaritan woman (John 4:7–42), and intentionally engaged a man possessed by a "legion" of evil spirits who lived east of the Sea of Galilee in Gerasene territory (Mark 5:1–20). Additionally, many of Jesus' closest associates were women; he first appeared after his resurrection to Mary Magdalene (John 20:11–18).

The path of inclusivity was continued by St. Paul. After his conversion, Paul was "assigned" the task of being the apostle to the Gentiles. Paul attacked his mission with great vigor. His three arduous missionary journeys throughout the eastern Mediterranean world, establishing numerous churches as he preached the message of Jesus, were a significant outreach beyond the Jewish world of his ancestry. His belief that the message of Christ went to all was manifested in two important ways. First, he specifically stated his belief in Jesus' vision of inclusivity: "In former generations this mystery was not made known to humankind, as it has now been revealed to his holy apostles and prophets by the Spirit: that is, the Gentiles have become fellow heirs, members of the same body, and sharers in the promise in Christ Jesus through the gospel." (Ephesians 3:5–6) Similarly, in Galatians 3:28, Paul writes, "There is no longer Jew or Greek, there is no longer slave or free, there is no longer male and female; for all of you are one in Christ Jesus."

The more inclusive message of Jesus and St. Paul began to be somewhat obscured after the Edict of Milan proclaimed by the Emperor Constantine in 313. Almost overnight Christianity moved from being proscribed by the Romans to becoming the normative religion for all in the empire. Christianity's acceptance provided it with a position from which it could leverage much greater influence in society, leading it to proclaim views that made the church more exclusive. While a more exclusive perspective, pitting Christianity against paganism, had been present from the time of St. Irenaeus (140–202), this more conservative attitude became common as Europe entered the medieval period.

QUOTE

St. Fulgentius de Ruspe (circa 500) wrote: "Not only all pagans, but also all Jews and all heretics and schismatics who finish their lives outside the Catholic Church, will go into eternal fire. . . . No one, howsoever much he may have given alms, even if he sheds his blood for the name of Christ, can be saved, unless he remains in the bosom and unity of the Catholic Church."

From the medieval period forward to the mid-twentieth century, the church's perspective as holding a unique distinctiveness and probity was maintained intact. This understanding was formalized at the Fourth Lateran Council (1215), which proclaimed: "There is one universal Church of the faithful, outside of which no one at all is saved." This council's declaration, often loosely communicated as "outside the church there is no salvation," was the base from which Roman Catholicism defended itself against the Protestant reformers of the sixteenth century and the various ideological challenges of the nineteenth century.

Yet, a better understanding of this principle began to evolve in the mid-twentieth century. Rather than intolerance and eliteness, the church's position was one that described the fullness of Catholicism as the goal to which all peoples of faith should strive, but not to an exclusive extent. In 1943 Pope Pius XII expressed in *Mystici corporis* this more nuanced perspective: "Today those who do not belong to the visible bonds of the Catholic Church . . . [we ask them to] strive to take themselves from the state in which they cannot be sure of their own eternal salvation; for even though they are ordered to the mystical body of the Redeemer by a certain desire and wish of which they are not aware, yet they lack so many heavenly gifts and helps which can be enjoyed only in the Catholic Church."

QUESTION

Why did the church hold fast to a tradition that had moved away from the inclusivity of Christ?
For centuries the concept that stated "Man must be changed by the church, not the church by man" was dominant. This was canonized at the Lateran V Council (1512). By the mid-twentieth century this perspective began to change.

Vatican II's Teaching on the Relationship of Catholics and Non-Catholics

The Second Vatican Council, described by some as a revolution in Catholic thought but considered by others to demonstrate continuity of tradition with reform, had much to say about the relationship between Catholics and non-Catholics. Indeed, this was one of the most contentious issues on the floor of the council for it raised the concept of the development of doctrine, one of the twin pillars of theological modernism condemned in 1907 through *Pascendi Dominici Gregis*. Thus, what the council said concerning the relationship of Catholics and non-Catholics, both ecumenism (Catholic and non-Catholic Christian dialogue) and interfaith dialogue (between Catholics and non-Christians) is extremely important and has largely determined the church's contemporary perspective on the subject.

The Dogmatic Constitution on the Church (*Lumen Gentium*)

"The Dogmatic Constitution on the Church," while introducing the concept of the church as the "people of God," made some important comments with respect to the relationship between Catholics and non-Catholics. Section #8 in part reads, "The sole Church of Christ . . . constituted and organized as a society in the present world, subsists in the Catholic Church, which is governed by the successor of Peter and by the bishops in communion with him. Nevertheless, many elements of sanctification and of truth are found outside its visible confines." Section #16 is equally revelatory: "Those who, through no fault of their own, do not know the Gospel of Christ or his Church, but who nevertheless seek God with a sincere heart . . . try in their actions to do his will as they know it through the dictates of their conscience—those too may achieve eternal salvation."

These two passages demonstrate how Vatican II returned the church to a more inclusive perspective concerning its relationship with non-Catholics. For the council to say that the Church of Christ "subsists in" rather than *is* Roman Catholicism acknowledges that, while the fullness of truth is found in the church, truth and the possibility of salvation can be found among other peoples of faith. The council's more conciliatory and less divisive language paved the way for the church to return to a more inclusive understanding of the relationship between Catholics and non-Catholics.

Declaration on Religious Liberty (*Dignitatis Humanae*)

While the "Declaration on Religious Liberty" did not directly address the relationship between Catholics and non-Catholics, it did, nonetheless, provide some important teachings that connect directly with this subject. This document, the only Vatican II text with any significant influence from United States bishops, uses the concept of human dignity as the base upon which it formulates its teaching. The document clearly states that the "one true religion continues to exist in the Catholic and Apostolic Church," but it also "declares that the human person has a right to religious freedom . . . [and] men should be immune from coercion on the part of individuals, social groups and every human power so that, within due limits, nobody is forced to act against his convictions nor is anyone to be restrained from acting in accordance with his convictions in religious matters in private or in public, alone or in associations with others" (Sections 1 and 2). Additionally, the declaration clearly states that people are not to act contrary to their conscience, especially in religious matters. This freedom is to be secured by civil authorities. Lastly, the document admits that at times in the past there has arisen in the church "a form of behavior which was hardly in keeping with the spirit of the Gospel and was even opposed to it" (Section 12). Several interpreters view this as a reference to the Crusades, Inquisition, and pogroms against Jews.

Decree on Ecumenism (*Unitatis Redintegratio*)

The principal document of the Second Vatican Council that addressed the concept of the church's relationship to other religions was the "Decree on Ecumenism." From the outset, the document (Section 1) affirms that the restoration of unity among Christian peoples "is one of the principal concerns" of Vatican II. The document admits that the separation between Christians can be blamed on both sides, Catholic and Protestant, but the church wishes to embrace those in separate communities as brothers. While many obstacles may exist, due to differences in doctrine, discipline, and structure, the desire to find common ground between all who are baptized is important. In a very important gesture, the council acknowledged that while "defects" exist in other communities of faith, these churches "have been by no means deprived of significance and importance in the mystery of salvation" (Section 3). Church members must acknowledge the good they receive from others; Catholics can learn from these faith communities. Still, Catholicism is seen as the one faith that holds the fullness of the means of salvation.

FACT

There are twenty-two (some say twenty-three) Eastern Rite Catholic traditions divided into five categories: Alexandrian, Antiochian, Armenian, Chaldean (Eastern Syrian), and Byzantine. Vatican II declares these churches to be autonomous. They are characterized by loyalty to the pope, yet there are many liturgical differences in celebratory rites. Additionally, Eastern Rites do not require priests to be celibate.

The practice of ecumenism, as articulated in *Unitatis Redintegratio*, falls upon the clergy and laity. There can be no true ecumenism that does not involve interior conversion. Therefore, not only actions but attitudes must be transformed. This may lead to common prayer services or worship, but this must not be done indiscriminately. The document suggests that theology should be taught from an ecumenical point of view, but Catholics must never compromise their beliefs for the sake of unity.

"The Decree on Ecumenism" addresses two major groups who are considered separate churches: Eastern Rite Catholics and Orthodox, and Protestants. The council affirms the special relationship between Roman Catholicism and the various Eastern Rites, all of whom are in communion with the Roman Church. The council speaks of the desire to seek greater unity with Protestants, but the significant differences between these collective churches and Roman Catholicism cannot be ignored. Still, common areas of discussion, such as belief in Jesus and concentration on the Scriptures, are seen as ways to begin appropriate ecumenical dialogue.

Declaration on the Relationship of the Church to Non-Christian Religions (*Nostra Aetate*)

While *Unitatis Redintegratio* addresses the concept of ecumenism, *Nostra Aetate* is specific to the concept of interfaith dialogue. The document's composition and publication were contentious for what was said concerning the Jews. The council rejects any idea that Jews should be charged with crimes associated with Jesus' crucifixion. Similarly, the document rejects any display of anti-Semitism. The document speaks of one human community that shares a common destiny, namely God. The council rejects as foreign to the mind of Christ any form of discrimination based on race, color, condition of life, or religion. More directly, the document speaks of the respect held for Muslims, suggesting that past history be dropped and promotion of common values be a common goal. In a general way, the document summarizes its teaching in a profound statement: "The Church rejects nothing which is true and holy in these [non-Christian] religions" (Section 2).

Ecumenical Dialogue Today

Ecumenical dialogue in twenty-first-century Roman Catholicism is first seen in the church's association with various Orthodox traditions. Although a break between the Roman Catholic and Orthodox churches began as early as the Counsel at Ephesus (431) and became formalized in 1054 at Constantinople, still, the few doctrinal differences are more terminology than substance. At the close of Vatican II, on December 7, 1965, Paul VI and Patriarch Athenagoras I signed a reciprocal act of justice and forgiveness. Both sides "regret the offensive words, the reproaches without foundation and the reprehensible gestures which on both sides marked or accompanied the sad events of that period [of separation]." More recently, on November 11, 1994, Pope John Paul II and Mar Dinkha IV, Patriarch of the Assyrian Church, negotiated a similar Common Declaration. In part the document stated, "We both recognize the legitimacy and rightness of these expressions of the same faith and we both respect the preference of each Church in her liturgical life and piety."

ESSENTIAL

Theologically, Roman Catholics and Anglicans are very similar. While differences exist, sacramental theology, the doctrine of grace, and the basis of ecclesiology (save the office of the pope), are ideas common to both communions. This should not be not surprising since the original break of the Anglican community from Catholicism was a political move of King Henry VIII.

The post–Vatican II period has been a time of great advancement in the relationship between Roman Catholics and the Anglican Church. This began under the leadership of Pope John XXIII and his foundation of the Secretariat for the Promotion of Christian Unity. In 1966, the Archbishop of Canterbury, Michael Ramsey, made an official visit to Pope Paul VI, which led the next year to the creation of the Anglican-Roman Catholic International Commission. Unfortunately, new tensions have arisen between Catholics and Anglicans over the issues of women's ordination, beginning in 1976, and most recently the ordination of openly gay priests to be bishops in New Hampshire and California.

Ecumenical dialogue with other Protestant groups has been rather sparse, save the Lutheran-Roman Catholic dialogue, which bore significant fruit in 1999 through a Joint Declaration on the Doctrine of Justification. This dialogue, inaugurated in 1965, has produced numerous documents, with the 1999 "Joint Declaration on the Doctrine of Justification" being the most prominent.

Interfaith Dialogue

Interfaith dialogue is a relatively new reality in Roman Catholicism. Prior to the publication of *Nostra Aetate* at Vatican II, formal association between the Church and non-Christian faiths was fragmentary at best. Because Christianity evolved from Judaism, there had always been an association between these two great monotheistic religions, but historically that relationship was filled with tension and, unfortunately, pervaded by a sense of anti-Semitism that forced Jews into urban ghettos. Thus, only in the last fifty years has there been official recognition by the church of non-Christian faiths and even more recently efforts to dialogue toward common ground and understanding. However, as previously described, Vatican II opened the door for dialogue on various fronts with different communities of faith.

The pontificate of John Paul II was marked by specific overtures toward non-Catholics. In 1988, the pope renamed the Secretariat for Non-Christians, The Pontifical Council for Interreligious Dialogue, and appointed Archbishop Michael Fitzgerald, a leading expert on Islam and Christian-Muslim relations, as its secretary. In October 2002, Fitzgerald was appointed president of the council. On a practical level, Fitzgerald promoted the view that interfaith dialogue is necessary due to the reality of religious pluralism and the ever-increasing contact between peoples of different religions throughout the world. Theologically, such dialogue and evangelization are part of the basic Christian belief in a God of love and God's love for humanity. This dialogue does not aim to produce a new world religion or to achieve some type of theological unity between faiths. Rather, the dialogue can help to eliminate false stereotypes and form a basis for openness whereby peoples of faith can learn from each other.

Catholic-Jewish Relations

The first significant outreach to non-Christians was toward the Jews. In 1993, John Paul II re-established diplomatic ties between the Vatican and Israel, which had been strained for several years prior. In 1997, a Legal Personality Agreement was signed between Israel and the Vatican that recognized church officials in Israel. In March 2000, the pope went to Israel for a five-day pilgrimage, the first visit to the Holy Land by a Roman pontiff since Paul VI's whirlwind eleven-hour tour in January 1964. In May 2003, the pope received representatives of the World Jewish Congress and the International Jewish Committee for Interreligious Consultations. The meeting was an opportunity to demonstrate good relations between Jews and Catholics and to demonstrate the dignity of humanity among all peoples of faith.

Catholic-Muslim Relations

As with Jewish relations, the Church's association with Islam has been recent in its developments. In the fall of 2007, Muslim scholars and clerics published "A Common Word Between Us and You." While not minimizing the differences between these two great world religions, the document had many positive aspects. It was seen as an argument against atheism in a religiously apathetic Europe. Additionally, it was found that both faiths ascribe to the two greatest commandments (Love God and your neighbor as yourself). Thus it was hoped that this could be a link between the Qur'an, Torah, and New Testament. Pope Benedict XVI's response was guarded but warm: "Without ignoring or downplaying our differences as Christians and Muslims, we can and, therefore, should look to what unites us, namely belief in the one God, provident Creator and universal judge who at the end of time will deal with each person according to his or her actions. We are all called to commit ourselves totally to him and obey his sacred will."

Contemporary Issues

Renewed relationships between Catholics and non-Catholics and Catholics and non-Christians have generated various issues associated with common worship. While common prayer is authorized with caution through Vatican II, two additional issues, intercommunion and interfaith marriages, are questions frequently heard in the general discussion of the relationship between Catholics and non-Catholics.

Intercommunion addresses the issue of Catholics receiving the Eucharist at non-Catholic services and vice-versa. This question often arises when Catholics and non-Catholics attend common functions, such as a wedding, funeral, or a baptism. With the exception of rites, which are in full communion with Rome and Catholicism, it is generally not allowable for a Catholic to receive the Eucharist in a non-Catholic church. Canon law, however, does allow a Catholic to receive the Eucharist from a non-Catholic when it is physically or morally impossible to approach a Catholic priest, when the danger of religious indifference is invisible, and most importantly when the church has valid sacraments. This last criterion is key, as it obviates all of the Reformation churches. Non-Catholics from the Reformation churches may receive communion from a Catholic priest if in danger of death, the individual cannot approach a minister of his or her own faith, the person asks on his own, manifests Catholic faith in the sacraments, and is properly disposed.

QUESTION

What does Catholicism teach with respect to Judaism and Islam, especially when considering a long history of animosity?
Vatican II set the tone by creating an atmosphere based on trust. While not ignoring differences, the church today seeks to find what is holy and good in all traditions and, as much as possible, common ground for future discussion. Thus, contemporary relationships are based on hope, not on fear and animosity as in the past.

Interfaith marriages are regularly celebrated in the Roman Catholic Church. According to church law, only two Catholics can be married without the need for a dispensation. Such legal permission, whether the union is a Catholic with a non-Catholic or a Catholic with a non-Christian, can be obtained through the appropriate office in any local diocese. While different diocesan policies are in place, it is generally the rule that the non-Catholic party of the marriage will agree to support the Catholic member in raising the children of the union in the Roman Catholic faith. Often, interfaith marriages between Catholics and other Christians are celebrated outside the context of the Eucharist, in deference to the non-Catholic party. However, others choose to celebrate marriages at a nuptial Mass with the understanding that non-Catholics in attendance will not receive the Eucharist.

Interfaith marriages can also be celebrated outside the Catholic Church, but special permission is required. In such cases a priest or deacon, as the official Catholic witness, may join with a minister, rabbi, or official of another faith community in the celebration of a wedding. With the proper permission obtained in advance, these marriages are considered sacramental. The role of the Catholic witness may vary, but his presence and participation in the wedding rite are essential.

A List of Significant Dates in Church History

Catholic history spans over 2,000 years and has touched the lives of millions of people. This timeline highlights a few major points that help set the progression of the Catholic Church in perspective. Please note that some dates here are approximate.

Timeline: An Overview	
3 B.C.–A.D. 30	Jesus' life
30–600	Patristic Church
35–311	Age of Martyrs
1350–1700	European Renaissance
1377–1415	Great Western Schism
1517–1648	Protestant Reformation
1542–1648	Catholic Counter Reformation
1697–1770	The Enlightenment
1760–1914	The Industrial Revolution
Timeline of Events	
3 B.C.	Jesus is born
A.D. 27	Jesus begins his ministry
30	Jesus is crucified; the Church is born at Pentecost
35	Conversion of Saul, who becomes St. Paul
49	Council of Jersualem
70	Roman Diaspora—destruction of the Jerusalem Temple
313	Edict of Milan
325	The Nicene Creed is created at the Council of Bishops at Nicaea
381	Emperor Theodosius declares Christianity the official religion of the Roman Empire
410	Rome falls
431	Council of Ephesus
451	Council of Chalcedon; Pontiff at Rome asserts supreme authority
480	Establishment of the Benedictine order, which gives rise to other monastic orders
800	Charlemagne, King of France, is named Emperor of Romans
1054	Split between Latin-speaking Catholic Church and Eastern Orthodox Church

Timeline of Events	
1073	Pope Gregory VII centralizes control of church with new theory of papal infallibility
1098–1099	First Crusade regains control of Jerusalem
1212	St. Francis creates the first of the mendicant orders, the Franciscans. The Dominicans, Carmelites, and Augustinians also arise in the 1200s
1224–1274	Life of St. Thomas Aquinas
1305–1377	Avignon papacy
1377	Papacy returns to Rome, but a second pope is elected at Avignon
1415	Council of Constance ends Great Schism, Martin V is elected pope
1517	Martin Luther post his Ninety-Five Theses
1540	Formation of the Jesuits
1543	Copernicus asserts that the Earth revolves around the Sun
1544	Jesuit missionary work begins among pagan people of Japan, Africa, and North America
1545–1563	The Council of Trent
1566	Pope Pius V standardizes Latin Mass
1632	Galileo supports Copernicus based on his observations through a telescope
1789	French Revolution fractures the church
1789	John Carroll becomes the first bishop in the United States and creates the first diocese at Baltimore
1869–1870	Pope Pius IX calls the Vatican I Council, declaration of papal infallibility
1891	Pope Leo XIII issues *Rerum Novarum*, an important encyclical on workers' rights
1959	Pope John XXIII announces he will call an ecumenical council
1962–1965	Second Vatican Council
1963	Pope John XXIII dies; Pope Paul VI is elected
1968	Pope Paul VI publishes encyclical on *Humanae Vitae*, birth control
1978	Pope Paul VI dies; Pope John Paul I is elected and dies shortly after; Pope John Paul II is elected
1983	U.S. Catholic Bishops publish a pastoral letter "The Challenge of Peace: God's Promise and Our Response" on nuclear war
1986	U.S. Catholic Bishops publish a pastoral letter "Economic Justice for All: Catholic Social Teaching and the U.S. Economy"
1995	John Paul II publishes *Evangelium Vitae*, reiterating his stand on abortion, euthanasia, and the death penalty
2003	Sexual abuse crisis in the United States
2005	John Paul II dies; Benedict XVI elected

APPENDIX B

Basic Roman Catholic Prayers

The Lord's Prayer (Our Father)

Our Father, Who art in heaven, hallowed be thy Name. Thy Kingdom come. Thy will be done, on earth as it is in Heaven. Give us this day our daily bread. And forgive us our trespasses, as we forgive those who trespass against us. And lead us not into temptation, but deliver us from evil. Amen.

The Hail Mary

Hail Mary, full of Grace, the Lord is with thee. Blessed art thou among women, and blessed is the fruit of thy womb, Jesus. Holy Mary, Mother of God, pray for us sinners now, and at the hour of our death. Amen.

Doxology (Glory Be)

Glory be to the Father, and to the Son, and to the Holy Spirit. As it was in the beginning, is now, and ever shall be, world without end. Amen.

Act of Contrition

O my God, I am heartily sorry for having offended Thee, and I detest all my sins, because I dread the loss of heaven, and the pains of hell; but most of all because they offend Thee, my God, Who are all good and deserving of all my love. I firmly resolve, with the help of Thy grace, to confess my sins, to do penance, and to amend my life. Amen.

Apostles' Creed

I believe in God, the Father Almighty, Creator of Heaven and earth; and in Jesus Christ, His only Son Our Lord, Who was conceived by the Holy Spirit, born of the Virgin Mary, suffered under Pontius Pilate, was crucified, died, and was buried. He descended into Hell; the third day He rose again from the dead; He ascended into

Heaven, and sitteth at the right hand of God, the Father almighty; from thence He shall come to judge the living and the dead. I believe in the Holy Spirit, the holy Catholic Church, the communion of saints, the forgiveness of sins, the resurrection of the body and life everlasting. Amen.

Prayer to the Guardian Angel

Angel of God, my guardian dear, to whom God's love commits me here. Ever this day, be at my side, to light and guard, rule and guide. Amen.

Memorare

Remember, O most gracious Virgin Mary, that never was it known that anyone who fled to thy protection, implored thy help, or sought thine intercession was left unaided.

Inspired by this confidence, I fly unto thee, O Virgin of virgins, my mother; to thee do I come, before thee I stand, sinful and sorrowful. O Mother of the Word Incarnate, despise not my petitions, but in thy mercy hear and answer me. Amen.

Nicene-Constantinopolitan Creed

We believe in one God, the Father, the Almighty, maker of heaven and earth and of all that is seen and unseen.

We believe in one Lord, Jesus Christ, the only Son of God, eternally begotten of the Father, God from God, Light from Light, true God from true God, begotten, not made, one in Being with the Father.

Through him all things were made.

For us men and for our salvation he came down from heaven: by the power of the Holy Spirit he was born of the Virgin Mary, and became man.

For our sake he was crucified under Pontius Pilate; he suffered, died, and was buried.

On the third day he rose again in fulfillment of the Scriptures; he ascended into heaven and is seated at the right hand of the Father.

He will come again in glory to judge the living and the dead, and his kingdom will have no end.

We believe in the Holy Spirit, the Lord, the giver of life, who proceeds from the Father and the Son.

With the Father and the Son he is worshiped and glorified.

He has spoken through the Prophets.

We believe in one, holy, Catholic, and apostolic church.

We acknowledge one baptism for the forgiveness of sins.

We look for the resurrection of the dead, and the life of the world to come.

Amen.

The Mysteries of the Rosary

Joyful Mysteries:

The Annunciation of Gabriel to Mary (Luke 1:26–38)

The Visitation of Mary to Elizabeth (Luke 1:39–56)

The Birth of Our Lord (Luke 2:1–21)

The Presentation of Our Lord (Luke 2:22–38)

The Finding of Our Lord in the Temple (Luke 2:41–52)

Luminous Mysteries

The Baptism of Our Lord in the River Jordan (Matthew 3:13–16)

The Wedding at Cana, when Christ manifested Himself (John 2:1–11)

The Proclamation of the Kingdom of God (Mark 1:14–15)

The Transfiguration of Our Lord (Matthew 17:1–8)

The Institution of the Holy Eucharist (Matthew 26:17–30)

Sorrowful Mysteries

The Agony of Our Lord in the Garden (Matthew 26:36–56)

Our Lord is Scourged at the Pillar (Matthew 27:26)

Our Lord is Crowned with Thorns (Matthew 27:27–31)

Our Lord Carries the Cross to Calvary (Matthew 27:32)

The Crucifixion of Our Lord (Matthew 27:33–56)

Glorious Mysteries

The Glorious Resurrection of Our Lord (John 20:1–29)

The Ascension of Our Lord (Luke 24:36–53)

The Descent of the Holy Spirit at Pentecost (Acts 2:1–41)

The Assumption of Mary into Heaven

The Coronation of Mary as Queen of Heaven and Earth

Index

We Have

EVERYTHING®

on Anything!

With more than 19 million copies sold, the Everything® series has become one of America's favorite resources for solving problems, learning new skills, and organizing lives. Our brand is not only recognizable—it's also welcomed.

The series is a hand-in-hand partner for people who are ready to tackle new subjects—like you!

For more information on the Everything® series, please visit *www.adamsmedia.com*

The Everything® list spans a wide range of subjects, with more than 500 titles covering 25 different categories:

Business	History	Reference
Careers	Home Improvement	Religion
Children's Storybooks	Everything Kids	Self-Help
Computers	Languages	Sports & Fitness
Cooking	Music	Travel
Crafts and Hobbies	New Age	Wedding
Education/Schools	Parenting	Writing
Games and Puzzles	Personal Finance	
Health	Pets	